WHAT SHOULD WE DO?

MORE PRAISE FOR *WHAT SHOULD WE DO?*

"What is the No. 1 reason service businesses fail? It is the lack of customers or sales. If you want to succeed, you must master persuasion and influence. These are the skills you can learn in *What Should We Do?* by Joe Crisara."

— Kurt Mortensen, author of *Maximum Influence*, *Persuasion IQ*, and *The Laws of Charisma* and founder of the podcast *Maximize Your Influence*

"As Uncle Joe says, 'Your ego is not your amigo!' If you're looking for a trusted playbook to run a successful home service company, Joe delivers. His years of experience, tactics, and beliefs put to use with successful outcomes are right in this book. He gives you the tools to help, but you have to take action because ambition without action is useless. No zero days!"

— Chris Yano, CEO of RYNO Strategic Solutions and host of *To the Point Home Services Podcast*, RYNOSS.com

"Joe starts with helping contractors mentally believe they can hit new goals, and then he spells out the practical steps to elevating the trajectory of their business."

— Tom Howard, vice president of customer experience at ServiceTitan

"Joe and his teachings have helped our business immensely! His approach to providing the best possible customer service is something that any business can benefit from and use to take their service to the next level."

— Chad Peterman, president and CEO of Peterman Brothers

"As the sales profession matures into the 21st century, selling with integrity has proven to create massive and sustainable sales results. With one simple question—'What should we do?'—Joe Crisara embodies selling with integrity in the modern age. Be comprehensive in your evaluation of your customer's problems, offer a variety of solutions, and allow the customer to make the best decision for themselves. Read this book and prosper in sales."

— Weldon Long, author of the *New York Times* and *Wall Street Journal* bestseller *The Power of Consistency*

"We may only serve at the highest level when we close the sale. This book shows home service technicians how to close the sale on the first visit at a higher-than-average sale and profit. Uncle Joe knows something all skilled tradespeople need to know to be successful. The skilled trades are as essential and precious as our soldiers and frontline workers; they keep life safe, stable, and comfortable. Our critical home systems are no longer a luxury. They are life-support systems, and we have a duty to help make it easier for buyers to buy and sellers to sell."

—Ryan Chute, partner at Wizard of Ads®

"Warning: This book contains valuable, actionable information. There are no fluffy 'guru' concepts here. Readers are advised to take immediate action and follow the steps laid out in this book. Over the years I've read and contributed to a number of articles and books related to the trades, business, and mindset and motivation. After a while, they all start to blend together and often become repetitive—even tiresome—reads. Joe's book is the first in a long time that actually makes me want to read more. Joe uses genuine stories to illustrate specific points that anyone can use to immediately improve their level of communication and persuasion. The result is more authentic and profitable conversations and a higher level of ethical service. So grab a highlighter and pen and take some notes while you read because this book will help you make more money."

—Landon Brewer, president and CEO of P.R.I.M.E. Platform

"Drawing from Uncle Joe Crisara's timeless wisdom, this book is a beacon for service professionals. It's a transformative guide echoing the Pure Motive Service principles I've imbibed in my entrepreneurial journey. Joe's training approach is both innovative and rooted in real-world wisdom, uniquely addressing the challenges, intricacies, and nuances of the service industry. It is essential reading for those seeking genuine growth in customer service."

—Tersh Blissett, owner of Service Business Mastery and Service Emperor and founder and cohost of the podcast *Service Business Mastery*

"This book has me turning the pages wanting to gather more information. Joe Crisara's great training approach puts the outcome in the client's hands by informing, educating, and building world-class solutions. Anyone will benefit, from a well-seasoned veteran to a green tech just getting out of trade school. He addresses challenges that people in the industry face daily, such as building options, asking for the order, closing, and how to handle red-, yellow-, or green-light situations. Joe breaks down the importance of Pure Motive Service and *why* being the best version of yourself is important to getting the highest return. Joe uses memorable comparisons, such as, 'Be a window, not a door.' And he highlights the magic moments that are the most powerful part of the Pure Motive Service system. *What Should We Do?* exemplifies how to serve your client to the highest level every time for the maximum results."

—Jason Walker (aka Jay Dub Money Maker), CEO of HVAC Masters
of the Hustle

"I've known Joe Crisara for more than 20 years, and I've called him countless times for advice. What's great about this book is that all of his advice is in here. As I read *What Should We Do?* I can hear his voice. It's packed with Joe's proven solutions that help people learn every day. This book is like having your own highly compensated consultant in your office. I know Joe's solutions are proven because he has helped me provide the highest level of service to my customers, resulting in sales and income I never dreamed were possible. I can't say enough about Joe's wealth of knowledge and the information in this book. Read it and prosper!"

—Rick Picard, HVAC specialist at Rodenhiser Home Services

"This book is loaded with actionable solutions and inspiring insights to help HVAC, plumbing, electrical, and other home service companies grow their businesses and achieve success."

—Mandeep Bhalla, founder and CEO of Grow Nearby and host of the
podcast *Born for the Trades*

"Uncle Joe has done so much for me, my team, and our trade as a whole. Now he gives us this manual for sales success that's within reach of anyone wanting to better themselves and their client experiences. Joe lives true to his word by providing six options for the best training in the trades. But you don't need six options when deciding among customer service training—there is only one solution for that, and it's Uncle Joe!"

—Travis Smith, president of Sky Heating, AC, Plumbing & Electrical

"Having known Joe Crisara for 20+ years, I can honestly say that he has created the definitive field guide in total alignment with his Pure Motive Service system. All the vital skills from his classroom and online training are here. This tactical handbook is an incredible resource to help home service technicians build and improve their communication skills with customers to provide a world-class experience. Joe's techniques, style, and heart come through the pages like a sincere educator wanting his students to take what they learn, go out in the world, change lives, and create the life they desire. Joe's passion for tradespeople is evident as he pours out a lifetime of knowledge in a quick and easy read that any technician can use to change their career and impact. Well done, Joe! It's an honor to call you a friend and brother."

—Drew Cameron, president of Flow Odyssey and Energy Design Systems and founder of EGIA Contractor University

"You judge a book by its content and a person by their character. In a world full of gurus motivated by the wrong things, Joe shows you how to do it from a heart of pure motive."

—Todd Liles, owner of Service Excellence Training and SPARK Success Group, www.ServExTra.com

"This book is a step-by-step guide on how contractors can differentiate themselves, increase value, and grow sales."

—Brian Bohannan, vice president of sales at JB Warranties

WHAT SHOULD WE DO?

HOW TO WIN CLIENTS, DOUBLE PROFIT & GROW YOUR HOME SERVICE SALES

JOE CRISARA

SERVICE MVP • CULVER CITY, CALIFORNIA

Name: Crisara, Joe, author.
Title: *What Should We Do?: How to Win Clients, Double Profit, and Grow Your
Home Service Sales / Joe Crisara.*
Description: Culver City, California: Service MVP, [2024]
Identifiers: ISBN: 979-8-9895534-0-2 (hardcover) | 979-8-9895534-1-9 (paperback) |
979-8-9895534-2-6 (e-book) | 979-8-9895534-3-3 (audiobook) | LCCN: 2023922044
Subjects: LCSH: Service industries—Marketing. | Self-employed—Marketing. |
Plumbing industry—Marketing. | Heating and ventilation industry—Marketing. |
Electricians—Marketing. | Small business marketing. | Repairing trades—Marketing. |
Small business—Management. | Dwellings—Maintenance and repair—Marketing. |
Mechanics (Persons)—Marketing. | Electric apparatus and appliances—Maintenance
and repair—Marketing. | Household appliances, Electric—Maintenance and repair—
Marketing. | Business presentations. | Customer relations. | Success in business. |
BISAC: BUSINESS & ECONOMICS / Industries / Service. | BUSINESS & ECONOMICS /
Sales & Selling / Management. | BUSINESS & ECONOMICS / Business Communication /
Meetings & Presentations. | BUSINESS & ECONOMICS / Customer Relations. |
BUSINESS & ECONOMICS / Freelance & Self-Employment. | BUSINESS &
ECONOMICS / Small Business. | BUSINESS & ECONOMICS / Industries / Energy. |
BUSINESS & ECONOMICS / Mentoring & Coaching. | BUSINESS & ECONOMICS /
Motivational. | BUSINESS & ECONOMICS / Personal Success.
Classification: LCC: HD9981.5 .C75 2024 | DDC: 658.8/0973—dc23

For information, contact:
Service MVP
www.servicemvp.com
877-764-6304

Hardcover ISBN 979-8-9895534-0-2
Paperback ISBN 979-8-9895534-1-9
E-book ISBN 979-8-9895534-2-6
Audiobook ISBN 979-8-9895534-3-3

Dedicated to my beloved wife,
Julie Crisara,
my rock and guiding light.

Your kindness, generosity, and unwavering support
have been a constant source of inspiration to me.
You've always put the needs of our family before your own,
and your moral compass has been a shining example for us all.
I'm grateful for your unwavering service to me and our family.
You've been with me through the darkest times, and your
support has helped me pull through. Your care and respect
for everyone is truly remarkable, noted by everyone who has
had the pleasure of working or living with you.

With all my love and gratitude.

If you give your mind a $10,000 problem,
it will come up with a $10,000 solution.
If you give your mind a $1 million problem,
it will come up with a $1 million solution.

—Jack Canfield, *The Success Principles*

CONTENTS

FOREWORD

As I sat down to read Joe Crisara's book on sales, I knew I was in for something special. I first met Joe a few years ago through a mutual friend who owned an HVAC company. Although my company was small at the time, my friend's was smaller, and I was surprised by how often they had Joe conduct on-site training. When I asked my friend how they could afford to spend that much on training, his response was that since working with Joe, their sales had doubled, so how could they afford not to? Based on his recommendation, I hired Joe and never looked back.

If you don't know me, I'm Tommy Mello, owner of A1 Garage Door Service and host of the podcast *The Home Service Expert*. With more than 35 locations and nearly 700 employees, A1 Garage has grown to become one of the largest residential garage door service companies in the United States.

If you've listened to my podcast, you know I appreciate a fresh, effective approach to sales. Joe's book delivers just that, and I'm excited to share my thoughts with you.

This isn't your typical sales manual. It's a journey through practical, tried-and-tested strategies that Joe has refined over the years. The chapters are filled with insights that will resonate deeply with anyone in sales. For example, his techniques for understanding customer needs aren't just theoretical; they're actionable and relevant.

When I applied some of Joe's strategies at A1 Garage, the results spoke for themselves. Our approach to sales transformed, becoming more customer-focused, and our numbers improved significantly. It's a testament to the effectiveness of Joe's methods.

Joe's writing style is straightforward and engaging. He breaks down complex ideas into manageable concepts that are easy to grasp and implement. Whether it's building lasting customer relationships or mastering the art of closing a deal, Joe covers it all with clarity and simplicity.

This book is a valuable resource for anyone looking to refine their sales approach. It's not just about selling more; it's about selling better, with a focus on building trust and delivering value to customers.

I'm grateful to Joe for putting his wealth of knowledge into these pages. This book is more than a guide; it's a tool that can help reshape the way you think about and approach sales.

To those about to read this book, you're making a wise decision. It's a resource that will likely change your perspective on sales and help you grow your business.

All the best in your sales journey!

Tommy Mello
CEO, A1 Garage Door Service

GET TOOLS FOR YOUR SUCCESS

SERVICE MVP

servicemvp.com/tools

Download worksheets, lists, guides, and more resources to help your entire team reach their potential.

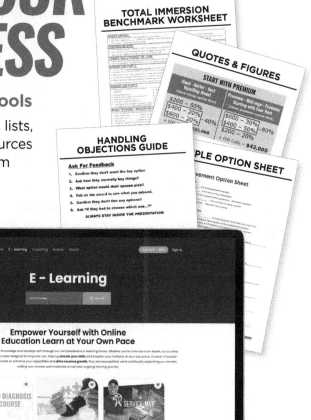

INTRODUCTION

I've been teaching Pure Motive Service for more than 30 years now, but I was once just like most service contractors. One who was deeply in debt, just scraping by, and undercharging everyone for everything.

I mistakenly thought that the only way to create higher value was to do the same service everyone else was doing for a lower price. That is, until I experienced a very big and painful blow to my ego that produced an aha moment that would change my life.

This is my story.

Back in 1992, I owned a heating, air-conditioning, and plumbing contracting business in Illinois, and I was also the president of the local heating and air-conditioning association. I became president because they voted me in while I was in the bathroom. (That's what happens when you are a member of these things.) I was young. In fact, I'd only been in business for about five years at that point.

The association meeting started at 7:00 p.m., so my friend Ron and I used to meet at the bar next door for drinks at about 6:30. Ron was the owner of another local HVAC company, and he and I went to trade school together so we knew each other pretty well. He was the vice president of the association.

Ron would drink his gin and tonic and I would have a beer, and we'd go on and on about how crazy low the competition's prices were and how hard it was to compete in that kind of environment. (I'll bet you talk about that with your fellow contractors too.)

One day, one of my techs, Glen, went to see a longtime customer—I'll call her Mary—because her furnace wasn't working. He inspected her furnace and discovered a big crack in the heat exchanger, which meant the unit was not fixable. Glen told Mary that the furnace needed to be replaced and gave her some prices. Mary told Glen she'd been doing business with us for five years now and wanted to talk to me because I was the owner of the company.

I got on the phone with Mary and said, "Hey, Mary, how's it going?" And she said, "Well, I wish it was going better. My furnace's heat exchanger took a dump." And I said, "Oh, that's too bad. Well, Glen gave you some prices. What do you think?" Mary said, "Yeah, he quoted me $2,500 for this new 90 percent efficient furnace that you guys are trying to sell. But you know what, Joe, you're the owner of the company, and I've been dealing with you for five years. So I wanted to know what *you* could do for me."

Naturally, I thought Mary was asking me to just lower the price for her.

So I said, "Well, here's what I could do, Mary. I have a furnace that we bought last spring as a floor model. I'll give it to you for

$1,800. Heck, I'll even put a humidifier in for you and include a one-year warranty and service."

I expected Mary to jump on this deal and say, "Yes, let's get it done." Instead, she said, "Well, Joe, thanks a lot. It's a great offer, but I'm going to have to talk to my husband, Tom. He's coming home at six tonight."

I said, "OK, that's fair," and we hung up. I wasn't worried because I knew we had this one in the bag.

The next morning, my crew loaded up the installation truck and the crew scheduler came to me and said, "We're ready to go, Joe. Where are we going?"

The problem was Mary hadn't called back yet. So we tried calling her. Four times. But Mary wasn't answering.

I told the guys to just work on cleaning the truck out for a while. I got busy with an appointment, and the next time I looked up it was noon. The crew scheduler poked her head in my door and said, "Hey, are we going to do an installation today? What's going on? I've got a 90 percent furnace to put in here."

I said, "Oh, jeez, let's call Mary and see if she's ready for this thing." I called again—no answer. So I sent the installers to lunch. The guys came back around 1:00 p.m., and I made another phone call. This time Mary answered.

I said, "Hey, Mary, what's going on? We've been waiting all day for you."

And then she said four words that broke my heart: "We found someone cheaper."

"I quoted you $1,800 for a 90 percent furnace—who the heck was as crazy as I was for doing that to begin with?"

"Well, there was a gentleman named Ron who came over."

"Wait a minute. Ron? Tell me his last name."

It was my friend, Ron, from the heating and cooling association. I couldn't believe it.

"What did Ron quote you? Like $1,750?"

"No, no, it was a lot cheaper than that. He's doing the whole thing for $1,250. The exact same thing you're doing."

"That's crazy. You can't make any money doing it for that price. Are you sure it's Ron? Did he have a funky sweater on? Black mustache?" She said he did.

So we lost that job to Ron's company. I was pretty upset because Ron and I had spent so much time bashing the competition before association meetings, and there he was massively undercutting my already heavily discounted price.

The next meeting was a few days later, and I could hardly wait to see Ron. I was going to hammer him in front of everyone and tell them how he undercut my prices and made me look like a fool.

I got to the bar early and had his gin and tonic all set up for him. At 6:30 p.m., Ron, his mustache, and his funky sweater came strolling up to the bar. He was carrying a little briefcase.

I said, "Hey, Ron, how's it going this week?"

"Oh, we had a very good week actually," he said. "You know what? We took one of your customers, Mary Smith."

"Yeah, I know. How could you quote $1,250 for a furnace? What's the matter with you?"

Ron gave me a funny look. "Joe, what are you talking about?"

"Ron, you should be ashamed of yourself after all the time we spend talking about how everybody's so cheap out there.

And here you are quoting $1,250 for a 90 percent furnace, a humidifier, and a one-year service plan. Why would you do that? The furnace alone is going to cost you like $900."

Ron interrupted me. "Joe, how long have you known Mary?"

"Well, I really don't know her at all. The CSRs took the calls and the techs serviced her furnace. I just talked to her once."

"How long have we known each other, Joe?"

"Since 1979."

"So that's about 13 years. And you're taking the word of somebody that you've never even talked to before over mine?"

I felt a little embarrassed. We had known each other a very long time.

"So what did you sell it for? Like $2,200, $2,500 maybe?"

"I've got the contract right here in my briefcase. You want to see it?"

He reached for his briefcase. Click, click, open. He pulled out a stack of papers, put them on the bar in front of me, sat back in his chair, and took a drink of his gin and tonic.

I looked down at them, and my future life flashed in front of my eyes.

The papers were the proposal, the contract, and a check stapled at the top. The check was for $9,857.

I was speechless.

It was Ron's platinum package and it was good for 10 years of service, including all the pads and filters, humidifier, air cleaner, and media—prepaid. Mary wouldn't have to write a check for the next 10 years. It was all covered. He reconditioned the outside unit and put the 90 percent furnace in the basement.

It was pretty unbelievable. And here I was bringing the price down to $1,800 for just the furnace and making almost nothing on it.

Ron didn't have to make me look like a fool. I made myself look like one.

That is how bad of a salesperson I used to be. I was running a failing business and almost $471,000 in debt, but no one—not even Ron—knew it.

It gets worse. I had built myself a pretty strong brand name by putting my face on the side of every truck, along with the words, "I will personally see to your satisfaction."

So when Mary was asking what Joe, the famous heating guy in Mundelein, Illinois, could do for her, what was she really asking? In essence, she was asking, "What would Babe Ruth do if he had a nice fastball right down the middle?"

I dribbled it back to the pitcher.

Ron hit it out of the park.

Paradigm Shifts

The combination of losing that deal and seeing what the customer was actually willing to pay was a life-changing moment for me.

The clinical description of what I experienced is a *paradigm shift*. I first learned about paradigm shifts in the book *The 7 Habits of Highly Effective People* by Stephen R. Covey. Covey said the true changes in our life only come when we see the same thing in a different way, even if the situation is the same. I saw my own situation through the eyes of a different version of myself.

If Mary had asked this different person, "What can you do for me?" I might have said, "Well, Mary, what would you like me to do for you?" I could have just asked her, right? Then maybe she would have said, "Well, Joe, I want a super-duper system! Could you come out and sell me the best one?"

That's what she was telling me, but I didn't know because I didn't ask. I just made an assumption about what she meant based on my own experiences and the people who had trained me. Those experiences resulted in me looking at customers through a certain lens. And that lens was shaped by the first person I rode with when I got into the trade.

What Lens Are You Looking Through?

If you are a contractor, you know this guy—let's call him Bob— because you probably rode with him as an apprentice like I did.

The first time I got in the truck with Bob, he said, "You're a schoolboy. You went to college, right?"

I told him I went to Harper College in Palatine for air-conditioning and heating.

Bob said, "Well, you can forget everything you learned in college because that doesn't apply out here in the field. Just forget it and take your books home because out here we do things a different way. We've got 'beer-can cold' for air-conditioning. We've got a little light stick to check the power of a system."

Bob became my teacher, and I took his knowledge as gospel.

So years later, when Mary asked what I could do for her, I naturally saw her question through Bob's lens, where the assumption was that the customer always wanted the cheapest option. The problem with that assumption? Nothing could be further from the truth.

To change the way you see selling your services, you have to use a different lens. This can be challenging because many of us in the contracting industry were brought up in a middle-class or lower middle-class environment. Nobody was rich or came from a family with millions of dollars, and a lot of us grew up in families that had money problems. Many of us might even be in debt, like I was. (Hopefully not as bad.)

Those family money values and your early experiences in the industry combine to create a certain lens that determines the way you see the world. For example, if you get in front of a customer and they say they're struggling financially, you assume they're being honest. But the truth is you don't know!

I've proposed six options, ranging from premium to economy, to people in some of the poorest areas in the country who still ended up choosing the premium option.

The bottom line is, if you're making the decision for your client based on your own conditioning and assumptions, you're not only losing money but also failing to serve that customer properly. And that's worse.

My goal is to get you to stop looking at life through a lens that is not serving anyone, and start looking through one that will allow you to act in a way where you can prosper and your clients can get the value they are looking for.

When you change your lens—when you shift your paradigm—you will change your life.

It's How You Respond That Matters

As you work your way through this book, you'll start to see places where you've failed, and that's OK. Just stick with me and remember there are two ways of looking at failure. You can say, "I quit. I failed, and that's it." Or you can see it as an opportunity, like I did.

When I saw Ron's contract with Mary and the check for $9,857, I felt terrible. I felt like I should not be the president of the association. In fact, I felt like I shouldn't even be the president of my own company. I left that meeting pretty depressed. I could have given up. Instead, I made a decision.

I told myself, "That's never going to happen again. Nobody's ever going to not buy from me because I didn't offer them my best stuff. From now on, I will make it a policy that everyone will at least see my best services. Even if it costs an astronomical amount of money, I don't care. I'm going to leave myself out of the price because I'm not going to get in the way of the best thing anymore. I will never again be a door blocking the view of the best services I could offer my customer."

"But wait a minute, Joe," you might be thinking. "I thought this book was going to teach me how to sell!"

The truth is people already need what you offer. They wouldn't have called you if they didn't. They don't need you to sell them on it. What they need is your help figuring out which solution to buy.

In fact, what I'm going to teach you is a system that allows you to *stop* selling and *start* doing what is necessary for your clients to discover and then buy the solution that's exactly right for them. That's right. I'm going to teach you how to help clients sell themselves on the solution that is the best option for them and their family.

The system is called Pure Motive Service, and it is how more than 100,000 contracting businesses all over the world now interact with customers in a way that results in more sales.

Are you ready to learn how you can become one of those success stories?

Great! Let's get started.

WHAT IS PURE MOTIVE SERVICE?

Chapter 1
THE FLAT TIRE STORY

As contractors, we are hands-on types who learn best when someone shows us how something works. So, whenever possible, I'm going to tell a story in a way that you can see the concepts in action. Then we'll unpack the concepts.

The following story is Pure Motive Service in action. What I love most about it is that it's not a home service industry example. It's proof that this system will work for any business that involves serving others.

By the end of this book, you will be able to come back to this story and not only recognize what I was doing but also be able to do some of it yourself. For now, just let the story flow over you.

Ready? Let's go.

Fixing a Tire Store

The regional manager of a tire franchise in California called me and said the company was having some problems with its consumer division. It was losing money because only 24 percent of customers who visited the shop would actually end up buying tires. The other 76 percent would just get a patch on the bad tire.

The commercial division, on the other hand, was keeping the company afloat. If one tire went flat on a FedEx truck, for example, the driver would always get four new tires.

Further complicating things, the consumer division was maintaining all this prime California real estate, about 10 garages with multiple bays. They also had plenty of inventory on hand, but hardly anybody was opting to get all four tires replaced.

So the regional manager said, "Joe, what can you do to help us out?"

And I said, "Well, the best thing to do is let me come and take a look."

I live in Templeton, California, so I went to one of the locations nearby. At first, I just sat in the office and watched what was going on. People would come in and say, "I woke up this morning and my tire was halfway flat. Could you see what's going on with this thing? I just need to get it fixed so I can get to work because I'm really busy today."

I watched 10 transactions and only two people bought a full set of tires. Two others bought just one tire to replace the one that was going flat. After transaction number 10, I pulled the store manager aside and said, "OK, let's try a different way. Tell me about all the different tires and services you do, then let me take the next customer."

LEARNING ABOUT LISA

The next customer who came in was a woman who had two kids with her. She came up to the counter and said, "Oh my gosh, I am so busy. I've got to get to work, and I've got to drop my kids at school, and I just saw that one of my tires is going flat. You can hear it kind of making a noise when we drive the car. So I need this thing to be fixed as soon as possible."

I smiled at her and said, "Who do I have the pleasure of speaking with?"

"Oh, my name's Lisa."

"Hi, Lisa. How many people drive the car?"

"Well, I'm a single mom, so it's my car, the only car I have. I really need to get these kids to school, and I need to get to work."

"OK, well, first of all, thank you for coming into the tire shop today. I appreciate the effort you're making, and it makes me feel good that you are worried about your kids getting to school and you getting to work. And I'll make sure we get everyone where they need to be, no matter what happens. Even if we have to hire an Uber driver, we're going to do that, OK? Let me take a quick look at the car to collect some information. I'll be right back."

I went to her car, a five-year-old SUV, and wrote down the VIN. Then I checked the odometer, which told me something more about the likely condition of the car.

When I got back to the office, I said, "Lisa, I just looked at the car and you've got 73,000 miles on it. Did you realize that?" She said she didn't. "You said you drove here. How'd you get here?"

"I drove on the 101."

"There are six lanes of traffic there. Do you usually drive on the outside lane or the inside lane?

"I drive on the inside lane, the one for high-occupancy vehicles."

"Well, we definitely want to make sure we fix it so there's no risk of that tire blowing out in traffic with the kids in the car. I don't mind fixing the tire, but I want to make sure we do it in a way that's safe for your kids and more reliable for you."

"So what can we do?" Lisa asked.

PRESENTING LISA'S OPTIONS

I said, "Well, I've written down some possible solutions for you, and I've got them right here. The top option is the platinum plus plan to keep Lisa and the kids safe and make their lives easier. That's a complete tire replacement and undercarriage renovation. The car's got 73,000 miles on it. We'll replace what you have with four European tires that have a self-healing Teflon liner. That means if the outer part of the tire gets a puncture, the liner in it will keep it from going flat. Your car will tell us that there's a problem, and we will fix that tire for the next five years and 75,000 miles for free. You're also going to get new brakes, struts and suspension because they're all 73,000 miles old. And then you're going to get an oil change for the next five years too.

"We just want to make sure we take care of you, so we're going to have an Uber driver take you and the kids to school and work today, then we'll bring the car back to you. And when we're done with that, like I said, whenever you need an oil change done, you just drop your car off and we'll bring it back to your office. And we're going to do that four times a year."

"How much is that going to cost?" Lisa asked.

"Well, here's the price right here. It's $5,792 for all of that. What should we do?"

"Oh my gosh. I'm a single mom. I don't really have that kind of money."

"That's OK. We've got another option. It's $3,498. That's just the tires and the oil changes without the brakes and suspension, with a four-year warranty for the next 60,000 miles. What should we do?"

"OK, that's better. Is there anything for less money?"

"Sure, the next one we can do is a set of four Goodyear or other standard tires and oil changes for the next three years or 36,000 miles. That would be $1,797. If you want to buy just one standard tire, it would have a 12,000-mile warranty and no oil changes. We've also got a retread for $249, no warranty, or we can just patch the tire for $89. So here are options from $5,792 all the way down to $89. Just pick the one that's right for you. I'm going to go bring your car in and put it up on the rack and then we'll do the one you want. When I come back, just tell me what we should do."

WHAT SHOULD WE DO?

I came back into the office and said, "OK, Lisa, what should we do?"

She said, "You know what, Joe, I want this car to be reliable. You said you'll take me to work and the kids to school?"

"Yep. We're going to Uber you there right now."

"OK, let's get that top option done today then."

"You sure? There are some cheaper options."

"I'm sure. I want the top option."

"Check or credit card?"

That was the first time that franchise had ever sold the premium tires, and the reason was that no one had ever offered that option before. The employees all assumed that no one would ever spend that much.

I explained to the employees that it might be true that they wouldn't, but that's something you have to find out when you put the options in front of them. Pure Motive Service isn't about profiling people and assuming they don't want something. It's about saying, "Hey, here's the best thing all the way down to the economy option." Let the customers see the whole range of solutions and choose for themselves.

Before I showed the store the Pure Motive Service approach, the consumer division was averaging just $264 per invoice. Thirty days later, they were at $2,417 in total revenue per invoice. It changed the entire franchise, and the consumers liked it more too. The tire shops had more customers because they were providing a lot of choices without people having to ask for them.

So, what's your flat tire story? Or, better yet, what would you like it to be? Whatever that story may be, Pure Motive Service can help you make it a reality. In the next chapter, I'll introduce you to the five values that are at the foundation of the Pure Motive Service system and explain the magic (and the title of this book) that is the question "What should we do?"

Next, you'll learn the five Pure Motive Service principles, which also serve as the section headings for the chapters outlining the Pure Motive Service techniques and concepts we'll be unpacking throughout the rest of the book.

So, without further ado, let's proceed to chapter 2, which is all about Pure Motive Service.

How Pure Motive Service Got Its Name

I had the pleasure of having Rick Picard in class at an early Total Immersion Summit. Back then (in 2004), he was a $1.8 million HVAC salesman. Now he has made $12 million per year for the last five years straight and counting.

At the break he came up to me and said, "Joe, this is so life-changing, what you're teaching. You should call this Pure Motive Service."

I looked at him, surprised, and asked, "What's that?"

"Well, that's the motivation," he said. "You're teaching people how to serve others without looking for something in return. You know the science tells you people will likely return that favor, but you shouldn't expect it. That's what you're saying, right?"

"Yes, that's exactly it," I said.

"You give people the opportunity to purchase more, but if they don't want to, they don't have to," Rick said. "You're just there to understand the problem and provide them with options so they have the freedom to purchase as much or as little as they want. Your motives are pure."

And the rest is history.

Chapter 2
PURE MOTIVE SERVICE

The purpose of this book is to capture the essence of my Pure Motive Service system, one that thousands of my clients have used to increase sales and customer satisfaction, as well as to shift their mindsets so they could go from just scraping by to unlimited prosperity.

At the center of the Pure Motive Service system are a series of specific actions that will help you create meaningful connections with your clients and provide them with a series of options that will allow them to choose exactly what is right for them so they will stay customers for life.

My goal is to teach you enough of the system so you can walk away with a solid understanding of it and some things you can do to make a difference in your company right away. It won't be everything I've got—there's a ton more where this came from—but by the time you're done reading or listening to this book, you'll have a good sense of what the system does and the things you need to start putting in place. So, what is Pure Motive Service?

Pure Motive Service System

Pure Motive Service is a sales system that puts clients first by making them aware of all the possible benefits they could receive from your services and then skillfully assisting them in selling *themselves* on the solution that is right for them. It is a principle-centered system that you can use to achieve:

- Better customer connections
- More customized solutions
- Higher revenue and ticket averages
- Higher closing rates
- Fewer callbacks

Here's what I know. If the only change you make is to let your clients know about all the solutions available to them, you will automatically become more successful than you are now. But "more successful" is not really my goal for you. My goal is for you to become successful beyond your wildest imagination. And this book is designed to start you on the path to doing just that.

The Eternal Conflict

The Pure Motive Service system was designed to overcome the eternal conflict that occurs between a poorly informed client and a high-level service professional (you). Managing conflict is part of our job. Think about it: no one would have a business if there were no problems that needed to be solved. Conflict is the reason a business exists.

An aversion to conflict is one reason why most service professionals diagnose only the immediate problem and propose the cheapest solution available. If the client doesn't disappear and go with a provider who took the time to diagnose the system and offer a top-of-the-line option (remember Mary?), they will negotiate the lowest price possible and pay only what they think is fair, which creates even more conflict.

The problem with this approach is that since the service professional was focused only on the problem at hand rather than looking at the system as a whole, there may be other undiagnosed issues. And when they crop up later, the client will hold the service professional accountable for the choice *the client* made because it was the only one they were offered.

The Pure Motive Service provider's approach is to diagnose not only the immediate problem but also the entire system, and then offer a range of premium, midrange, and economy solutions. They then skillfully navigate any conflicts (aka objections) that may arise, allow the client to choose the option they like best, and complete the work listed in the option the client selected. This way the *client* is accountable for the choice they made because the service provider has left no stone unturned in terms of the range of services offered to them.

The graphic on the next page shows you the (big) difference between an uninformed client's buying system and the Pure Motive Service provider's system.

THE CONFLICT
Between Clients and High-Level Service Pros

The Uninformed Client's Buying System				
Provider diagnoses only the immediate problem	Fixes only the immediate problem so it's cheap	Client negotiates the lowest price possible	Client pays only what they think is fair for fixing problem	Holds provider accountable for future problems

The Pure Motive Service Provider's System				
Provider diagnoses the entire system and the problem	Offers a range of premium, mid, and economy solutions	Allows the client to choose the solution they like best	Completes the work on client's choice of solution	Client is accountable for the choice they made

BE A WINDOW, NOT A DOOR

To manage this conflict, you need to become a window that clients can look through to see all of their options rather than a door with only one option. The tire franchise stopped being a door labeled "$89 tire patch" and became a window where clients could see all the available options and choose the one that was right for their family.

Most providers act like a door, which blocks the view of all the client's options except the cheapest one. Another part of being a window is putting all the options in writing so the client can see everything in one place. Telling people about the options is lip service; real service is writing everything down in clear language so they can make an informed choice.

Pure Motive Service is grounded in a genuine concern for the client around universal topics that nobody can argue with, such as health, wellness, safety, and comfort. For example, if you're an HVAC contractor, you're concerned about the air quality and whether or not the existing system is safe and capable of keeping the client as warm or cool as needed. If you're a plumbing contractor, you want to make sure the toilet, piping, and drains are working properly so sewage goes where it's supposed to go. If you're a garage door service provider, you want to make sure the door is working properly so the client can get in and out of the garage as needed.

Your concern about the health, wellness, safety, and comfort of your client and their family provides a rock you can stand on while creating interest and desire for your services. This genuine deep concern about your client is expressed through the five Pure Motive Service values.

You need to become a window that clients can look through to see all of their options rather than a door with only one option.

The Five Pure Motive Service Values

The five Pure Motive Service values are enhancing quality and reliability, protecting the client's safety and health, providing customer-service choices, customized relevant solutions, and honesty (even when it's not popular).

ENHANCING QUALITY AND RELIABILITY

The key to this value is diagnosing the whole system, not just the main component. For example, the average home plumbing system is probably 15, 30, or even 50 years old. Maybe the client needs to replace the sewer pipe from their house to the street. What about the rest of the pipe under the house or the stack that goes through the structure? In your top offering, why not provide clients with the option to modernize the infrastructure that supports the system in place? This is a huge differentiator. Everybody else is just doing what the client is asking them to do. In your premium choice, you're providing options you know will boost the system's quality and reliability. Your economy option is to do only what the client asked you to do.

PROTECTING THE CLIENT'S SAFETY AND HEALTH

The goal is always to eliminate whatever the threat to the client's safety and health is at its root, and this should be reflected in your top option.

For example, if your client's child has asthma, clean air is essential to their safety and health. An air-filtration system would clean the air before it got into the structure so it wouldn't get dirty in the first place. Or, if you're putting in a tankless hot-water system, why not offer the client the option to replace all the old pipes that lead to it so the debris from the old pipes won't ruin the new component?

PROVIDING CUSTOMER-SERVICE CHOICES

This value is about anticipating and offering what customers need before they ask us for it.

It's not enough to do only what they ask us to do. It's important to do more than they ask us for. In fact, if somebody says, "Could you do something for me?" you could answer, "What do you want me to do?" And then say, "You know what? I can actually do better than that." That gives the customer a heads-up that you tend to do this job *better* than they expected.

Let's say you're an HVAC provider and your top option calls for a 12-year warranty and service plan. The customer might expect the warranty, but they probably wouldn't expect a 12-year service plan where you come to their house twice a year to check the system and replace all the filters. It's not just about protecting the client's investment; it's also about protecting them from the filters becoming obsolete and more expensive. You're anticipating things that could be a problem in the future and offering them tomorrow's service at today's price. That's customer service.

CUSTOMIZED RELEVANT SOLUTIONS

This value is about getting to know the client and their family so you can make sure the options you offer are customized and relevant to their needs.

The knowledge you collect will allow you to talk to your client about those options in a way that shows you care. For example, instead of talking about the air purifier, talk about why it is relevant. Here's what that sounds like: "I included this [air purifier] because of your son, David, so he will have clean air to breathe and your house will be a safe place for him." (You'll learn exactly how to talk about the options in chapter 25—where we'll cover presenting on-code solutions.)

HONESTY (EVEN WHEN IT'S NOT POPULAR)

Finally, you must be committed to being honest about what you find, even when it's not popular. This value can be tough. It is a commitment to tell customers about everything you found during your diagnosis of the whole system—no matter how bad it is.

It's not popular to tell people things they don't want to hear. It creates discomfort, which leads to conflict. Your job is to manage that conflict and communicate both the problems and the solutions in a way that the client can see the solution as an enhancement rather than something negative.

It's also a mindset. You need to be connected to what you want from the work, meaning what does the system need to have so you can be proud of it when you're done? You also need to be committed to that customer and what you want for them, which is to be able to get back to their life and not have to worry about this problem because it's fixed permanently.

As a Pure Motive Service provider, you must make a decision before every call to stand firm on these five values—regardless of what the customer says—to the point where you are willing to walk away from the job if you aren't permitted to live by them. (You'll learn how to confidently deal with challenges to these values in chapter 27, which covers dealing with client objections.)

What Should We Do?

I titled this book *What Should We Do?* because that question, posed at every step of the buying process, is central to the Pure Motive Service system.

If I do my job right, by the end of this book the question "What should we do?" will be embedded in your sales DNA. It is our way of asking the client to make a voluntary commitment. The client's answer to this question is what will allow the call to move forward.

A PERFECT QUESTION

"What should we do?" is a perfect question and here's why. If I say to you, "So, what do *you* want to do?" it puts pressure on you. It's making you do work. In the Pure Motive Service system, I create the solutions and then you pick one. So it's something we're doing together. It's a collaboration. Thus, "What should *we* do?"

I'm creating a series of solutions that I think are right for you, and you're picking the one you think is best. You wouldn't be able to pick one if I didn't offer it. So both people are necessary. I can't be more committed than you are, since you're spending your money. But you can't make the solutions that I can because you don't know everything that's available.

It's a true collaboration between consumer and provider.

Another great thing about it is that it's a neutral question. I'm not telling you what to do or which option to choose. I took the time to learn about your current system or problem and about how you want to live, and I used that information to put together solutions that I believe are a fit for you and your lifestyle. Your part of the collaboration is to give me the information and then choose the option that's best for you.

"What should we do?" should be your go-to question at any point when the consumer seems stuck in the decision-making process. For example, you present the top option and they respond, "It's a lot of money." You progress to the next option, and when you've laid out all of them you say, "So, what should we do?"

Maybe they get overwhelmed by all the choices. They might say, "I've got to think about this." So you can start paring the choices down for them. You might say, "So this top option, can we agree you're not going to do that one?" They might say, "No, I'm not going to do that one." You say, "OK. Let's get rid of that one. What should we do?"

Or they might say, "I like the top option because it has a 10-year warranty, but it's a lot of money." You can say, "It's a high investment, but it's an investment in your family. So, what should we do?" And it keeps going from there.

I've also noticed that the question kind of clears the decision-making mechanism. Having to decide on something creates tension, and that can be uncomfortable. At this point, some people might be thinking, "How can I get rid of this guy?" Saying "What should we do?" catches them off guard. It calls out that subconscious voice that's saying, "This is too much money. I can't afford this. I'm not worth it"—which is what a lot of people mean when they say they can't afford it.

Here's the reality. Anyone who owns a house most likely is able to figure out how to afford a repair on that house. When the plumbing is leaking, or the air conditioner is broken, or the garage door doesn't work, they can't live their normal lifestyle and it's constantly on their mind. Then they start thinking, "Who can I call to help me with this thing?" They are looking for someone they can trust to take control of the situation, figure out what's wrong, tell them what their options are, and then turn control back over to them to make the choice.

Asking "What should we do?" is how you turn the control back over to the client, along with the accountability for whatever they decide.

If they pick the top option, you, as the provider, take more responsibility for the outcome over a period of time. If they pick the bottom option, they, as the client, are accepting the responsibility for the outcome. If it breaks again, or something else goes wrong, they know they will have to pay for it again because there's no warranty.

With the Pure Motive Service system, you truly don't care which option they go with, as long as they feel it's right for them.

You're like a card dealer in Vegas. You can't influence how the cards are played. You just deal, and the client takes it from there. If you tried to help them, that would be like the house gaming the player. You'd be cheating on behalf of the client. So card dealers in Las Vegas have to stay neutral. And that's the way service providers should be too: "Here are the solutions, pick the one you want, what should we do?" And that's pretty much it.

"What should we do?" are four perfect words that create the expectation to move forward while making sure the accountability for the decision remains with the client.

A STRONG FOUNDATION

The five Pure Motive Service values and the question "What should we do?" are at the center of the Pure Motive Service system, but there's much, much more to learn. After all, it is a system, and there is an order in which things should occur.

The good news is that the information in this book is actionable. That means you can apply it to your calls right away.

Obviously, I'm not able to share all of what I teach in my Total Immersion Summit or this book would be 1,000 pages long! My goal is to give you enough of the basics so you can get results right away.

"What should we do?" are four perfect words that create the expectation to move forward while making sure the accountability for the decision remains with the client.

The Five Pure Motive Service Principles

The remainder of this book is organized into sections based on the five Pure Motive Service principles, which are five things you need to *be* in order to have success with this program.

BE A STUDENT

As a student of the Pure Motive Service system, you will need to focus on three things:

1. Learning from your clients through the interview process as you're doing your evaluation. Don't worry about being perfect. Just apply the system as best as you can, and we'll build on it as we go along.

2. Recognizing and putting your old beliefs aside and trying out the new thinking you'll be learning here. To clarify, avoid freestyling by combining parts of your old thinking with parts of the new stuff. It's called a system for a reason!

3. Learning and then practicing the new techniques in this book as much as possible until you can do them without even thinking about it. There will be plenty of examples and opportunities sprinkled throughout the book.

By the end of this section, you will understand that the willingness to continuously learn and change is the key to success.

BE ON CODE

At the foundation of Pure Motive Service is the connection with the client. In this section you will learn:

1. How to communicate with your client in a way that will resonate with them by uncovering their unique buying code.

2. How to create an instant connection with your client with magic moments.

3. How to use the law of verbal packaging to focus the client on the value of your service, rather than on the broken parts.

By the end of this section, you will understand what buying codes are and how to identify them; how to create powerful magic moments that will establish an immediate emotional connection; and what words and phrases to use to position your offering properly—and which ones to avoid!

BE SKEPTICAL

Pure Motive Service is unique in that we use all the tools available to us to assist our client in selecting the service option that is right for them and their family. This includes:

1. Leveraging the laws of scarcity and dissonance to create and release tension, which releases the client from the prison of indecision so they can take action.
2. Requiring the client to engage in a "convince-me step," which confirms they are ready to get the work done before we invest our time diagnosing the system.
3. Surfacing any potential competitors or other people whose interference might tank the call by testing the danger line.

By the end of this section, you will understand how to confidently guide your client through this part of the Pure Motive Service process so they are well on their way to becoming customers for life.

BE ETHICAL

Pure Motive Service is an ethical sales system with values that govern the way you do the call, from the diagnosis to creating the options to preparing and delivering the presentation. In this section you will learn:

1. The hierarchy of persuasion, including which type of persuasion we use in Pure Motive Service and why.
2. Why we diagnose not only the client's stated problem but also the entire system related to it.
3. The science of pricing and how to use it to effectively price your options.
4. How to effectively use the laws of association and contrast to talk about the options in a way that will properly position their value in the mind of your client.
5. How to use all of what you've learned to create the right proposal, one that states the problems and provides six solution options, and why that proposal must be in writing.

By the end of this section, you will have deeper insights into how to ethically use this powerful knowledge to create an effective proposal that provides the client with multiple options for solving the problems you've uncovered.

BE DETERMINED

As Pure Motive Service providers, we offer our unconditional friendship first. That means that once the client has indicated to us that they want to get the work done, we are going to hang in there and assist them in selecting an option because we know that no one is going to care as much about the work as we will. In this section you will learn:

1. How to get your client's attention and then present the problems you've found and how to then use the laws of dissonance and scarcity to increase their desire to hear your solutions.

2. How to present your on-code solutions and why you only present the top option even though you've got six written down.
3. How to deal with client objections, along with my ultimate closing technique.
4. A fail-safe way to eliminate buyer's remorse even though it's counterintuitive.
5. The best way to get referrals and reviews before and after you leave the call.

By the end of this section, you will know everything you need to know to run a Pure Motive Service call successfully from the beginning to the end.

Uncle Joe's Rules

I'll also be sprinkling what I call Uncle Joe's Rules throughout the book. These are quick, one- or two-sentence statements designed to help you stay on course and internalize all the new thinking you'll be doing as a result of this book. Let's start with this one:

— UNCLE JOE'S RULE 1 —
Pure Motive Service is the knife that cuts through the fog of uncertain value.

Ready to learn more about Pure Motive Service? Great. Let's go!

 BULLSEYES

- Pure Motive Service is a sales system that puts clients first by making them aware of all the possible benefits they could receive from your services and then skillfully assisting them in selling themselves on the solution that is right for them.

- Pure Motive Service requires you to become a window that clients can look through to see all of their options rather than a door with only one option.

- Your genuine deep concern about your client is expressed through the five Pure Motive Service values: enhancing quality and reliability, protecting the client's safety and health, providing customer-service choices, customized relevant solutions, and honesty (even when it's not popular).

- "What should we do?" are four perfect words that create the expectation to move forward while making sure the accountability for the decision remains with the client.

- The book is organized into five sections based on the Pure Motive Service principles, which are be a student, be on code, be skeptical, be ethical, and be determined.

TOOLS FOR YOUR SUCCESS

servicemvp.com/tools

✳ TEST YOUR HOME SERVICE SALES IQ
Do you know what it takes to win clients, double your income, and grow your home service sales? Answer 10 questions and find out!

✳ PURE MOTIVE SERVICE BASIC TRAINING COURSE
Your first online coaching course is on us! Unlock your full potential by finding out how America's service sales coach uses pure motives to create higher value for clients.

Scan to get your online course

BE
A STUDENT

Chapter 3
BE A STUDENT—OVERVIEW

Remember Lisa from the tire shop? You'll remember she told me she had to get to work, she had her two kids with her, and one of her tires was half flat and making noise. She also said she wanted it fixed as soon as possible. You may have noticed that I didn't launch right into offering her the options. I took the time to learn more about her and her vehicle first.

1. I asked who I had the pleasure of speaking with and found out her name.
2. I expressed my appreciation of her efforts to get the car fixed.
3. I asked how many people drove the car and found out she was a single mom and it was the only car she had.
4. I looked at her car and found out it was a five-year-old SUV with 73,000 miles on it, which told me the likely overall condition of the vehicle.

5. I asked her what route she took to get to the store and found out it was a busy 12-lane freeway.

6. I asked what lane she drove in and found out it was the one for high-occupancy vehicles, an inside lane, which told me the risk level of having a tire go flat or blow out.

Then—and only then—did I present the options, starting with the top one. Taking the time to learn about her allowed me to create and effectively present six options—two premium, two midrange, and two economy.

What I didn't do was profile her or make a decision for her. I could have decided that, as a single mom, she wouldn't want the top options. I didn't do that. I took the time to learn about her, I created the options, and then I allowed her to pick the one that was right for her family—and, in this case, that turned out to be the top option.

Most people won't pick the top option, but given six options, even fewer will pick the very bottom one. Learn about your client, provide the options, and let the customer buy. That's what Pure Motive Service is all about.

To be successful with this system you have to be a student, but your clients are just one of three categories of things you'll need to be open to learning about. Number two is the willingness to learn new ways of thinking, and number three is to learn and then implement new techniques. Let's discuss each of these categories in more detail.

Learning about Your Client

If you're in the home service business, the first part of the call is devoted to learning about the customer, the system and all its related components, and how the people in the home are interacting with the system.

The second part is about creating the right proposal, making an on-code presentation, and getting the job. (You'll learn all about how to do this part in the last two sections of the book.)

Some clients will follow you around and ask a ton of questions about what you're finding. The problem with that is it's not time for you to talk yet. You still have more to learn. So you could say, "Well, John, I will tell you about it. Let me go ahead and get my information together and I'll get to that toward the end. Let me finish this part of it first."

If they keep it up, give them a reason to start talking about themselves. This will allow you to continue to learn more about them as you evaluate their system. This is important because it will give you clues about the most effective way to present your options. What you want to do is focus on talking about their accomplishments. Accomplishments are things that we feel good about, and talking about them puts us in a positive mindset.

THE NINE MAJOR ACCOMPLISHMENTS

There are nine major accomplishments you can ask clients about. Spread these questions throughout the entire call. You don't have to be stationary while you're asking the questions. You should continue to work, move, and get your gauges out. If you have these questions in your back pocket, the pressure is off to talk before you're done collecting the information you need to gather in order to create your options.

Home: You can always talk about the home. You could start by saying something like, "How old is this part of the system? How old is the electrical (or air-conditioning) system? How long have you lived here?"

Job: Usually the question about the home leads right into the job. You could ask, "What kind of job do you have?"

Education: Talking about someone's job can lead to learning about their educational background. You could ask, "Where did you go to school for that? Was it difficult? How many years did you go? What kind of degree did you get? What did you major in?"

Family: People love talking about their families. You could ask, "How many kids do you have? How old are they? What grades are they in? How many people live here? What are their names?"

Fun: Another great topic is what the client does in their free time. You could ask, "What do you do for fun?" Once they tell you, riff on it. "How'd you get into that? What's that like?"

Pets: People love to talk about their pets too. Once the pet train begins, let it roll. You could ask, "What kind of dog is that? What's his name?"

Hobbies: Look around the house and see if you notice any clues. Is there a nice garden in the front yard? You could ask, "Who is the gardener?" Stuffed moose head on the wall? "Who's the hunter?" Golf club and miniature putting green in the family room? "Who plays golf?" You get the idea.

Travel: Another topic people love to discuss is their vacations. If you go somewhere, it feels like an accomplishment. You could ask, "Where'd you go on vacation? What was that like?"

Opinions on Select Current Events: Find out what they think about things that might give you insights into what they care about as it relates to your services. A good example is a question about the environment: "So, what's your opinion about this new green movement that everybody's talking about?" Then listen to the answer. If the client says they think it's a crock, you'll know not to focus on the green solutions you have available.

Remember, you're just the interviewer. It's OK to ask the customer his opinion without interjecting any of yours.

As you're doing your interview, you also want to be learning what you can about the system and the client's relationship with it, especially what it is not doing right now that you think might be important to them. The best way to accomplish this goal is to alternate between personal and technical questions, asking no more than three of one kind before you switch to the other.

ALTERNATING THE QUESTIONS

So what might that sound like? Here's an HVAC example:

You: Hey, Tom, how long have you lived in this house?

Tom: Nine years.

You: Oh my goodness. You're from this area?

Tom: Yep. Born and raised.

You: What was it like when you were a kid in this area? It must have been pretty cool.

Tom: Oh yeah. Not nearly as many houses around then.

Now, switch to some technical questions that will give you information about how the customer is experiencing and interacting with the system.

You: Hey, Tom, I've got a question for you. Would you say this house is pretty much dust-free, as in there's no dust problem in the house?

Tom: Oh, no. My wife says it's dusty all the time.

You: Have you heard about the newest thing that just came out about air quality in the home? It was in *Popular Mechanics*.

Tom: No, I didn't read that.

You: Well, I'm just here for the tune-up today, so I won't talk about it.

Tom: Well, let me know what it is.

You: You sure?

Tom: Yes.

You: Well, let me finish my tune-up and I'll send you a link.

I not only learned more about the client but also created desire and curiosity. (That's how I sold an upgrade. I asked three personal questions, then all of a sudden switched to the technical questions about the air quality.) But remember, you can't ask more than three of one type of question before switching to the other.

You: What kind of allergies do you have, Tom?

Tom: Well, mine are better than my wife's.

You: Oh my goodness. Has she gone to the doctor for that kind of stuff?

Tom: She's suffering bad enough without the doctor.

You: I just realized I never asked you what you do for a living.

Tom: I'm an auto mechanic.

You: What kind of education did you get for that?

Tom: I started as an apprentice at a dealership.

You: Really? What was that like?

Have you ever seen a scripted list of questions, where everything is on a scale? For example, on a scale of one to 10, how important is air quality? On a scale of one to 10, how important is reliability? You don't have to do that. Mix it up. Ask two personal questions and one technical question, then go back to another personal one. It should be a natural sequence. You just respond to what's going on. The client might volunteer one, or one might present itself to you.

Let's say the client answers the door and their kids are all going crazy. You could say something like, "John, it looks like right now is a bad time for you. Is it? I could reschedule the call."

And he might say, "No, it's OK. I've got three kids here. I tell you, it's tough with these kids. I'm home with them all day today." He's telling you stuff about the kids now, right? That's personal. So just respond to that prompt with kid questions. "Oh, how old are they? What school do they go to?" and then switch to your technical questions when it makes sense. "What kind of allergies do they have?" You get the idea.

I offered a list of personal accomplishments you can ask about, but just know the customer may come up with some on their own without you having to bring them up in that order. Be creative and flexible.

Remember, people buy more when they like themselves, and they will like themselves more when you show that you're interested in them.

Learn about your client, provide the options, and let the customer buy. That's what Pure Motive Service is all about.

Learning New Ways of Thinking

A good portion of this section is going to involve me asking you to let go of some old beliefs and embrace some new thinking. You'll learn how your beliefs create your reality, which will help you understand not only where you are now but also how to get unstuck and move forward.

Another thing I'll be asking you to do is leave your mother in the truck. What I mean by that is setting the money beliefs you learned from your family aside and providing your customer with a range of options—from premium to economy. That way they can pick the one that's best for them rather than going with the one cheap choice you've made for them based on your own beliefs.

I'm also going to talk about how to visualize your goals, a great way to identify those goals (do-be-have), and how to get others on board to support them by throwing a "goal party."

You'll also learn why taking responsibility for the outcomes of each call you go on is critical to your success and how to use the equation E + R = O to navigate toward the outcomes you desire.

Finally, I'm going to talk about how to recognize what I call "yellow lights" so you can slow down or stop and potentially turn around a call that's going south. The more willing you are to entertain these new ways of thinking and try them on, the easier and more natural doing the techniques I'm teaching will become.

NO CHEATING

Don't attempt to cheat the system by trying to combine your old thinking with this new thinking. It won't work. You'll want to blame the system, but when someone has a problem, it usually turns out they're not applying the system faithfully. If they were, they would be succeeding!

There's a story at the end of chapter 4 about a Service MVP client who was struggling with this process and what happened when I finally got him to apply the program "as written." There's a lot of room for creativity in the system, but it needs to happen through the application of the thinking and techniques you'll be learning here.

— UNCLE JOE'S RULE 2 —
You're either growing or dying. Nothing stays the same!

Learning New Techniques

You've already learned a couple of new techniques in this chapter. You learned that you should not talk much on the first part of the call. You learned the major accomplishments you can discuss with the client and how to alternate personal and technical questions with no more than three in a row.

In the previous chapter, you learned how to use the question, "What should we do?" when a customer seems to be stuck on making a decision.

There's always something new to learn, but just learning it is not enough. You have to practice it. It's the practice that will create the success you're after.

Sometimes learning a new technique will require you to understand a certain "law" that governs it. So let me introduce you to the 12 universal laws of persuasion. Just let them flow over you for right now. I'll give you plenty of examples of each one in action as you move through the book.

THE 12 UNIVERSAL LAWS OF PERSUASION

The following laws originated with a book titled *Maximum Influence: The 12 Universal Laws of Power Persuasion* by Kurt W. Mortensen, one of America's leading authorities on persuasion, motivation, and influence. They have been adapted for the Pure Motive Service system.

Law of Dissonance: Solutions are worthless without a problem.

Law of Connection: People like to buy from people they like and trust.

Law of Contrast: When you show people a range of options from premium to economy, most people will pick an option somewhere in the middle.

Law of Social Validation: People follow the crowd. They like to do things that people have done before them. It makes it easier for them to decide.

Law of Balance: It's important to balance the emotional and technical aspects of your work.

Law of Esteem: People often buy better when they feel good about themselves.

Law of Association: There are premium, midrange, and economy choices, and people know which one they want to buy in 2.7 seconds.

Law of Scarcity: Scarcity creates value. When things are too plentiful, they are perceived as worthless. That's why sometimes the best thing to do is stop the call and say "no" to the client.

Law of Obligation: When you do something nice without expecting something in return, people love to return that to you. They feel obligated.

Law of Involvement: A bored mind says "no"; involving your client creates commitment.

Law of Verbal Packaging: Use words to either create higher value or reduce the value.

Law of Expectation: Put all the choices in front of your client and then ask, "What should we do?"

Familiarizing yourself with these 12 universal laws will help you better understand what's behind the techniques and information I'll be sharing throughout the book and why they work so well.

In the next chapter, you'll learn how your beliefs create your results and how shifting them can literally change your life.

BULLSEYES

- To be successful with this system, you have to be a student who is willing to learn about your clients, learn new ways of thinking, and learn and then implement new techniques.

- When learning about clients, tap into the nine major accomplishments: home, job, education, family, fun, pets, hobbies, travel, and opinions on select current events.

- Getting unstuck is going to require you to let go of old beliefs and embrace some new thinking—no cheating!

- There's always something new to learn, but just learning it is not enough. You have to practice it. It's the practice that will create the success you're after.

- Awareness of the 12 universal laws of persuasion will allow you to more easily understand how Pure Motive Service works and why it works so well.

Chapter 4
YOUR BELIEFS CREATE YOUR RESULTS

When I was about 17, my grandfather had an old blue Ford Fairlane. He had about used it all up, so it was perfect for me. It was a little rusty on the back, but that was OK. I could take it to auto shop in high school and fix it. For months, all I could think about was that car. Grandpa eventually sold it to me for a hundred dollars because he had to make me pay something.

That was my first experience with visualization. At that point, I didn't even know that's what I was doing. I just knew that once I had my brain focused on something, I would always get it.

Whether you realize it or not, it's the same with you.

When it comes to building a business, however, there's often an unwillingness to visualize what we want. Here is an example of what two guys in one of my Total Immersion Summits said they wanted:

Tom: I want to get our prices up to a point where we can make a healthy profit and our whole company can prosper together so I can get my company where it needs to be and treat my guys the way I want to treat them. I want to be able to explain to customers the service they are getting for the price they are paying so they feel good about what they're getting.

John: I want to fine-tune our sales program to be able to sell our services for what we need to make. Otherwise, you're basically just moving money around. I also want to learn how to sell. Most of my other work was just service and the price was what it was—I never had to sell anything—but times have changed. That's why we're all here, right? To make a better life for ourselves and our families.

I'm betting you want what they want too.

Obviously, you've already accomplished some things. You wouldn't be where you are if you hadn't. Early on, when you were in training, I bet you couldn't wait to get your own truck. You imagined yourself driving to the customer's house without another tech hanging over your shoulder. You visualized that, and it came to be. If you're an owner, at some point when you were still a tech, you started dreaming about what it would be like to not have to go knock on someone's door and ask for a raise.

On a personal level, maybe you bought a house, or got married, or had some kids.

The point is, do great things in life happen without us knowing they're going to happen? No. We have to visualize these things. The first place new and better things happen is in our imagination. To live the life you've always dreamed of, you have to see it first in your mind.

Visualization is the first step, and I'll give you some exercises for that in chapter 6, where I explain the goal party. Right now what you need to know is that making your dreams a reality is a lot easier if you aren't constantly fighting against your inner beliefs.

I used to think that beliefs were set in stone, but I learned nothing could be further from the truth. I know this is true because I've not only had to change a lot of my beliefs to get where I am today but also seen what happens when the contractors I've coached make that jump.

To change your beliefs, you first need to understand how they work. Your beliefs are creating your results.

The first place new and better things happen is in our imagination.

The Rope around Your Ankle

When an elephant is born in a circus, it weighs about 500 pounds. As soon as possible, the trainers tie a 15-foot-long, three-quarter-inch rope around its ankle. That rope is then tied to a stake. And from then on, the elephant's whole existence takes place within that 30-foot circle.

Let's say the elephant grows up to be 10,000 pounds. Do you think he can still be controlled with the rope?

Sadly, yes. The elephant believes the rope will hold him, no matter how big he gets. And eventually, the trainers don't even need to use the rope anymore. They show the elephant the stake, and he automatically thinks he has to stay within 15 feet of it. The physical rope is now a mental rope.

In the contracting industry, many of us are a lot like those elephants. We start out with a fresh mind. We don't know what to think yet. As we undertake training in our trade, however, we start to be conditioned by the people who are training us, who were conditioned in the same way by the people who trained them.

Acknowledging that there is a mental rope limiting your success is the first step toward freedom.

As a young HVAC contractor, I had a mental rope that tied me to the idea that my services were only worth a certain amount. For example, I used to think the cost to install a gas valve was $300 to $400. Before I left the trades, I was getting about $2,500 for every one of those calls.

You might be thinking, "That's crazy. You must have been ripping people off!" And if I was just selling the customer a gas valve, you'd be right. But I didn't just sell them a gas valve. I also looked at the age of the system, the level of neglect, the service it had received over its lifetime, and the customer's awareness. I knew enough about their whole system to be able to offer the customer at least three options. One at the very bottom, and at least two at the top.

Unfortunately, the industry doesn't look at things as creatively as I do. We're going to talk about how to take the rope off your ankle so you can charge what you need to charge to not

WHAT SHOULD WE DO?

only provide the service customers really want but also be able to live the way you want to live.

We'll examine ourselves and how we see things. We'll look at the reason one technician could have a drain call where he hopes to get $250 and another technician averages $2,300 on every drain-cleaning call he goes on. Or why one technician can only pick up $200 to $250 to fix a bad refrigerant leak and a different technician might pick up $1,500. Or why one HVAC technician sells a furnace for $2,500 and another sells the furnace plus some other services for an average of $10,000—every time.

I don't even want you to take my word for it. I want you to try it for yourself. You don't have to have faith in me, but you do have to have faith in your customer.

Acknowledging that there is a mental rope limiting your success is the first step toward freedom.

Here's what I want you to do on the next call you go on. If you get a call tomorrow for a refrigerant leak, go ahead and give the client a choice to fix the leak, but also search the rest of the system for leaks and offer those services too. If you happen to see evidence of a brand-new condensing unit outside with an old evaporator coil inside and an old line set that has never been replaced, you're going to offer to enhance that too. If you want extra credit, go ahead and offer five years of service—a five-year leak-free warranty on top of it. If you're an electrician, install or fix the electrical box like the customer wants you to, but offer a light bulb change every year for the next 10 years. In other words, promise to come out to their house every single year, or even twice a year, before the bulb is burnt out and change it for them.

Here's what I've found. Statistically speaking, the majority of people, 65 to 75 percent, will purchase right in the middle. Roughly 15 to 20 percent will buy your top offering. The rest, about 8 to 12 percent, will purchase the lowest offering—the very thing you normally sell.

Given the choice, most people will pay more for more service.

If you've never tried this method before, you don't know if I'm right or just making stuff up. So don't trust me. Just offer at least three options to your customer next time and see what happens.

I'll wait.

On second thought, keep reading. Before I go on, though, let me just say this. The people in your company are so lucky to have someone like you who is taking steps to grow personally and professionally. It makes me feel good to know there are owners like you out there who will invest the time to learn a new way of thinking.

Now, back to that mental rope. There are five truths I've found that make us so vulnerable to having that mental rope placed around us.

Given the choice, most people will pay more for more service.

WHAT SHOULD WE DO?

The Five Truths

WE LIVE IN AN INNER-BELIEF PRISON

This prison is created by our own history. It's composed of a series of beliefs that we've accepted as truths, which are based on the conditioning we've received from other people in the industry and the different places we've worked.

One of the beliefs we've accepted is that we believe people do things for *our* reasons and not *theirs*.

Those beliefs might not be the best for us, but they are familiar. Following them is comfortable. And those beliefs are twisted together to form that rope on your leg.

When we think and do something different, we feel uncomfortable. Uncomfortable is not a good feeling. There's a reason they call it a "comfort zone." But comfort is not our friend.

THE PRISON WE HAVE CONSTRUCTED IS NOT BASED IN REALITY

The prison is based on the lens that we see life through, and we refuse to look at it a different way. We think the lens is accurate, but it's not. It's more like a filter that shows us only what we are used to seeing—instead of the various possibilities, which are based in reality.

This filter is what allows you to believe that doing the same exact presentation for every customer is the right move. The problem with that approach is that people are different.

For example, let's say you're selling a green solution for air-conditioning to a guy who doesn't believe in global warming.

He thinks you're a moron, but he lets you finish your spiel because he doesn't want to embarrass you. When you're done, he thanks you for your time and shows you out of the house. And when you're gone, he thinks, "What an idiot. This guy actually believes in this stuff and thinks I'm going to spend extra money on a green solution?"

Or, maybe you think the most important thing in making a decision about an air-conditioning unit is return on investment, so that's what you always lead with. But maybe the prospective customer is sitting there thinking, "What's this guy talking about? My utility bills are $85. What am I going to save? I told him I don't like air-conditioning and I'm looking for the most environmentally friendly solution possible, but he's not listening. I need to get him out of here!"

WE RARELY CHALLENGE THESE BELIEFS

Let's go back to that gas valve that would normally be around $300 to $400. Do you know that on that kind of call, with the right offering, you could get up to $5,000?

How can you do that? You have to be good at coming up with creative solutions for people. You have to be good at listening. You have to be good at finding upgrades, even beyond the thing that's wrong. You also have to be good at offering people things they might not even know they need, such as improved air quality, life-safety systems, or flood-protection systems. Explain the things you have to offer that will improve the customer's life a lot more than just a working gas valve.

There's always $5,000 on the table for that type of call. But why don't we see it?

A lot of us think it's a badge of honor to make something cheaper for a customer. We feel smart that we were able to reduce the price even if it also reduced the amount we got paid. But how smart are you really? Remember my $1,800 furnace for Mary? I thought I was pretty smart to come up with the idea to sell the floor model. But I was about $8,000 off of what the ticket price could have been.

You can be as stupid as I was, and keep repeating the same mistake over and over again and thinking the way you see things is actually true. But what I'm telling you right now is that the belief prison you have created is not based in reality.

I get it. I was just like you. There was a time when I didn't challenge that reality either. See if this sounds familiar. I prided myself on being the best technician. Nobody could outdo me. As a matter of fact, that pride (also known as ego) led me to do lots of things that were not very good. When someone had an out-of-balance blower wheel, I was the kind of guy who would put a two-by-four on it so it would stop vibrating rather than put in a new one.

Or when I was first out in HVAC, my mentor, Bob, told me, "Don't replace the gas valve. We can fix it. That's even cheaper." Or, instead of buying a new bracket, we took it back to the shop and manufactured the part ourselves.

In my defense, I grew up in the 1970s in Illinois dairy country, and if you know farmers, you know that they make everything themselves. So to me, the desire to DIY instead of buy was standard operating procedure.

The problem is that our pride doesn't allow us to challenge these limiting beliefs.

WE HANG ONTO THESE BELIEFS FOR DEAR LIFE

You don't want to let go of your beliefs because you've believed them for a long, long time. You're afraid that admitting your beliefs are wrong would mean part of your life has been wasted.

The truth is everything you learn in life is just a step. Being willing to change your beliefs is another learning step. Maybe you've been doing your trade for 10 years and you've learned a lot along the way. That doesn't mean what you were doing 10 years ago was invalid. Making mistakes is part of learning. We've all made them. With our marriages, with our children, with our homes, with our parents. Mistakes are a part of life. The important thing is to learn from those mistakes or past beliefs. It's an honor to learn from a mistake and be able to say, "I'm smarter than I was before."

WE WON'T CHANGE UNTIL WE ARE WILLING TO LOOK AT THINGS DIFFERENTLY

Let me ask you a question. What is the rope around your ankle? What is the inner-belief prison that you've constructed around yourself? What kind of prices are you charging? What kind of situations do you find yourself in?

If you're an electrician, are you saying to yourself, "Well, it's only a broken switch. Who's going to pay more than $150 for that kind of a call?" When customers bought my electrical service, I told them the parts were free. That's because what I was selling them was my service. I would go over the whole electrical system, look at the load balance, and check every single outlet in the house to make sure they were all safe.

If I was an air-conditioning guy, I'd check the superheat, the compression ratio, and the duct sizing. I'd check the humidity-removal capacity of the system. That's what I'd do with a refrigerant call. What does the refrigerant cost per pound? To the customer, it's free. It comes with my service. You buy the service; the parts and materials are free.

Your results won't change unless you release your old beliefs. And so whatever old-school beliefs you have, you have to be willing to look at things differently. You have to be able to say, "My ego is *not* my amigo."

The first step in releasing yourself from your inner-belief prison is recognizing that you've been operating with an imaginary rope around your ankle—a rope that isn't attached to anything except in your mind. Once you identify those beliefs that are not based in reality, the next step is to consciously open your mind to seeing things differently. That's what will allow you to begin letting go of those beliefs that no longer serve you.

— UNCLE JOE'S RULE 3 —
Your ego is not your amigo!

New Beliefs, New Results

Think you're the only one struggling to embrace the idea of changing your beliefs to achieve more success? Here's an example of a client who was hanging onto his old thinking for dear life until he saw the system in action.

David was an experienced tech at an HVAC company in Bakersfield, California, that I'd worked with the previous summer. One day, he called me up and said he was struggling with the program.

He said, "Joe, I've been working with your program for three months and I'm not selling anything. I'm only closing one call every two weeks."

I asked him how much he was used to selling and he told me $2.5 million. He also said he was the best salesman the company ever had. Now, to me, $2.5 million was mediocre. Anyone should be able to do that amount in sales just by being there and listening to what people want because there's so much that people need. I asked him to tell me more.

"I used to close two or three jobs a day," he said. "Now that I'm using the program, I close like one job every 10 days. The last one was for $8,000. Everybody else is averaging $20,000. I've run 20 calls in the last two weeks, and I've lost all but one. I'm going to wind up losing my house and my wife is going to divorce me, Joe!"

"Well, David, I can't control whether you lose your house and I can't control what's happening in your marriage, so if you called me for real estate or marital advice, you called the wrong person. But let me ask a question. You went on 20 calls and you probably failed on the first 10, right?"

"Yeah. Then I lost nine in a row this week alone. The very last one I sold was yesterday. And that was the first one out of 20."

"Well, did you try going back to your old way? What happened then?"

"Oh yeah, right about the fifth one, I realized I wasn't getting it with this new program. So I went back to my old way of doing it."

"What happened there?"

"I still lost the calls."

"How were you doing before you changed to this program?"

"I was starting to suffer," he admitted. "I was on a bad streak even then."

"You're saying you were doing bad before and you're still doing bad while you're in the program. Is that right?"

"Yes."

"Well, let's talk about the program. But first, tell me about some of the option sheets you've made and the prices you've done."

"Well, I don't have anything on me right now."

"You don't have anything right now or you don't have anything at all?"

"Well, uh, I don't have anything at all because I didn't even bother writing some of the stuff up. I just said it verbally. I figured why write it up if I'm going to lose the job?"

"You're already imagining losing the job, so you're not even willing to do the service the way you learned it. What if you didn't care if you lost the job or got the job, but just did the service first? And what if you stopped worrying about what's going to happen to you at the end of the call? Right now, you're creating a self-fulfilling prophecy. You're going into calls thinking they are going to fail, so you're making that a reality. Your beliefs create your results."

Crickets.

"It might be easier for me to just show you how Pure Motive Service works," I said. "Let's try something. The next call you go on, I want you to text me the first names of everybody in the family—the husband, the wife, the kids, the dog. I'll give you bonus points for the grandma. You text all the names to me and let's just see how that call goes."

Probably to get me off the phone, David agreed.

The next day, he texted me, "I'm on the call right now. The names are Pamela and Donald. They have two kids, Michael and Anna."

I texted him back, "What do they do for a living? What kind of business? What do they do for fun? Find that stuff out."

"Pamela works at the emergency room. Donald works as a consultant in the medical industry. He travels for business. They go on vacation to Disney World every year with the kids."

So now we knew her job, his job, that they have two kids, and where they go on vacation.

I was just walking him through the interview process using the nine major accomplishments.

About 30 minutes later, David texted me, "Joe, these people really do need the ductless solution in this house because what they want is not going to work with the current ductwork. I'm going to write up the option sheet."

I texted back, "Good call."

Another 15 minutes went by, then David texted me a picture of the option sheet.

I texted, "Put the names of the people on there so they can see the platinum plus plan means more time for the family, and it's a complete solution. Put the kids' names on there, and then tell them how the air quality is going to be good for the kids.

And then just show it to them. Say, 'Here are all the options. The premium one is designed just for your family. The midrange one has a lower warranty. The economy one is basic. Take a look at all these options and choose the one that's right for your family.' Then before you present, call me and put me on speaker so I can listen to what happens. Tell them I'm a technician in training."

When he called, I heard David deliver the options exactly as I had outlined them. Great!

Then I heard Pamela say, "So that top option is the one we really need, though, isn't it?"

David replied, "Well, it's the premium option. It's got the best service and the best warranty, so if you want to save the most money on utilities, that's the best one. So, what should we do?"

Pamela said, "OK, let's just do that one."

David said, "Are you sure? We've got some cheaper options."

Pamela said, "Nope, we don't want those. We want the premium one."

And so she bought a $59,000 job, and David made the sale with just that little bit of coaching.

Once he was back in the truck, David called me. Before I could say anything, he said, "You got lucky on that one. It was just a good customer."

I said, "Well, OK, then let's try another one."

We did another call like that, and he sold $24,000.

"Are you starting to see how this works?" I asked him. "What are we doing now that you weren't doing before?"

"I'm getting everybody's names. I'm starting to learn about the people, and it's making it easier to make the option sheet.

People are selling themselves; I'm not selling anything. I feel like I'm lucky on every call now."

"Well, what do you think of that?"

"It's a game changer. Thanks a lot, Joe."

And sure enough, he went from selling $8,000 in two weeks to $120,000 in one week. And ever since then, he's never had a week under $120,000. Even when he had fewer calls, he still sold more stuff because he knew how to connect with the customers.

When I asked him what shifted for him, David said, "I've got more time to connect with people now because I'm not really worried about what I'm going to write up. I know to go ahead and make a connection first. That makes it easy to write the options up, and that's it."

This is a classic case of how worrying too much about possible negative outcomes actually leads to failure. Your beliefs create your results. People who are successful don't let their fears stop them; they use fear as a barometer. Fear is a signal that you have to change something or pivot and stop thinking about yourself. Stop thinking about selling the job. Start thinking about connecting with people first. Then, let the system create the solutions. You're just the facilitator.

— UNCLE JOE'S RULE 4 —
To change your beliefs, you first need to understand how they work. Your beliefs are creating your results.

In the next chapter, you'll learn why you must leave your own inherited anxieties and beliefs about money in the truck so you are free to create and present the high-ticket options that your clients deserve—even if you would never consider buying them yourself.

 **BULLSEYES**

- Your beliefs create your results.

- The mental rope we inherit is the biggest obstacle to creating the results we want.

- There are five truths that we've accepted that keep us stuck: we live in an inner-belief prison, the prison we have constructed is not based in reality, we rarely challenge these beliefs, we hang onto these beliefs for dear life, and we won't change until we are willing to look at things differently.

- Stop thinking about selling the job. Start thinking about connecting with people first. Then let the system create the solutions.

- Your ego is *not* your amigo.

Chapter 5
LEAVE YOUR MOTHER IN THE TRUCK

Most contractors don't come from rich stock. Most are from Middle America, and many are people who used to be factory or restaurant workers. If you or your parents ever worked one of those jobs, working in a service contracting business seems like going on vacation, doesn't it?

My Family's Money Story

My dad was a plumber in the Chicago area in the 1960s and retired in 2000. He worked industrial and commercial types of jobs—big projects like at O'Hare International Airport.

The 1970s were a terrible time of recession. If you were in the trades, you were out of work—a lot. My dad would work one half of the year and be laid off the other half. I remember the first time it happened. My dad came home the Friday after Thanksgiving in 1972 and told my mom, "Yep, I got the pink slip. We'll have to wait until April when the project starts up again."

About the middle of December, we had a family meeting. Dad said, "Guys, Christmas isn't going to be very good this year." Christmas at our house was never really about material possessions; nonetheless, the tape of that conversation plays in my head to this day.

Around that same time, my dad worked as a bartender and a school janitor for $3.50 an hour. He took a job for half the pay just to make ends meet. I still remember the look of dejection on his face when he got home each day.

I'll bet you have a story like this one somewhere in your life, a time when you or your parents went through financial struggles or when you heard your mom and dad argue about money. What invariably happens is that your mother (or father) sets some rules—spoken or unspoken—about how the family deals with not having enough money.

Here are five ways a family can react to their money problems, how they may affect your ability to serve your clients, and why you need to leave your mother in the truck when you go out on calls.

The Five Family Money Taboos

TALKING TO STRANGERS ABOUT MONEY

In my family, money was always tight. So we never, ever talked to strangers about money because we never wanted to embarrass our parents.

When we finance or do a payment program for a client, we're going to have to talk to them about money, right? But it's only natural that you'd be uncomfortable asking people something like what they paid for their home.

DIY MENTALITY

Another thing that happens when you grow up with no money is that you are used to doing things yourself. So what do you expect your customer to do when he says he wants an electrician? You're expecting him to react the way you would and want the easiest solution and cheapest price. It's in our heads!

RESEARCH ADDICTION

Having no money also forces you into doing a lot of research to make sure you are always getting the most value for the lowest possible price.

Are you a big researcher? What are you projecting onto your buyer about the way they should purchase? I'm not saying you should expect them to make a snap decision, but why do we always assume they wouldn't?

IT'S A BADGE OF HONOR TO BUY (AND SELL) CHEAP

You love to find a good deal, even if it's not the best quality, so you see it as a badge of honor to make things cheaper for people. Is that really valid? If you do find a way to make things cheaper, will the quality be higher? (The answer is no.) You get what you pay for, right?

YOU'RE STRAPPED SO YOU ASSUME EVERYONE ELSE IS TOO

If you're in debt, what does that say about your ability to talk about money in a neutral fashion? If you have bill collectors calling, how does that affect your ability to negotiate? How does it affect your ability to price things out when you see other people struggling as much as you?

It's hard to sell a high-end solution if you're in debt. It's easy to start overempathizing with people, thinking, "They are just like me. They don't have the money either."

The bottom line is we shouldn't concern ourselves with our client's financial state because the truth is we don't know what it is. Write this on a Post-it note and put it on your mirror: "Money is not my master. I don't focus on money. I only focus on quality, reliability, safety and health, and the service I provide."

When it comes to engaging with clients, you need to leave your mother—her concerns, her values, her fear, her anxieties, and her beliefs about money—in the truck. You're the person who has been trained. You're the professional who knows how to handle people, who is going to be successful on this call.

*Money is not my master. I don't focus on money.
I only focus on quality, reliability, safety and health,
and the service I provide.*

No More Buyer Profiling

Profiling buyers is not effective. It never has been. Would you want to be profiled? If you walked into a place and someone said, "Don't show them the pricey stuff," would you think that is good customer service? How many of us hold back that service right now from our customers?

You're like a card dealer in Las Vegas. You're not making any judgments. You just deal the cards—that is, the six options—then let the client decide what to do. Leave your mother in the truck because success starts right now.

In the next chapter, you'll learn the techniques I use to not only create the right big goals but also enlist others' support in visualizing them into reality.

— UNCLE JOE'S RULE 5 —
*Leave your mother in the truck!
Don't sell the way you'd buy.*

 **BULLSEYES**

- At some point your parents set some rules—spoken or unspoken—about how the family deals with not having enough money.

- There are five common money taboos: talking to strangers about money, DIY mentality, research addiction, the belief that it's a badge of honor to buy (and sell) cheap, and the assumption that because you're strapped everyone else is too.

- Profiling buyers is not effective and prevents you from providing the best service.

- You're like a card dealer in Las Vegas. You're not making any judgments. You just deal the cards—that is, the six options—then let the client decide what to do.

- Leave your mother in the truck! Don't sell the way you'd buy.

Chapter 6
THE GOAL PARTY

In the 1970s, there were two young men who roomed together at a Texas university. One was a great golfer who said he wanted to win the Masters Tournament someday. His roommate wanted to be an announcer for CBS. "I'll probably be the guy interviewing you after you win," he said. They would go back and forth, practicing for their future interview at the Masters.

The golfer's name was Fred Couples and the journalist's name was Jim Nantz.

Years later, Couples did win the Masters and Nantz was the guy who interviewed him. After it was over, they embraced each other and said, "We did it. We made it together."

Those two had very high goals, right? They not only knew exactly where they wanted to go but also believed it was attainable. And their beliefs allowed them to create those results. The point is, you're more likely to reach your destination if you have one.

The idea of a goal party is about figuring out exactly which destination you're after.

Creating High Goals

You're reading this book because you want to grow your business by learning how to sell and create more value. Let's see how we can make that goal crystal clear.

Remember, I knew I wanted my grandfather's Ford Fairlane. I couldn't wait to get behind the wheel and drive it. I thought about how I was going to clean up the rust on the back fender, and I even got the materials to do it. I knew that car—the shade of blue, what the interior looked like—down to the last detail.

The same thing happens when you buy a house or rent an apartment. You walk into it and love it, and suddenly nothing else matters except how you're going to get that place. I could teach you the basics of the Pure Motive Service system and you could say, "OK, I'll give it a try," but I know the effect would be only temporary because you don't yet understand how operating within the system is connected to your own goals.

If you did know how to create more value for your customers, if you did know how to get more consistency, what impact would it have on your life? If it doesn't positively impact your life, there's no point in doing it.

You're more likely to reach your destination if you have one.

THE POWER OF CLARITY

To understand what impact learning the Pure Motive Service system is going to have on your life, you'll need a clear picture of what accomplishing your goal might look like, feel like, and even smell like.

Remember, once you had that burning desire inside of you to get that house or car or whatever you wanted, nothing was going to stop you. You need to feel the same way about what you're doing every single day out there in the field. You can't just go on calls and say, "We'll see what happens." You have to have a crystal-clear vision for what *will* happen.

Justin, an HVAC tech I know in Memphis, Tennessee, averages about $40,000 a week doing the exact same job that many of you do. That's nearly $8,000 a day on average. He's also serving the exact same types of clients you do. He's able to bring in these amounts because he has high goals and is clear on what he wants to accomplish each and every day.

If I spontaneously said to you, "Tell me your life goals," that would be pretty scary, wouldn't it? So I'm not going to ask that. I'm going to frame it a little bit differently. I'm going to show you how to have what I call a goal party.

GOAL PARTY

A goal party is where we get together with others and share what each of us wants to do. You can have this "party" with just one other person, or with a group of people. The reason I call it a party is because it's about getting together with other people to celebrate one another's goals.

You might be thinking, "I don't want to share my goals with others. I'm afraid someone might try to kill my dreams." I understand why you might think that. When I told people in Chicago that we were moving to California, there were a few who said, "Why the heck are you moving there? You're crazy. It's all earthquakes out there. It's going to fall off the planet, for God's sake. It's terrible!"

Today I'm living among palm trees in endless 80-degree weather so I don't know how terrible it is, but a lot of people warned me I shouldn't do it. Luckily, I had decided a long time ago to live my dreams and not pay too much attention to the people who try to kill them.

BE AN INVERSE PARANOID

In reality, the majority of people I told about my goal wanted to help me get there and wanted to see me make my dreams come true.

Think about how powerful it would be if everyone in your company or family knew exactly what you were trying to accomplish, and if your own belief was that people were always trying to help you reach your goals. I call that being an "inverse paranoid." Rather than being paranoid that people are out to get you, be sure that they want to help you achieve whatever you want. If I tell you what I want to do and I haven't done it yet, you're more determined to help me get there. That's the power of the goal party.

Inverse paranoia applies to your relationship with your client too. A guy named Clotaire Rapaille wrote a book called *The Culture Code*. Rapaille studies the way people purchase and does a lot of research on persuasion. I interviewed him a while back for my website. In the interview, he said he wanted my clients to know this: "Everybody who calls a service provider to work in their home is opening up the heart of their family to an outsider. So when they select you, they think you are a 12/10 already, or else they wouldn't have exposed you to their family."

Your clients want to help you succeed. Your job is to make sure you're running the call in such a way that you'll stay a 12/10 throughout the entire thing. This book will show you how.

— UNCLE JOE'S RULE 6 —
Become an inverse paranoid who believes everyone you meet is trying to help you.

FROM 100 GRAND TO MILLIONAIRE

When I decided to start consulting, my goal was to see how many people I could help earn $100,000 a year. My next goal was to see how many millionaires I could create. Now my goal is to see how many people I can help become millionaires based on the information in this book alone.

I am clear on what I want, and I've surrounded myself with a whole lot of people who know my goals and are actively helping me achieve them. That's how powerful this concept is.

The goal party starts with . . . goals! Goals are things you want to do, be, or have, and I'm going to teach you the process of figuring that out.

Do, Be, Have

This goal-setting approach was made famous by an author named Jack Canfield, a success coach who wrote the *Chicken Soup for the Soul* books. He also wrote a book called *The Success Principles*, which contains 67 timeless principles. I followed them, and they took me from being someone who was $471,000 in debt to being completely out of debt within about five years. And I've gone on to achieve a lot more success than I ever dreamed possible.

At first, I was just trying to keep my nose above water. As it turned out, I could do a lot better than that. And I know you are capable of more as well.

Take a minute and think about some of the things you want to do, be, or have. What do you want to *do*? That's all about the action you have to take. What do you want to *be*? That's more of a concept, like being a better father or getting out of debt. The things you want to *have* are probably pretty easy. They could be material things, like having a new car or a new home.

Think big! The clearer you are about the things you want to do, be, or have, the more likely it is that those goals will eventually become real.

Take out a sheet of paper and draw three columns. At the top of the first column, write the word *do*. At the top of the second column, write the word *be*. At the top of the third column, write the word *have*. Then, in each of the columns, write 30 things you want to do, be, or have.

Make the first 10 for yourself, the next 10 for your loved ones, and the last 10 for your community or church organization. They might be intermingled. The thing you want to *do* might be purchase a new home. What you want to *be* is a homeowner. What you want to *have* is a brand-new house. And that's fine because the point of this exercise is to find out those commonalities.

As you make your list, some themes should start to float to the top, where the do, be, and have items are essentially the same thing. Out of those core things (usually five or six), pick three.

Think big. The clearer you are about what you want to do, be, or have, the more likely it is that those goals will become real.

SMALL BIGS

Let's say the first thing you want to do, be, or have is centered around your relationship. You want to *do* more for your wife, *be* a better husband, and *have* a great marriage. This type of goal is a great place to apply what I call "small bigs." Small bigs are small things you can do that produce big results.

For instance, maybe it's Friday after work and your wife says, "Hey, Mike, what do you want to have for dinner tonight?" And you answer, "Whatever," because you don't care. So that's like a Ping-Pong ball that goes back to her.

When it comes to achieving the things you want to do, be, or have, I want you to say no more "whatevers." If your spouse asks your opinion about what you want, tell her what you want! If, for example, you want a steak tonight, you may or may not be able to afford one right now, but nonetheless, still tell her, "I really want a steak, but I'll settle for a pizza." The small act of consistently honoring her requests can make a big impact on your relationship.

Let's say what you want to do is purchase a new home. A "small big" there might be to go on Zillow to explore the type of home you'd love to live in so you can begin imagining you and your family living in that kind of space.

I always start with the *do* column because that's the hardest one. I can want to *have* things and I can want to *be* a certain thing, but taking the actions required to get those things is the hardest part.

Goal Party: The Interview

The first step is to imagine what it would look like, feel like, or even smell like to do, be, or have all of those things. You want to imagine it as though it's already happened.

The problem is if you try to do this by yourself you probably will not be able to think big enough. Having someone interview you about what you want can help you unlock your big dreams. Pick someone who will really cheer you on. The sky's the limit.

Here's an example of what that sounded like when I interviewed a client named Mike whose *do* was to purchase a home, *be* was to be a homeowner, and *have* was a brand-new house.

I said, "Mike, imagine it's five years from now. I've invited you to my beautiful home in Los Angeles. You arrive in a limo because you're doing that great. You ring the bell. I answer the door. We sit down at my kitchen table, and I offer you some sparkling water. Here we go."

Joe: Mike, my God, I haven't seen you in five years. What have you been doing?

Mike: Well, I'm married now, and I'm doing pretty well at work. I was just voted the best technician/salesman in my company.

Joe: Really? That's great! Are you still living in the same house you lived in before?

Mike: I moved out of there, and I'm living in a much nicer part of town now.

Joe: Really? What part of town is that?

Mike: North side. Libertyville.

Joe: What kind of house do you have now?

Mike: It's a brand-new house in a new neighborhood. Really nice. It has an in-ground pool in the back.

Joe: That sounds great. What does it look like?

Mike: It's a two-story red brick house with black shutters.

Joe: How many bedrooms?

Mike: Four. The primary suite has a vaulted ceiling and sliding doors that lead out to a private porch.

Joe: Wow. How about the kitchen? What does that look like?

Mike: It's huge. White cabinets, granite countertops, stainless-steel appliances. There's an island, and a table and chairs in front of a bay window where I can read the paper and drink coffee in the morning. You can't beat it.

Joe: How about the backyard? What does it look like?

Mike: It's big enough for kids and there's a fence for the dog. Huge patio. And we ran gas to the grill so no more hauling those heavy propane tanks around.

Joe: That sounds great. Now tell me about the garage. Knowing you, I bet it fits three cars.

Mike: You're right. Besides the two new SUVs, I've got a brand-new Mustang in there.

And we could keep going on and on. The interviewer asks the questions, and you just give the answers based on what you want, visualizing your future.

*Having someone interview you about what you want
can help you unlock your big dreams.*

DON'T HOLD BACK

The whole point of this party is to not hold back. Let us have it. Lay it on as thick as possible. The goal party is your chance to visualize what it will look like, feel like, or even smell like when you attain your goals.

You should spend some time every day visualizing your goals because the clearer they are in your mind, the more likely it is that you'll take the steps needed to bring them into reality.

Another important aspect of achieving your goals is to begin taking responsibility for everything that happens to you. In the next chapter, you'll learn why that is and a formula that you can use to generate the results you want.

BULLSEYES

- To understand what impact learning the Pure Motive Service system is going to have on your life, you'll need a clear picture of what accomplishing your goal of creating a thriving service business will look like, feel like, or even smell like.

- Enlist someone to interview you about your goals so they can help you think bigger.

- Know that the majority of people you tell about your goals will want to help you get there and see you make your dreams come true.

- Leverage the power of "small bigs," which are microinvestments of your time and energy that add up over time to produce big results.

- Invest time every day to imagine what it would look like, feel like, or even smell like to do, be, or have your goals, as though it's already happened.

Chapter 7
YOU ARE RESPONSIBLE

Think about the great quarterbacks: Joe Montana, Troy Aikman, Tom Brady, and Patrick Mahomes. Their poise in the pocket is a function of their ability to respond effectively to whatever situation that may arise. They are responsible.

Once that ball is snapped, the responsibility for whether or not the team goes forward on that play is literally in the quarterback's hands. He sees a blitz coming and responds with a laser-focused pass to the tight end for a touchdown. Another quarterback might see a blitz coming and run the opposite way, like my favorite team, the Chicago Bears. That unfortunately has described our quarterbacks for a while—guys who run the opposite way when they see what's coming. It's funny, isn't it? (Unless you're a Bears fan.)

You're the Quarterback

When you're out there running calls, you're the quarterback. When you lack the ability to respond appropriately, that's when you start blaming and complaining about the customer. You start saying, "It's their fault. It's their problem. They're the ones who caused this situation, not me." You're putting the responsibility for that call on the customer. You're looking outside of yourself for the reason things are happening, but the answer is not there.

There are people facing the exact same situations you do every day who would walk out of a call with $1,500 from the same guy who just told you he won't pay $150. You weren't wrong. He won't pay $150. But he will pay $1,500. That's the tragedy.

WILLINGNESS IS KEY

There is some good news. Your willingness to take responsibility for your results is the key to your success.

I'm not talking about taking responsibility for things you don't have the power to change. I'm talking about your willingness to change the way you respond to different situations so you can get an outcome you want.

For the purposes of this explanation, let's agree that we can change the way we choose to respond to a given situation. Now that we've agreed on that, there's an equation I want you to know: $E + R = O$, where E stands for an event, R stands for your response, and O stands for the outcome. I first discovered this equation in the book *The Success Principles* by Jack Canfield, which I mentioned in the last chapter.

An outcome is the same thing as a result, but it would have been confusing to have two Rs in the equation. So when you see the word outcome, I want you to think *result*.

Your willingness to take responsibility for your results is the key to your success.

Event + Response = Outcome

What kind of events happen on the calls you go on—things customers say that just blow you away, or make you feel small or like a failure?

Here's an example. You go on a call where there's a problem with the air-conditioning unit and you fix it. Then, you go find the customer and hand him a bill. He looks at it and says, "That was $300? You've only been here 15 minutes! That's $1,200 an hour! What the hell is wrong with you guys?"

The customer's reaction to the bill is the event.

If I was going to blame the event, I'd blame the customer for reacting that way. Maybe I'd counter with my own reaction and say something like, "I'm busy, and it's 98 degrees outside! I had to go fast."

But what if you considered this situation in a different way?

15 MINUTES TO FAILURE

If you only took 15 minutes on a call, how much time did you have to look at the airflow in that system to see if the ductwork was even sized correctly? How many cubic feet per minute (CFMs) are really needed per ton of cooling—400 CFMs per ton? Did you look at the ductwork to see if the return air size was good? And what about the subcooling and the superheat? You made that analysis already, right? I know I'm using a lot of HVAC examples, but you get the idea. Just substitute the elements from your own industry.

Could you do all of that in 15 minutes? No!

So, if you were to take responsibility for that call, what would you have to say?

You'd have to acknowledge you did this call wrong. You didn't take the time to diagnose the entire system, nor did you provide the customer with any other problems or solutions beyond the one you were called out for.

Customers often complain about the price. In that case, the *event* is a customer saying, "What are you, crazy, charging me that much to fix this thing?" Unfortunately, you're not going to change this event. It happened. You might have changed it by creating more value earlier in the call, but once it happens, it's over. You could say something like, "You're paying for a service. You're paying for my knowledge. Parts cost a lot of money." You could talk about the cost of your insurance, trucks, uniforms, tools, education, and overhead, or how you aren't a charity. But the more you say, the more you will lose people. By the way, losing people is an *outcome*—and not one you want.

You can't change an event, but you can influence the outcome of it by the way you respond. A better *response* in this situation is to ask questions. So if somebody says, "You're crazy. That's too much money," my response will be, "Well, John, listen,

I understand. But it's an investment in the comfort of your family. Isn't your family worth the investment?"

And he'll probably say, "Yeah, that's true."

And then I'll say, "All right. What should we do?"

You can't change an event, but you can influence the outcome of it by the way you respond.

STAYING QUIET

Whenever you ask "What should we do?" don't say anything else until the customer answers. The first few times there might be 15 to 20 seconds of silence, and if you're not expecting that it can be nerve-racking. The customer probably isn't used to it either, but if you stay quiet, they'll use that time to decide what they want to do. So give them that space.

Very often they will say, "Well, let's just do this thing. Let's get it over with."

Many times we just talk too much. We talk ourselves out of the sale.

Another thing that happens when a customer challenges you on price is that you just want to go do the job and get the hell out of there as soon as you can. It's the "flight" part of the fight-or-flight response. But if you give in to that response, it won't lead to an outcome you want.

Here's what you need to know. There's no need to justify yourself. You are a professional. The client can see your experience. To turn the situation around, ask the customer a question.

You could say, "Well, John, let me ask you a question. You say it's extremely expensive, and I understand it is a high investment, but when's the last time you bought any service where it was the best quality and the best expertise at the cheapest price?"

And he's probably going to say, "Never."

And you're going to say, "What should we do?"

Here's another example. I'm at the point in a call when I'm asking for the sale. I've shown the client the options and I've said, "So, what should we do?"

They say, "Well, Joe, we need some time to think about this. We'll call you back next week."

A lot of technicians would respond by saying, "OK, just give us a call when you're ready." But they know in their heart that the customer is never going to call back.

The outcome in that scenario is lose-lose. The client didn't get their problem fixed and you spent an hour at that job but didn't sell anything. You're not going to do that. You're going to take that event and add a response that will create the best outcome.

Let's try it again, this time with a customer named Mary. This example assumes you've presented the customer with three options. (Don't worry; I'll explain in detail how to create the full six options later in the book.) For now, just focus on the series of responses that are going to lead Mary to the solution that is right for her.

Mary: Joe, can we take the weekend to think about it?

Joe: Well, sure. The weekend might be of some value. When are you thinking, like until Monday?

Mary: Yeah. Monday would be great.

Joe: OK, let me ask you a question. This top option—we can both agree you're not going to do that one on Monday, right? No matter what, we're not doing that one?

Mary: No, we don't want that one.

Joe: OK, let's get rid of that one. What about the bottom one? The one that's cheapest.

Mary: No, not that one either.

Joe: So you're considering the one in the middle?

Mary: Yes.

Joe: Well, what should we do?

Mary: We might as well go ahead and get it done right now.

See how quick that was? One minute ago, I was not getting the job. Two minutes and a few questions later, I'm getting the job.

There's no need to justify yourself. You are a professional. The client can see your experience. To turn a situation around, ask the customer a question.

BE LIKE TOM BRADY

Like Tom Brady, I'm poised and confident and I'm not leaving. I'm moving forward. I'm marching this team down the field. I am focused on responding to each event in a way that will produce the best outcome for both me and my client.

Remember, one of the Pure Motive Service principles is to be determined. So you have to hang in there. You've got to be that quarterback who is unflappable in the face of conflict. You can't be running away from the line of scrimmage trying to save your own life. You've got to be marching forward, eyes on the field. Even if you got sacked or hit real hard last time, you've got to get up and then change the way things are going on the next call.

That's just one quick example. We'll talk a lot more about being determined and handling objections later in the book.

— UNCLE JOE'S RULE 7 —
Taking responsibility is the gift you give yourself so you can begin improving.

Five Things You Must Give Up

Taking responsibility will also require that you give up five things right now: complaining, saying "I can't," being sarcastic, blaming others, and making excuses. These things are from your inner-belief prison, and they don't serve you anymore.

COMPLAINING

Complaining about someone or something tells me there must be a way you could have changed things. Either change the mind of the person who is in the way of your success or change your involvement. Don't participate in negativity.

SAYING "I CAN'T"

The client may say, "Can you lower the price?" Of course you can. Get them to agree the top option is too much and direct them to the next lowest option you've created for them. Let's say they ask if you can bump the warranty up from 9 to 12 years on that one. If you are willing to do that, say, "If we said we could do that, what would happen then?"

BEING SARCASTIC

Sarcasm is the language of losers. It drives people away from you in a business that depends on your ability to bring them closer. Give people your unconditional friendship and support. Even people who are negative need your help, so stay the course! Stop trying to get out of the call and get into it by finding out more about the customer and raising their self-esteem. (I'll show you exactly how to do that in chapter 10, through creating what I call magic moments.)

BLAMING OTHERS

Think about it this way. Would you blame your kids for not doing their homework if you didn't give them rules and instructions about how and when it needed to happen? No. Well, when it comes to running calls, you are the parent of that call, and it's up to you to take responsibility for guiding the client through the sales process.

MAKING EXCUSES

Let's say you lost another call to a competitor and you're thinking, "It can't be me. I did nothing wrong. It's (always) the customer. They just don't see it the way I think they should see it. They always want it cheaper, and they're always going on the internet to shop."

— UNCLE JOE'S RULE 8 —
Complaining about problems takes time away from what we need to do to solve them.

What if I told you every good technician or salesperson does at least $20,000 to $40,000 a week?

But then there's Rick, who sells HVAC services in Rhode Island. He and his team did $12 million last year—that's $240,000 a week in HVAC equipment sales, just door to door, doing free estimates. This guy has the exact same customers you have, except maybe worse. New Englanders are committed do-it-yourselfers. I mean, everybody's got their own woodshop and built their own house with pegs—they didn't even use nails. So if Rick tried to sell them a new furnace the same way everyone else did, they'd think, "I could probably do it myself. It's just a little sheet metal. No big deal."

But Rick regularly goes in and sells a $20,000 or $30,000 job with services that these customers have never seen before. How? Because he's not focusing on the same thing that everybody else is focusing on. He's looking at himself and saying, "What can I do differently from everybody else?"

Winners Take Responsibility

Great athletes who failed early in their careers but turned it around didn't blame their team or the referees. They blamed themselves. And they focused on learning to play at a higher level, one that would allow them to win a championship.

The same is true for you. Shifting the responsibility for outcomes onto other people makes you a hostage. It gives other people—your clients, your boss, your instructors—the power to determine whether you succeed or fail.

Taking responsibility for everything that happens, and practicing E + R = O, will allow you to make success happen every single time you go on any kind of call, so you can close those deals and bring home the bacon every time.

— UNCLE JOE'S RULE 9 —
Thinking the problem is something or someone else is the problem.

A New Set of Tools

What I'm doing in this book is giving you a whole new set of tools. I expect you to put the tool belt on and give it a try. I'll take responsibility from there.

Here's the catch. You can't use half of what you know and half of what I know and then blame my half if it doesn't work. But if you use 100 percent of what I tell you to do, I'll take full responsibility. And if you fail with the stuff I tell you to do, you'll be the first person in history to have ever failed with it. Use 100 percent of what I'm telling you to do, and I promise it will work.

In the next chapter, you will learn how to spot potential problems early on in the call and exactly how to address yellow lights before they turn into red alerts that will tank the call.

 **BULLSEYES**

- E + R = O stands for Event plus Response equals Outcome. You can't change an event, but you can influence the outcome of it by the way you respond.

- Focus on responding to each event in a way that will produce the best outcome for both you and your client.

- The best response to an event is to ask the client a question.

- The five things you must give up are complaining, saying "I can't," being sarcastic, blaming others, and making excuses.

- Taking responsibility for everything that happens, and practicing E + R = O, will allow you to make success happen every single time you go on any kind of call.

Chapter 8

DON'T RUN THROUGH YELLOW LIGHTS

What does a yellow light mean?

Slow down!

If that brings up images of the character Jim Ignatowski taking his driver's test in the 1970s sitcom *Taxi*, you're welcome. If you're too young, Google it. It's hilarious.

But what is a yellow light in sales?

Slow Down or Stop

A yellow light is a microconflict that arises when a client does something that isn't what we want. It's an important signal that we need to slow down or even stop the call. For example, let's say you've gone through the process and created your six options ranging from premium to economy. You're ready to present them, but only one of the two spouses is home.

Blink, blink, blink goes the yellow light.

The right thing to do is schedule a time to present when they both will be there. Otherwise, they are going to say, "I have to talk it over with my spouse," and your chances of making the sale just got cut in half.

Or maybe you show up at a call and the client says, "Just take a look at the air-conditioning unit and tell me what you think." She told you right away she wasn't going to buy anything, but you think you heard, "I want to fix the air-conditioning unit."

Blink, blink, blink.

You look at the air-conditioning unit and discover it needs freon. You go tell the client and offer to put some in. She says, "I've had this problem before. The last guy who came out was from XYZ company. That guy was a rip-off artist. He charged me $95 to put freon in."

She thinks $95 is too high, and your normal price is higher than that!

Blink, blink, blink.

Now you're getting annoyed. You think, "This call sucks!" To try to salvage it, you say you'll do it for $90. She says, "OK. How about I get back to you on that?"

Blink, blink, blink. The yellow warning lights were blinking big time, but you blew right through them.

There are two types of yellow lights you need to be able to identify: external and internal.

A yellow light is a microconflict that arises when a client does something that isn't what we want. It's a signal that we need to slow down or stop the call.

EXTERNAL LIGHTS

External yellow lights are things that other people say. They're not coming from us. Both spouses not being home when you are ready to present is an external yellow light.

Mary telling you that all she wants is for you to look at the system and how she felt ripped off by the last company is also an external yellow light.

Any objection or conflict that is initiated by something other people say or do is an external yellow light.

External yellow lights should cause us to pause and determine what happened to the client's commitment to getting the work done (if there was one) and then use Pure Motive Service techniques to reengage them in the process.

INTERNAL LIGHTS

Internal yellow lights are wired to the way we feel inside about the things that are being said. Picking up on internal yellow lights can be tougher, especially if you're not very in touch with your feelings.

Luckily, there are some clues. An internal yellow light typically starts flashing when there is some kind of event that makes you feel bad and start thinking things like, "This call sucks."

Like when Mary told you the last guy charged her $95 for freon and she felt ripped off, but then she didn't even agree to the work after you dropped your price.

You already know that Event + Response = Outcome. And you also know how you decide to respond will determine the outcome you get.

Let me show you one way to handle that situation with Mary.

— UNCLE JOE'S RULE 10 —

Thinking "this call sucks" is a signal that there's a yellow light ahead. Slow down!

Handling Yellow Lights

Let's say you did stop and verify that Mary wanted you to fix the air conditioner (not just look at it) and you discovered it needed some freon.

Before you lower your price, you could say, "Well, Mary, I'm not sure what the situation was last year. But if you are saying that if it will cost more than $95 to fix your air conditioner, that eliminates me because there's not anything in my price book below $95. So if you'd like, we could end the call right now. On the other hand, I'd be happy to continue if you are willing to be flexible about the investment being higher to make your family more comfortable. So, what should we do?"

Would somebody who just waited three hours for you to show up at the door eliminate you right now? Probably not. And if they do, then it's probably the best thing for both of you.

What does a yellow light mean? Slow down.

This may be the end of the section about being a student, but believe me, we are just getting started. In the next section, I'll be explaining exactly what it means to be on code and why it is crucial to the way you interact with your client at every phase of the Pure Motive Service system.

BULLSEYES

- A yellow light occurs when the client does or says something that gives us pause.

- External yellow lights are triggered by things that other people say or do. Any objection or conflict that is initiated by something other people say or do is an external yellow light.

- Internal yellow lights occur when something happens that makes you feel bad or uneasy, so you start thinking, "This call sucks."

- A yellow light is an event. And now you know that E + R = O. So the key to handling yellow lights is to recognize that you have influence over the outcome by the way you respond.

TOOLS FOR YOUR SUCCESS

servicemvp.com/tools

* GOAL PARTY WORKSHEET
Think bigger! Get a clear picture of your thriving future starting with this list of questions.

* PERSONAL CONNECTION WORKSHEET
Learn about your clients. Tap into their major accomplishments using these 48 handy connection starters.

* LEAVE YOUR MOTHER IN THE TRUCK WORKSHEET
Evaluate your money mindset. Answer questions to identify your beliefs, ditch buyer profiling, and change your focus to the service you provide.

Scan to download your tools

BE
ON CODE

Chapter 9
BE ON CODE—OVERVIEW

The sun and the wind saw a man on the street in Chicago who had on a jacket.

The sun said to the wind, "I bet I can get that man to take his jacket off before you can."

And the wind said, "No way, I can get him to take his jacket off a lot easier than you can."

"OK," said the sun. "You go first."

The wind cranked up to 90 miles an hour. But the harder he blew, the more the man on the street clutched his jacket. Afraid he'd knock the guy over, the wind stopped blowing and said to the sun, "OK, you're so smart, you try it."

And so the sun cranked up its radiant energy. The clouds started to evaporate and the temperature shot up to 110 degrees with 95 percent humidity. The guy immediately took his jacket off, and the sun won the contest.

The moral of the story is this: Are you going to sell your services just by talking and blowing air, or are you going to use your radiant warmth to get clients to take their jackets off and open their minds and hearts to you?

Selling through Radiant Energy

Think about a time you've felt an instant connection to someone you've just met. That's their radiant energy drawing you in. Now think about a time when you couldn't wait to get out of someone's space because you didn't feel connected. In fact, their energy seemed to be repelling you.

When someone feels connected to you, they are comfortable around you. They feel like they've known you a long time and can easily relate to you, which makes them not only happy to have you in their home but also much more willing to listen to what you have to say. This is called the law of connectivity, and it says that people like to buy from someone they like and trust.

The good news is you don't have to leave whether or not you feel connected to a client to chance. There's a way to consciously create that connection with a client by taking the time to find out who they are so you can uncover their unique buying code.

The law of connectivity says that people like to buy from someone they like and trust.

Uncovering the Buyer's Unique Code

You know how there are building codes you have to follow so your work is safe and will pass inspection? Well, buying codes are basically people codes.

There are also a few universal laws at work here. One is the law of obligation. The law of obligation says that when you do something nice for someone without expectation of anything in return, people love to return that to you. They feel obligated. When your client realizes you have invested in learning about them, it creates an obligation to, at the very least, look at your solutions in a different light.

The other law is the law of balance, which says we need to strike a balance between the emotional and technical aspects of our work. Here's why.

EMOTION VS. LOGIC

We all use a combination of emotion and logic when deciding to purchase something. In fact, the typical purchase decision ratio is 99 percent emotion and one percent logic. That's right, our purchase decisions are based almost entirely on how we feel and just a little bit on how logical the decision is.

And if our clients are making their purchase decisions following that ratio—99 percent emotional and one percent logical—then we need to respect it to stay in balance.

But, as contractors, how are we trained? We're 99 percent logical, and left to ourselves, that's the way we would communicate with clients about what we're doing. I'm not saying you should stop using logic; there has to be some, or you'll have an imbalance the other way. It's just about how you communicate.

So, in addition to diagnosing the problem, we have to diagnose the client because we know that 99 percent of any purchase decision they make is going to be based on their emotions.

You have to find out just enough about how the client and their family members are suffering as a result of the problem they called you about, expressed in their own words.

That way, when you make the presentation, it sounds like, "Oh my goodness, this guy nailed it!" There is no better presentation than one that has the client's words built right into it. But you won't know exactly how to make that presentation until you diagnose the people you're going to present to and find their code.

In addition to diagnosing the problem, we have to diagnose the client because we know that 99 percent of any purchase decision they make is going to be based on their emotions.

Diagnosing the Client

Let's say you got called out to John Smith's house because his garage door wasn't working. You've already introduced yourself. You've also scanned for yellow lights, and the coast seems clear. (There are actually a few more steps to do, but don't worry about those right now. We'll cover them in the next section.) You begin to diagnose John by asking him a series of five questions. His answers will give you some clues about the emotional reasons for your service so you can determine his buying code.

1. How many people are using the system?
2. Who was the person who requested us to come out or found the problem?
3. What did that person say?
4. What did other people say?
5. What was that like? (Don't ask how they feel. It's too direct.)

Here is what this process sounds like in practice:

You: So how many people are using the garage door in this house?

John: Me, my wife, Susan, and my two kids, Jeff and Amy.

You: Who found the problem?

John: My wife. She said she had already loaded the kids in the car, but when she clicked the button to open the garage door, it made a loud noise and the door opened about three inches and then went back down. She pulled the emergency cord hoping she could push it up manually, but the door wouldn't budge.

You: What did she say?

John: I was driving to work when she called. She said she was starting to panic because the car was trapped in the garage, and she had to get the kids to school and get to work for an important meeting. She sounded pretty stressed out.

You: What did your kids say?

John: Jeff is an anxious kid to begin with, so having to get back out of the car and change his routine really upset him. Amy had a test in first period today, so she was worried about missing that.

You: What was that like?

John: It was frustrating to say the least, and everyone was stressed out because the kids were late for school and my wife was late to her meeting at work.

By asking these questions, we force the client to face not just the technical part of the problem but also the emotional part of it. In fact, the client may ask why you're asking so many questions. And the answer is that a system is worthless without the people who use it. To design the right system, you have to know about the people using it.

From Worry to Worry Free

John told you his wife is frustrated and stressed, so that could be a buying code, but he and his wife are also worried about their son's anxiety, so worry is probably a better choice. Here's an example of what that might sound like when presenting: "The top option is called John and Susan's Stress and Worry-Free Garage Door System Repair. I created this option because I didn't want your family to be stressed, frustrated, or have to worry about your son's anxiety."

Uncovering the buyer's unique code is about finding out what the person you're selling to cares about and then adapting your presentation and the title of your top option to align with that. When you find the unique code, you are no longer asking them to spend money on you. You're asking them to invest money in getting their family's life back on track.

Common Buying Codes

Remember, being "on code" means using the client's language to describe the solution to their problem in a way that resonates with them. Here are some sample statements to listen for and their corresponding buying codes. The easiest codes to identify are emotional ones, such as stress, worry, frustration, anger, and fear.

- **Stress:** "Not having hot water is really stressing me out."
- **Worry:** "I'm worried that my son is having such a hard time breathing with no air-conditioning."
- **Frustration:** "The fact that this system has never worked right is really frustrating."
- **Anger:** "I am so mad because I thought this was fixed by the last guy, but here it is broken again."
- **Fear:** "My mother-in-law is visiting this weekend, and I'm afraid she will be uncomfortable."

Other codes have more to do with the client's current state of mind.

- **Time:** "I'm too busy to keep taking time off work to deal with this problem."

- **Hassle:** "I just don't need the hassle of this problem with my family going on vacation."
- **Work:** "I've got to get back to work. I don't have time for this right now."
- **Family:** "My mom's coming in to visit us this week so we have to get this work done."
- **Health:** "I have emphysema, and not having air-conditioning really makes it hard to breathe."
- **Safety:** "I just can't go up in the attic anymore with my knee replacement. It's not safe."
- **Service:** "I've got a lot going on because I'm cooking for the chicken dinner at my church."
- **Comfort:** "We bought this house for $250,000, and it's just not as comfortable as our last one."
- **Caring:** "My wife is coming home from the hospital, so I've got to make sure I can take care of our newborn."
- **Alone:** "Ever since Frank died, and the kids went to school, I'm here in this house all alone."
- **Money:** "I'm not made of money. I'm retired, and I'm on a fixed income."
- **Pride:** "I want Julie's mom to be proud when she comes to visit our house on the Fourth of July."

You can also pull client buying codes from things you discover during the call, either from things they offer during the conversation or items you observe in the home.

- **Sports:** You notice the client is a golfer, hunter, or football, baseball, or basketball fan, so the code would be a sports analogy. For a golfer, the premium option might be called Dave's Masters Electrical System Renovation. You could say, "It's like the green jacket of solutions."

- **Travel:** You see family pictures of different travel destinations, so the code would be a travel analogy. For example, the premium option might be called John's Peace-of-Mind-When-He-Travels System Renovation.

- **Kids:** You notice all the toys and children's books (and actual children) around the home, so the code could be focused on the children. For example, the top option could be called Platinum Keep-the-Kids-Safe-and-Healthy Water-Quality Solution.

- **Military Service:** You notice an American flag and other military decorations in a curio cabinet, so the code could be related to the military. For example, the top option could be called Premium Plus Give John Freedom Complete System Renovation.

- **Environment:** You notice there are wastepaper and recycling bins in their kitchen. The top option might be called Our Signature John's Earth-Friendly Electrical Renovation.

Naturally, there are more nuances to this process, but this is the basic structure. Don't worry; you'll see this process demonstrated again and again in future examples.

— UNCLE JOE'S RULE 11 —
I've talked my way out of an opportunity, but I've never listened my way out of one.

In the next chapter, we're going to learn the most powerful part of this program, which is how to create what I call magic moments. Magic moments create powerful, positive emotional experiences that make it easier for clients to choose a more expensive option.

Out of everything I teach, when it comes to human connection, magic moments move the needle the most.

 **BULLSEYES**

- You begin diagnosing the client by asking five specific questions: How many people are using the system? Who was the person who requested us to come out or found the problem? What did that person say? What did other people say? What was that like? Their answers will give you some clues into the emotional reasons for your service so you can determine their buying code. (Don't ask how they feel. It's too direct.)

- A system is worthless without the people who use it. To design the right system, you have to know about the people who use it.

- Being "on code" means using the client's language to describe the solution to their problem in a way that resonates with them. There are dozens of potential codes. The easiest ones to identify are emotional ones, such as stress, worry, frustration, anger, and fear.

- When you find the client's unique buying code, you are no longer asking them to spend money on you. You're asking them to invest money in getting their family's life back on track.

Chapter 10
MAGIC MOMENTS

I once went on a call in Philadelphia. The client, Eleanor, said there was a problem with the baseboards on the second floor. We were standing in front of the door when, all of a sudden, a man came into the room and hollered, "Get him out of here!"

I took a deep breath and said in a low voice, "Eleanor, it seems like it's not a good time for me to be here."

Eleanor waved me forward and said, "Come on upstairs. I'll tell you what's going on."

Once we were upstairs, she said, "Joe, my husband, Harry, he's a brilliant guy. He was a professor at Princeton University, but now he's got Alzheimer's and he is suffering from dementia. So I'm sorry about that. It has been tough. I love him so much, but I'm not sure what I should do."

I replied, "I'm sorry. I hope if I'm ever in Harry's condition someday my wife loves me as much as you love him because you are going through a lot. It's certainly great to see you take care of your husband and honor him so much."

Eleanor took a tissue from her pocket and dabbed the tears from her eyes. "Thank you, Joe. That means a lot."

Magic moments allow you to quickly establish a powerful emotional connection with your client (or any other human being for that matter).

In this case, the magic moment was me honoring the effort that Eleanor was putting in related to the challenge of taking care of a spouse with Alzheimer's and making her feel seen.

Magic moments raise the esteem of your clients or those around you and create those warm feelings and an experience the client will always remember.

Every call has the potential for a magic moment like this one within it.

What Is a Magic Moment?

Magic moments are the most powerful part of the Pure Motive Service system, which calls for us to keep the customer's best interests front and center at all times.

A magic moment is that point in time when another person's self-perception becomes more positive as they receive your genuine praise of their efforts.

The law of esteem says that when clients feel good about themselves, they feel more entitled to better-quality solutions and are more magnetically drawn to you. They look at you in a different light. They experience you as someone who not only sees them but also makes them feel good about what *they* see. This is important because there's a subconscious part of all of us that tries not to spend a lot of money, especially when it comes to home services.

If you've followed this program and have provided the client with premium, midrange, and economy options, they may be thinking, "Wow, I really would like to have that premium option," but it will be hard for them to decide because of the subconscious part of them that says they don't really deserve it.

A magic moment affirms that they do in fact deserve it because of the efforts they make with their kids, spouse, or career. And that when they put in that kind of effort, they deserve to have a service provider put forth effort for them too. That way they can focus on what they are good at and you can focus on what you're good at (heating, air-conditioning, plumbing, garage door repair, etc.).

A magic moment is that point in time when another person's self-perception becomes more positive as they receive your genuine praise of their efforts.

Magic Moments and You

Magic moments are actually the hardest thing I teach because I'm asking you to change as a person, to upgrade yourself to be more generous with your listening abilities, to take the time to show people you really care by making them feel seen and heard, and to make that human connection.

When you master magic moments, your calls will become much easier because any clients you make feel better about themselves will automatically feel better about you too.

Magic moments can happen at any time—at the beginning of the call, in the middle, at the end, or even after you've sold a service. Any time you feel the client's mood shifting or their attention drifting is a good time for a magic moment.

Victories and Challenges

Magic moments are built by praising efforts related to people's victories and challenges. They're authentic responses to finding out something special about your client or their family, particularly about their courage, care, sacrifice, dedication, determination, or bravery related to a victory or challenge they have experienced.

Examples of victories are coaching a Little League team, a daughter graduating from college or getting married, a recent exciting vacation, or a promotion at work. Examples of challenges are a son with ADHD, a wife with cancer, a parent who just passed away, or a husband with Alzheimer's.

Letting them know how you feel about their efforts tells the client you have heard what they said and can see the impact of those efforts.

Praise the Efforts

The key to magic moments is to praise the efforts of the person you're talking to. Don't praise material things because that's dangerous. If you say, "Oh, nice piano you've got there," what are you going to do when you find out that it's the ex-wife's piano?

Praising effort is the only thing that won't be offensive because you're using information that came directly from them.

You also have to be careful not to pass judgment. Think about it. If you say something like, "You're a good mom," in a way you're judging that person by saying they're good. You're only seeing what's in front of you. You have no idea what's going on behind the scenes. It's the same if you say, "You're a great dad." Maybe he thinks, "Right. He doesn't know that I'm an alcoholic." In both cases, you lose credibility because you don't know the truth.

Here's an example of the type of thing you can safely say, which will have the desired effect. Let's say the client, Mike, told you he had to take time off work to be there to let you in. (Making time is always a challenge.) You could say, "Can I just say something? I really appreciate the effort you're making to take time off work to try to get the heat back on for your family. They're very fortunate to have a husband and dad like you. It makes me feel good that you're taking that time for your family, so thank you for sharing that with me."

So the formula is to praise and then validate a specific effort they are making rather than praising who you think they are as a person. Because it might not be true! It's also important to share how their effort makes *you* feel. Tell people, "It makes me feel good when I see people who [insert effort you're praising]." And then thank them. Say, "Hey, thanks for sharing that. It makes me feel good. It's going to help me do better service."

You'll remember from the tire shop example that the first thing I did after I learned Lisa's name was praise her efforts by saying, "OK, well first of all, thank you for making the effort to come into the tire shop today." And then I told her how I felt by saying, "I appreciate the effort you're making, and it makes me feel good that you are worried about the safety of your kids and about getting to work and school on time."

Even if you just do one of those last two, either say how you feel or say thank you, that will go far in raising the client's self-esteem and creating the connection you're after.

— UNCLE JOE'S RULE 12 —
Praise the effort, not the outcome.

The Four Steps of Magic Moments

Let's revisit the magic moment with Mike so you can see the steps in action.

CREATE THE MOMENT

You: Can I just say something?

WHAT SHOULD WE DO?

Now, wait for him to give permission. By asking permission to share something, you are communicating to the client that something is about to happen. This is how you create the moment.

Mike: Sure, what is it?

PRAISE THE EFFORT

You: I really appreciate the effort you're making to take time off work to try to get the heat back on for your family. They're very fortunate to have a husband and dad like you.

The client, Mike, is the source of this magic moment, so it's not like you're saying something phony. He was the one who told you about it and brought it up. You're just commenting on the effort you noticed he's making.

SHARE HOW YOU FEEL

You: It makes me feel good that you're taking that time for your family.

Here you are using the universal law of social validation to affirm that someone else sees the value of the effort the client is making.

SHARE GRATITUDE

You: So thank you for sharing that with me.

Mike: You're welcome.

Two other things you can recognize and thank people for are the opportunity and their kindness.

Praise and Self-Perception

Why do we focus so much on magic moments? Because praise has the power to change our self-perception. No matter how low or down we feel, when somebody praises our efforts, it makes us feel better. We want to do business with people who make us feel good.

Big brands, like Apple and Nike, are aware of this concept and spend millions in marketing to raise your self-esteem. They know the better you feel about yourself, the more likely you are to treat yourself to their premium product or option. When you buy their premium product, they want you to say to yourself, "I feel I deserve the best." They also know when someone else sees you with that product, that person will perceive you as someone with high self-esteem.

Big brands like Apple and Nike know the better you feel about yourself, the more likely you are to treat yourself to their premium product or option.

When you buy an Apple Macbook for $4,000 versus a no-name PC laptop for $400, or when you spend $200 for a pair of limited-edition Nike sneakers instead of $50 for the knockoffs, that says something about you. The same is true if you go to Starbucks instead of making your coffee at home or buy a Tesla Model X instead of a domestic SUV.

The problem is that the self-esteem of the majority of Americans is very poor. In fact, several studies indicate 85 percent of us suffer from some kind of diminished self-esteem. And people who don't feel good about themselves will find it very difficult to spend more than the bare minimum on anything—even if it isn't in their best interest long term.

That's why you need to learn how to praise your customers in the right way so they will be in the mindset that will allow them to make the best decision about which option to buy from you—even if they do not choose your top option.

Very few people will go for the top option, maybe 15 percent. Most people who are in the positive frame of mind you helped create will choose the middle option. Just a few will choose the cheapest option, which I found is the sole option most techs were used to offering before learning this method. The good news is that once you learn this system, you will become skilled at putting your client in a positive frame of mind by building up their self-esteem with the right kind of praise.

Make a Magic Moment Exercise

When I teach magic moments at the Total Immersion Summit, we immediately start practicing. You need another person—a spouse, child, friend, waitstaff, or retail associate. Go attempt to create a magic moment with them and see what happens.

Remember, you are acknowledging the efforts of the person's courage, care, sacrifice, dedication, determination, or bravery related to a victory or a challenge. Here's an example you can use as a template. The next time you go to a restaurant, take the waitperson aside, ask their name, and say the following:

- [Name], can I share something?
- I wanted to tell you how much I admire the effort you are making to serve our table and make sure we have everything we need.
- It makes me feel good to see someone as dedicated to customer service as you are.
- Thank you so much for all your efforts to ensure we have a good experience.

Can I Give You a Hug?

Here's a powerful example of a magic moment that Rick Picard, longtime Service MVP client and $12 million (and counting) earner, shared with me:

"I went to a house to do an HVAC call, and the first thing I noticed was New York Giants stuff all over the place. That's unusual in Massachusetts because the New England Patriots are the local football team.

"After I introduced myself, I said, 'Who is the Giants fan?' The client, an older woman, said, 'Oh, that was my husband,

Bill. He had cancer and passed away last year. He just loved the New York Giants, so I keep that stuff around to remember him.'

"I said, 'Well, can I just tell you something? Bill was so lucky to have a woman like you who still honors his memory even after he is gone. And in a way you're making him live on through those memories. He's here right now because we're talking about him, right?' She had tears in her eyes. And then she said, 'Can I give you a hug?'

"As I looked around the house more, I started to notice everything her husband had done, like the deck was heavy-duty. That told me what she was used to, which helped me when it came time to create the options.

"In presenting the top option, I told her, 'I looked at some of the stuff Bill did around the house. I want to make sure we do it to the standard he would have wanted. I want to honor his memory by doing a premium job. I don't want you looking at the work we do and thinking it's substandard compared to what Bill would have done if he were still here.'

"Of course, I did find a way to make it affordable for her. I knew she was on a fixed income, so I did a monthly payment plan on it. I knew it would increase the value of the house, save her money on utilities, and save her money on repairs down the road.

"The Pure Motive Service approach changed my whole mindset from having to 'close' people during a sale to making sure every single thing I did had a pure motive behind it. My closing rate went from about 23 percent to about 86 percent when I shifted my focus from closing the customer to providing Pure Motive Service and creating magic moments."

— UNCLE JOE'S RULE 13 —

*The way you make other people feel tells people
everything they need to know about you.*

In the next chapter, we are going to begin a deep dive into the power of language and the law of verbal packaging where you will learn about the positive and negative qualities of certain words and how to use those words to communicate effectively with your client.

 **BULLSEYES**

- Magic moments allow you to quickly establish a powerful emotional connection with your client (or any other human being for that matter).

- Magic moments are built by praising efforts related to people's victories and challenges. They're authentic responses to finding out something special about your client or their family, particularly about their courage, care, sacrifice, dedication, determination, or bravery related to a victory or challenge they have experienced.

- The four steps of magic moments are create the moment, praise the effort, share how you feel, and share gratitude.

- Praise has the power to change our self-perception. No matter how low or down we feel, when somebody praises our efforts, it makes us feel better. We want to do business with people who make us feel good.

- When you master magic moments, your calls will become much easier because any clients you make feel better about themselves will automatically feel better about you too.

Chapter 11
THE POWER OF LANGUAGE

I was once on a plane that was in line to take off when smoke started billowing out from one of the jet engines. Suddenly the plane was surrounded by fire trucks and other vehicles with emergency lights and sirens. The flight attendant got on the intercom and told us we were "experiencing a delay in our departure due to slight mechanical difficulties." I wondered at that time what a major difficulty would look like!

Every word a flight attendant says has been carefully selected to manage passengers' emotions, including the potentially lifesaving health and safety instructions they must give before the plane takes off. For instance, if your flight is going to take you across a body of water, the flight attendant will say, "Your seat cushion may be used as a flotation device in the event of a water landing." Imagine the distress it would cause if instead they said, "If the plane is getting ready to crash in the middle of the ocean, start tearing your seat apart and then hold onto the seat cushion for dear life so you don't drown."

Institutions of every kind—from hospitality to health care—have learned how to use words to manage the emotions and expectations of their customers. Those who do it successfully are following the law of verbal packaging, which states that the more skillful a person is in the use of language, the more persuasive they will be.

It's time for us, as service professionals, to take a page out of their playbook and use this law to benefit both our clients and our businesses.

The Broken Wire

I was working with a master electrician named David in Denver, Colorado, and we were dispatched to a call where half of the house had no power. David was very proud of his license and told me about the years of effort he had put in to become a master in his trade.

When we got to the home, the client, Susan, told us there was no power in all the bedrooms in the entire house. She said she was worried because she was a single mom and her kids couldn't use the TV or play video games, and no homework was getting done because there were no lights on. David did a great job of telling Susan how fortunate her family was to have a mom like her who was taking the time to restore the power in the home.

After seeing David do a magic moment, I felt confident this call was on the right track. We headed downstairs, and David took apart the panel cover and found that all the circuits in the home had power. Then we moved into the bedrooms. David examined the voltage to each outlet and switch, which were completely dead.

As an observer, I was already mentally putting together options to restore the power in this 50-year-old house, where the premium option would be to restore all the circuits and conductors and the bottom option would be a diagnostic fee to just find the broken conductor.

As we walked from the bedrooms toward the kitchen, Susan stopped us to ask what we had found so far. I thought David, who knew our system, would realize that it was too soon to talk about his findings since we hadn't even come close to writing up our options.

I was wrong.

FROM 12/10 TO 0/10

As a master electrician, David had walked into the call as a 12/10. But he started to tell Susan, using the weakest language possible, what we had found so far in our diagnosis.

"I found the power at the panel, and that's working fine, but there's no power in the bedroom, which means there's a broken wire somewhere," he said. David went on to tell Susan that he didn't know where the wire was broken, and that he'd need between $500 and $1,000 to take apart some of the drywall in the finished basement to search for it.

Susan asked him about what we could do right now to get the power back on.

David, again using weak language, replied, "I have no idea until I take apart the drywall, and then we'll see what I find. It could be anywhere."

The uncertainty of David's language forced Susan to start looking for another source of information. She said, "I'm going to call my father who's a general contractor in Iowa. Maybe he can help me figure this out." Then, even though Susan was literally telling David that he was confusing her, he agreed that calling the father would be a good idea.

David's weak language had changed Susan's opinion of him from a 12/10 to a 0/10 in less than five minutes.

The law of verbal packaging states that the more skillful a person is in the use of language, the more persuasive they will be.

RECOVERING HIS VALUE

Before Susan could call her father, I called a time-out. In front of Susan, I said, "David, as a master electrician, can you tell us exactly what you do know at this point?"

"Yes," he said, "I can definitely tell you that the wire is broken between the panel and the bedrooms."

I asked Susan, "Could David and I take some time to go over the system findings and come up with some solutions before we call your father?" David and Susan both agreed that was a great idea. We could get our facts together in case we needed to call her father for his opinion. David and I went back down to the basement, and that's where I coached him about sharing only what we *do* know and what we *can* do rather than focusing on the things we don't know yet.

This was David's aha moment. I asked him, "What's a way we could fix the circuit without actually finding the problem?" David said we could just replace the circuit from the bedrooms all the way to the panel, and that would solve the problem. I also mentioned we could have a bottom option where we just diagnose the problem but make sure Susan understood that there were no guarantees.

— UNCLE JOE'S RULE 14 —
Only say what you can do, not what you can't do.

David and I wrote up six options, starting with the premium one at the top, which would solve the problem completely, all the way down to the economy option of just looking at it to determine the problem. After I finished coaching him on how to present all of the options, we went back upstairs and David began to present the solutions to Susan as we'd discussed.

David said, "Susan, I don't like what I'm seeing here. We have a fracture on the conductor between the panel and all the bedrooms on the second floor. Now, my greatest fear is that the home is 50 years old and that the conductors will continue to fail in the future due to age. So I worked up some premium, midrange, and economy options to get the problem fixed. The premium option will fix the problem not only now but also in the future so it never happens again. The midrange and economy plus options will also fix the problem, but with fewer enhancements, and the basic economy choice will look at the problem and fix any accessible fractures we can find in those conductors."

David then asked Susan if she still wanted to call her father so he could hear the information before he started explaining it to her. But Susan said, "We don't need to call him. It sounds like you know what you're talking about. Just go ahead and get this thing fixed the right way."

If the client has called you to provide them with service, in their mind, you are already a 12/10. Using power language ensures that it stays that way throughout the call.

David went on to make a masterful presentation of all the problems and solutions. He called the top option the Gives Susan Peace of Mind Complete Electrical Conductor Renovation option. He said, "I did this for you, Susan, because by replacing all the 50-year-old conductors in the home, it eliminates any problems that may happen in the future."

As you can imagine, things turned around for the better as David exuded new confidence in his tone and delivery of the information, leading to Susan purchasing the premium option.

If the client has called you to provide them with service, in their mind, you are already a 12/10. Using power language ensures that it stays that way throughout the call.

POST-CALL REVIEW

In the truck after the call, David and I discussed what had happened. In the first part of the call, David chose to talk about the problem before he had any solutions to offer. This confused Susan to the point that she wanted to call her dad—who was 500 miles away and wasn't even an electrician—to diagnose the problem over the phone!

In the second part of the call, David talked about what he did know and what the different solution options were. He came across as more confident and committed in his approach, which allowed Susan to feel confident in David's capabilities and to commit to purchasing the best solution we had available.

Instead of winging it, David began to leverage the law of verbal packaging, which, as a reminder, states that the more skillful a person is in the use of language, the more persuasive they will be.

Telling the client what you can do versus what you can't is one aspect of verbal packaging. Another aspect is knowing when it's best to say nothing at all.

Silence Is Golden

Have you ever heard somebody talk way too much when they were trying to sell you something? I was on a call once where the service provider went on and on so much that the client got up in the middle of his speech to switch their load of laundry. To remedy this situation, I got him to commit to using only two phrases to close the deal after he gave the prices: "I understand," and our benchmark question, "What should we do?" The idea was he would say only one of these two phrases and then shut up until the client talked next.

Upon implementing this new strategy, his closing rate went from 22 percent to 63 percent. He remarked how many jobs he must have lost because he talked too much. He said he couldn't remember losing any jobs when he just shut up.

Once you give the client the prices, the best thing you can do is stay quiet and let them think it through. When you do need to talk, however, I want you to become aware of some of the weak words you've been using and start replacing them with power words.

Once you give the client the prices, the best thing you can do is stay quiet and let them think it through.

Power Words vs. Weak Words

There are three pairs of common words where one is a power word that will make your client feel more confident in you and your service and the other will basically do the opposite. They are when versus if; can versus try; and will versus hope. There are also two single words that are considered superpower words—but and because. Let's unpack each example.

WHEN VS. IF

We use the word *when* to refer to the time of a future situation or condition that we are certain of. Are you certain you can fix the problem? Yes! The word *if* is a weak word that implies a possible situation or condition. If you say, "If I could get this fixed for you," or "If we can get the parts," the client is thinking, "Can this guy fix my problem or not?" *When* is your power word. Say, "When we get these parts, when I get this thing fixed for you, when I renovate this equipment, it will work perfectly fine. It will be just like brand-new."

CAN VS. TRY

As Yoda once said, "Do or do not; there is no try." There's only the word *do*. We don't try to do something, we do it. We state when we can do something and then we follow through on that commitment. So instead of saying, "I'll try and get this in tomorrow for you," say, "I will get it in tomorrow for you." And then make sure that happens. Another word I want you to replace is *could*. *Can* is your power word. Instead of saying "We could do that," or "We'll try to do that," say, "We can do that."

WILL VS. HOPE

The word *will* describes our plan for getting something done. "We will get that furnace in for you by Wednesday." If you say, "We hope to get that furnace in for you by Wednesday," that leaves the client up in the air as to when something is actually going to happen. *Will* is your power word. Using this word will require you to make sure you can deliver on your promise, but your client wants to know when you will do something, not when you hope you can do it.

BUT

The word *but* is the biggest eraser in the English language. It can either work for you or against you. (That's power!) If I said, "Hey, Mike, you've done a great job here at our company, and I appreciate your services. But do me a favor and bring your tools into the office. We need to talk." Do you think he even heard the first two things I said? Or did the word *but* erase that information so he only focused on why I wanted him to bring his tools into the office and what I wanted to talk about?

You can use the word *but* to your advantage. Let's say we're handling an objection like this one:

Mary: The price is too high.

You: Well, listen, I understand it is a high investment. When you deal with a company like Convenient Air-Conditioning and Heating, you're definitely going to pay more money. But let me ask you a question. When's the last time you bought something where you got the best service and the best quality but the price was the cheapest? So, what should we do?

Mary: Let's go ahead and do the top option.

What did you just do? Mary said the price was too high and you agreed with her. Then you used the word *but*, and all of a sudden that whole segment was gone. As soon as you said, "But let me ask you a question," suddenly you were in a different reality.

BECAUSE

The next superpower word I want you to grab onto is *because*. The word *because* is an instant benefit generator. Let's say you're sitting down with the client and presenting your top option to them: "Joe, I went ahead and gave you this quality package, which includes ultraviolet technology as well as an air-filtration system *because* you mentioned your kids have an issue with their allergies."

Whatever comes after the word *because* is all about the benefits. This works for advertising too: "ABC Heating and Air-Conditioning is the best in the area because we offer 24/7/365 service, our techs are fully trained, and we get there on time." You get the idea.

Value Words vs. Wild Words

Wild words are words that are unclear, have dual meanings, or otherwise repel the client. You should replace them with words that clearly communicate value whenever possible. Here are five common examples and how to best use each value word, plus three additional word pairs you need to know and how to use them to your advantage.

AGREEMENT OR PAPERWORK VS. CONTRACT

What to say: "I need your autograph on this *agreement*."

AUTOGRAPH OR OK VS. SIGN HERE OR AUTHORIZE

What to say: "I need you to *OK* this paperwork."

VALUE VS. COST

What to say: "It definitely has a higher *value* to it. I understand what you mean."

INVESTMENT VS. PRICE

What to say: "The *investment* for the premium option is $9,500."

PREMIUM VS. EXPENSIVE

What to say: "It is a more *premium* solution, no doubt. I know what you mean." (Note: Don't disagree; just reframe it as "more" by using the value word.)

MORE VS. LESS

Always tell the client what they are going to get more of, not less of, even if whatever is going to be less is a good thing. For example:

■ You'll have *more* money to spend on yourself versus this option will end up costing you less money over time.
■ You'll have *more* hot water faster versus less time waiting for the water to warm up.
■ You'll have *more* fresh air in the house versus there will be less dust and dander in the air.

ECONOMICAL VS. CHEAPER

These two words can be weak or strong depending on how you're using them. By itself, the word *cheap* implies lower quality. And if I say, "You're cheap, aren't you?" it's an insult.

However, just like the word *but*, the word *cheap* is a double agent. *Cheap* or *cheaper* are great words to use when you don't want to sell something. And *economical* is a great word to use if you do want to sell a less expensive option. Let me give you some examples. Let's say a customer wants to go with the third option. Let's start with the word *cheaper*.

Mike: Joe, I think I like that third option. Let's go with that one.

Joe: Are you sure, Mike? Because I do have cheaper ones. You didn't even consider those.

I repel him from the bottom options by saying they're cheaper. Now, let's look at the same example using the word *economical*.

Mike: Joe, these are all expensive. They are way more money than I thought they were going to be.

Joe: Well, Mike, can we do something for a second? Can we just focus on the more economical ones at the bottom?

You'll learn more about how to leverage words such as *cheaper* and *economical* when I talk about the convince-me step later in the book.

COMPONENTS VS. PARTS

How much do I charge for parts? Nothing. A client buys the service and the parts are included. After I charge for all that service, why would I charge for a part too? In fact, strike the word *parts* from your vocabulary. You're a service provider, not a parts salesperson.

Instead of using the word *parts*, use the word *components*. A component is one of the many things that make up a system. Say, "Let me go get the components I need, and I'll get this thing wrapped up."

— UNCLE JOE'S RULE 15 —
Explain what your solutions do, not what they are.

Trade Jargon

Jargon is a group of special words or expressions that allow you to communicate precisely and efficiently with other people in your industry. It also includes the specific names of components that make up a system.

For example, contactor, compressor, refrigerant, evaporator coil, and condenser coil are all technical names for the parts of an air-conditioning unit. If you're in the HVAC industry, you know what they do. Every industry has these specialized terms. Feel free to use them if you're talking to another service provider.

But should you use those terms when talking to a client? No!

You might think throwing around those terms makes you sound smart, but it actually does the opposite. In the best-case scenario, you'll confuse the client. In the worst case, they'll think you're double-talking them or talking down to them.

Words like condenser, evaporator, and refrigerant R410A are too inside baseball, and they have no meaning to the customer. No meaning equals no value, and no value leads to the client saying no, every time. You have to eliminate trade jargon from your client interactions. It is killing your sales.

In the next chapter, you'll learn how to speak to your client in terms of system faults and components instead of broken parts and how to verbally package them so your client can stay focused on the solution options you've created.

 # BULLSEYES

- Institutions of every kind—from hospitality to health care—have learned how to use words to manage the emotions and expectations of their customers.

- The law of verbal packaging states that the more skillful a person is in the use of language, the more persuasive they will be.

- Use power words *when*, *can*, and *will* instead of weak words.

- The word *but* is a superpower word that automatically erases the impact of the phrase that precedes it.

- Whatever comes after the word *because* is all about the benefits.

- Wild words are words that are unclear, have dual meanings, or otherwise repel the client. You should replace them with words that clearly communicate value whenever possible.

- Trade jargon and part names have no meaning to the customer. No meaning equals no value, and no value leads to the client saying no, every time.

Chapter 12
VERBALLY PACKAGING SYSTEM FAULTS AND SOLUTIONS

I was in Cleveland, Ohio, visiting an HVAC client and doing a ride along on a maintenance call with a service tech named Steve. We were talking about verbal packaging, and Steve mentioned he was reluctant to use the part where we talk about problems in terms of system faults. He said he felt funny about using different words than the part's actual name. I tried to explain to him that by talking about system faults we were just emphasizing the benefits of the parts instead of naming the individual parts, but I could tell he was still resistant to the idea.

We got to the client's house, and Steve did the introductions and interactions as he was trained to do. We then headed down to the basement to begin our diagnosis. There we found a furnace filter that was completely packed with dirt, a capacitor that was weak, and a drain system that was restricted because it was using vinyl tubing instead of standard PVC piping.

We wrote up the six options, and when I looked at Steve's sheet, I saw that he had used standard trade jargon to describe the problems and solutions. Even though I tried to get Steve to reword the options, he said, "Don't worry, Joe, I'll show you why that doesn't really matter."

System Faults vs. Parts Problems

Steve began presenting the problems and solutions to the client.

Steve: Brian, how important is indoor air quality to you?

Brian: I've lived in this house for 35 years, Steve, so everything seems fine with the air quality.

Steve: Well, I just want to show you the filtration restriction fault in the dust and entrapment system. This system captures the dust in the air so it doesn't get drawn into the heating system.

Why verbally package the problem as a "filtration restriction fault in the dust and entrapment system" instead of telling Brian he has a dirty furnace filter? Well, most clients don't realize that the purpose of a furnace filter is to prolong the life of the furnace—not to clean the air. Reducing the problem to the furnace filter doesn't allow us to address the root cause of why the filter is filling up so fast, which is that the dust in the air within the home is being drawn into the system. Which is probably why Steve led with the question about air quality!

Brian: Oh my gosh, I've never seen anything like that before! Can we fix that?

Steve: Yes, I have some solutions for you.

That got my attention. Maybe Steve had a change of heart as a result of our conversation? Then he continued.

Steve: Brian, I also want to show you the condensate drain with the vinyl tubing that's clogged.

Oh no. Condensate drain is trade jargon, and vinyl tubing is a part name!

Brian: I know. That drain clogs up all the time. I've been meaning to get to the hardware store so I can buy some new tubing.

Steve shot me a concerned look. He knew that wasn't the path we wanted the client to go down. He quickly shifted the conversation from talking about condensate drains and vinyl tubing to talking about the humidity-removal system and wastewater system instead.

Steve: Uh, OK. So, Brian, how important is it to remove the maximum amount of humidity from the air inside the house during the summertime?

Brian: Well, of course it's the most important thing of all when it comes to air-conditioning.

Steve: I know. That's why we want to upsize the humidity-removal system so your home will be more comfortable in the summer and the wastewater system won't ever get restricted again.

As we moved through the call, Steve was able to see in real time how his use of trade jargon and part names caused Brian to downplay the significance of those issues and reduce his interest in having us fix them. Steve also acknowledged that when he explained what a system component did by verbally packaging it, Brian willingly moved forward with the solutions we wanted to perform every time. In the end, we installed a complete dust-entrapment system, humidity-removal system, and voltage-absorption system to enhance Brian's system for the summer.

TAKEAWAYS

There are three things I want you to take away from this story about Steve and Brian:

1. When communicating the status of the system during the presentation, don't talk about the problem. In fact, I want you to strike the word *problem* from your vocabulary. From this day forward, when you explain a system problem to a client, you are going to use the word *fault*.
2. When you explain the problems in terms of system faults, the client recognizes that the problem is bigger than a single part and is more likely to choose to have an expert like you get the system back on track.
3. Specifically explain each system and what it does so clients can see the maximum benefit of enhancing or fixing it.

— UNCLE JOE'S RULE 16 —

Don't use trade jargon. It confuses the client and reduces their interest in having you fix the problem.

Faults and Systems

Hopefully, I've convinced you to stop referring to parts or using jargon in your presentations. You need to start talking about faults and systems instead. The template for this process is, "We have a [insert specific problem] fault in the [insert system name] system." Let's talk about faults first.

FAULT TYPES

There are five main types of faults: design, fracture, electrical, restriction, and installation.

Design Faults: A design fault is when the system was designed with the wrong capacity or application, or if the design is obsolete and doesn't apply to today's standards for the current equipment.

Let's say you're an electrician and you notice the municipal drip loop isn't there, and there's also water coming into the municipal entry system. Something isn't there that should be, so that is a design fault. The system is the municipal voltage-delivery system. So you could say, "We have a design fault in the municipal voltage-delivery system."

Fracture Faults: Let's say you're a plumber who has discovered a leak in a boiler pipe. Anything that is leaking, broken, or fractured is a fracture fault. Boiler pipes deliver heat. So you could say, "There is a fracture fault in the heat-delivery system."

Electrical Faults: An electrical fault is when power is present, but the system doesn't operate, whether due to a short or open wire or bad component.

Let's say you're an HVAC contractor who determines there's a bad fan motor in the outdoor air-conditioning unit. Problems with electrical components are electrical faults. The air-conditioning unit is a heat-rejection system. So you could say, "There's an electrical fault in the heat-rejection system."

Or maybe you're an electrician who sees a wire that's completely burnt off the contactor. Relay and contactor mean the same thing. It takes two wires in and distributes electricity to many different parts of the equipment. It's like the brain of the system. So you could say, "There's an electrical fault in the voltage-distribution system."

Restriction Faults: A restriction fault is when water, voltage, or air is restricted by either the design application or deterioration.

Let's say you're a plumber who finds a clogged drain during your inspection. Anything that is clogged or blocked is a restriction fault. So you could say, "There's a restriction fault in the wastewater-disposal system."

Installation Faults: Installation faults are caused by inadequate installation practices, such as using the wrong fittings, reducers, connectors, or seals. Anything installed in a substandard way is an installation fault.

Let's say you're a garage door technician who is called out to fix a newer garage door that is not opening and closing correctly and you discover the springs are damaged. So, you could say, "There's an installation fault in the garage door torsion-counterbalance system."

The template for the process of talking to a client about faults and systems is, "We have a [insert specific problem] fault in the [insert system name] system."

SYSTEM TYPES

The systems you are going to use will depend on what trade you are in. Generally, each trade has at least two systems going on in the client's home. There are also a bunch of subsystems, some of which you've already seen, some are listed here, and there are more where those came from.

For plumbers, there are water-delivery systems and wastewater-removal systems. For instance, if water is leaking from a hot water outlet, you could tell the client they have a fracture in the hot water–delivery system. At the main valve, you could say you have a fracture fault in the main water-delivery system.

For HVAC service techs, there is the air-intake system and air-delivery system. When it comes to airflow for heating, you have the air-delivery system and ignition-combustion system. For air-conditioning, there's the indoor heat-transfer system and indoor humidity-removal system. There's also an outdoor heat-rejection system and a refrigeration system.

For electrical service techs, there's the municipal entry system and the high-voltage distribution panel. There are also voltage-conduction systems and voltage terminals and controls.

If you're in a different trade, just identify what the major systems are for what you do and map the faults to them. Remember, the goal is to communicate what the system does and the benefits the client will get from fixing or enhancing it. Avoid confusing them by using jargon or talking about specific parts.

Here are some other examples of systems: a circuit board is either a motherboard or computer control system; a transformer is a voltage-conversion system; a fan motor is an air-delivery system; an electrical fault in the air-delivery system is what you would call a burnt-out fan motor; and a toilet is a porcelain waste-removal system.

Let me explain that last one in more detail. I get about $2,500 on average for a new toilet because I offer it as part of a light commercial porcelain waste-removal system. Here's exactly what that includes:

■ Two light commercial units that can flush down 32 golf balls with one flush. We replace both of them in the house. The client may only have one bad one right now, but both of them are

30 years old so I give them a price on replacing both of them at the same time.

- Clearing out all the drains in the house because it hasn't had any drain cleaning done in the last 20 years, along with a five-year warranty.
- Soft-closing heated seats.
- New sewage-connection system (wax ring).
- Lifetime component warranty. As long as the client owns this house, any leakages with the toilet are guaranteed for life.
- A five-year, no-drip, no-clog warranty. If the client's kids send their new toy soldiers for a swim on Christmas Eve and they clog up the toilet, there better be more than 32 of them because it takes a lot to clog it up. But if they did clog it up, who would be out at the client's house at 3:00 a.m. on Christmas Eve? I would be. Free. For the next five years, they're fully covered.

How often do I sell that package? Not very often. Every now and then people shock me and actually buy it. But you still need to give people the option to purchase everything you have available.

— UNCLE JOE'S RULE 17 —
Always communicate that clients get more of something, not less of it.

In the next section, you will learn the power of the third Pure Motive Service principle—be skeptical—including how to get your client to convince you they want to get the call done by using the convince-me step and the laws of scarcity and dissonance. You'll also learn about the danger line, and how to use it to keep a call moving forward while clearing out anyone or anything lurking in the background that could sink the call.

BULLSEYES

○ Using trade jargon and part names causes clients to downplay the significance of those issues and reduce their interest in having you fix them.

○ Explaining what a system component does by verbally packaging it increases the chance that clients will move forward with the solutions you present.

○ There are five main types of faults: design, fracture, electrical, restriction, and installation.

○ Identify what the major systems are for what you do and map the faults to them. Remember, the goal is to communicate what the system does and the benefits the client will get from fixing or enhancing it.

○ Always give people the option to purchase everything you have available even if very few people ever purchase the top option.

➤➤

TOOLS FOR YOUR SUCCESS

servicemvp.com/tools

✳ MAGIC MOMENT MASTERY
People want to do business with people who make them feel good. Quickly establish a powerful emotional connection with your client with this step-by-step guide.

✳ VERBAL PACKAGING DICTIONARY
The more skillful your use of language, the more persuasive you'll be. Use this dictionary to focus the client on the value of your service.

Scan to download your tools

BE
SKEPTICAL

Chapter 13
BE SKEPTICAL—OVERVIEW

One day in early summer I was working with an HVAC company in Memphis, Tennessee. It was the middle of the first week of June, and it gets pretty warm in Memphis at that time of year. I was doing a ride along with Justin, a technician who had recently attended one of our training programs. We got a prepaid maintenance call for an air-conditioning unit, so we headed over to the customer's home. When we arrived, the customer opened the door, and this is how it went:

Justin: Hi, Carol, how are you doing? I'm here to do the maintenance call, right?

Carol: Yes, you're here to do the maintenance call.

Justin: OK, good. So all we're doing today is the maintenance call. Nothing else, right?

Carol: Actually, I don't even like air-conditioning. I don't know why we do these things anyway.

Justin: Well, Carol, why don't we do this? If you don't think you need the maintenance, why don't we go ahead and cancel this call and save you the $95? I can have the office issue a refund. You don't have to do this today. We can just cancel the whole thing.

Carol: Well, no, I need you to take a look at it. We've got to get the unit fixed because it's not working very well. I don't like air-conditioning, but my husband has emphysema. He has to have it.

By the end of that call, we wound up selling a $14,000 system because Justin was operating in accordance with Pure Motive Service principle number three: be skeptical.

This Pure Motive Service principle has a few parts to it, so I'm going to take the next few chapters to explain it. First, let's talk about what being skeptical is and why it's one of the key principles at the foundation of Pure Motive Service.

Being skeptical is the act of suspending judgment (that is, the opposite of jumping to conclusions) when evaluating an explanation or claim. Or, in this case, it refers to whether or not the customer really wants a solution to the problem they said they wanted you to fix.

As soon as Justin offered to cancel the maintenance call and save the client $95, two things happened. First, his credibility went way up. Second, since he had offered the client a way out, she felt compelled to convince us that she actually did want us to fix the unit.

So, why would we ever offer a customer the option of canceling a call? Think about it. The customer probably arranged their whole day around you showing up in the morning to do this call. When your office tries to cancel a call at the last minute, what happens? The customer says, "Oh no! We took off work today. You better show up." And if you don't show up, the company is going to pay the price.

If you offer to cancel when you're already there and you've got your tools and everything ready to go, the odds of somebody who really wants the service agreeing to cancel it are almost zero.

As a matter of fact, if they do cancel it, you're probably doing them a favor, and it probably is good service. You shouldn't be doing work for them if they cancel when you get there, right? I mean, who wants to provide a service to somebody who doesn't really want it?

You're a professional. You've gone to school, and you have tons of experience. You don't need to spend time begging someone to use your services.

Being skeptical is the act of suspending judgment about whether or not the customer really wants a solution to the problem they said they wanted you to fix.

Clients Must Convince You

One aspect of the be skeptical principle calls for you to make your client convince you that they are serious about getting the work done. This is called the "convince-me step," and it involves getting two commitments from the client to get the work done. Making these commitments propels the client past their indecision and fear and reconnects them to their original goal.

The convince-me step works by connecting the laws of scarcity and dissonance to get the client to either make those commitments or allow you to stop a call that will not result in a sale.

Let's look at Justin's call again through that lens:

Justin: Hi, Carol, how are you doing? I'm here to do the maintenance call, right? (He asks for a commitment.)

Carol: Yes, you're here to do the maintenance call. (He gets the commitment, but he remains skeptical about whether that really is all and asks again in a different way.)

Justin: OK, good. So all we're doing today is the maintenance call. Nothing else, right? (He asks for the second commitment.)

Carol: Actually, I don't even like air-conditioning. I don't know why we do these things anyway. (The customer revokes her initial commitment.)

Let's Cancel the Call

Justin is paying attention, so he recognizes Carol's knee-jerk response as an event. He also knows that Event + Response =

Outcome and that the response most likely to produce the outcome he wants—Carol recommitting to getting the work done—is to offer to cancel the call. By offering to cancel the call, Justin is invoking the laws of scarcity and dissonance. The law of scarcity says that when you create scarcity with your services, it creates value. The law of dissonance says that if you create dissonance and provide a path to harmony, you and the customer will then search for that harmony together.

Justin: Well, Carol, why don't we do this? If you don't think you need the maintenance, why don't we go ahead and cancel this call and save you the $95? I can have the office issue a refund. You don't have to do this today. We can just cancel the whole thing.

Carol: Well, no, I need you to take a look at it. We've got to get the unit fixed because it's not working very well. I don't like air-conditioning, but my husband has emphysema. He has to have it. (The customer exposes her real need and makes the second commitment.)

By offering to cancel a call, you are invoking the laws of scarcity and dissonance so the client will either make the required commitments or allow you to stop a call that will not result in a sale.

Working the Danger Line

Justin has Carol's commitment to move forward with the call, but there's another place he needs to apply this principle. He needs to make sure there is not another provider lurking in the background who could tank the call. This could be a competitor, Carol's uncle, Charlie, or a neighbor who is a handyman. The only way he'll be able to find out is to work what I call the danger line.

The danger line is literally a line that separates you from the thing that could jeopardize the call. In this situation, Justin needs to know who else Carol has hired previously to fix her air-conditioning and how they failed, partly so he doesn't make the same mistakes and partly so he can make sure they aren't still in the running to do the call.

Justin will work the danger line by following a specific process where he will ask Carol who she has used before and why she didn't call them back to do this new work. And without ever saying a bad word about the previous contractor, relative, or neighbor, he will guide her through the process of eliminating them as competitors.

I'll go into more detail about that process in chapter 16. The point I want to make here is that we must remain skeptical about whether or not we are actually going to end up doing the call until the client convinces us otherwise.

— UNCLE JOE'S RULE 18 —
Assuming is a fast track to the graveyard of lost opportunities.

In the next chapter, we'll talk about the laws of scarcity and dissonance in more detail, and then in chapter 15, you'll learn how to apply those laws effectively while doing the full convince-me step. Finally, in chapter 16, you'll learn how to work the danger line to make sure you eliminate anyone who could possibly pop up and tank your call.

BULLSEYES

- Being skeptical is the act of suspending judgment about whether or not the customer really wants a solution to the problem they said they wanted you to fix. It is one of the key principles at the foundation of Pure Motive Service.

- The client must convince you that they are serious about getting the work done.

- The convince-me step involves getting two commitments from the client to get the work done. The process of making these commitments propels the client past their indecision and fear and reconnects them to their original goal.

- Another aspect to being skeptical is making sure there is not another provider lurking in the background who could tank the call.

- Offering to cancel when the client can't commit gives you a chance to stop a call that will not result in a sale.

➤➤

Chapter 14
THE LAWS OF SCARCITY AND DISSONANCE

When carmaker General Motors first put the Cadillac Escalade on the market in March of 2003, they gave only one to each showroom in the United States and instructed salespeople to tell customers the dealership wouldn't be receiving more until June.

Not knowing any of this, I headed to my local Cadillac dealer to see the vehicle. A salesman approached me and asked what I was looking for. "Show me the Escalade," I said. He pointed to the showroom. The vehicle was beautiful. I asked to take a test drive, but the salesman said I couldn't take it out on the street because they only had one and couldn't get it dirty. He couldn't sell it to me anyway because then they wouldn't have anything to show. I said, "Are you kidding me?" (He was not.)

I said, "Well, what can you do?" He said he could put me on the waiting list. I was number 1,201 at that dealership. I drove to a couple other dealerships, but their lists were even longer.

The other thing was that the vehicles came loaded. You could have the dealership add an aftermarket sunroof, bigger tires, or a better stereo system, but that was it.

It was one of the best car-sales moves in history. They sold every single Escalade for $50,000 flat.

General Motors knew scarcity was a huge purchase trigger in American culture. Scarcity made people want the Escalade so much that they were willing to pay a flat fee and wait months to take delivery of the vehicle. The early Mini Cooper, and more recently some Tesla models, also leveraged the law of scarcity for similar results.

The good news is that creating scarcity works for the service industry too.

The Law of Scarcity

The law of scarcity says that when you create scarcity with your services, it creates value.

Everyone's got a piece of equipment sitting in the warehouse that was either ordered in the wrong size or is there because of a customer cancellation. So let's say you're in HVAC. One day at your morning standup meeting, the boss says, "Hey, we've got an air-conditioning unit just sitting there in the warehouse. Who thinks they can move it?"

On your first call, you're putting together options for the client, and you realize that the equipment in the top option is the exact brand and model of the air-conditioning unit in the warehouse. You mention this to the client, and their eyes light up, so you ask, "Should I call the office and see if we still have it?"

The client says, "Oh, yes! Please find out. I hope you still have it!"

Suddenly, she's afraid someone else is going to get it first and she'll have to wait for another unit to come in.

You were using the law of scarcity without even realizing it.

Many sales-training programs shy away from leveraging scarcity even though it is the most powerful thing we can do. Creating scarcity creates urgency and desire, as well as an obligation to get the job done.

Creating scarcity can also be about excusing yourself from the call rather than agreeing to a client's demand to cut corners. Your willingness to walk away rather than perform substandard service communicates to the client that you are a professional who is committed to doing the call in a way that is ultimately in the client's best interest.

Creating scarcity with your services creates value, urgency, and desire, as well as an obligation to get the job done.

As a home service contractor, there are three things you can make scarce: service, time, and information.

SERVICE SCARCITY

Here's how most of us were taught to sell our services:

You: So, Rich, what are we here to do today?

Rich: I need a price on getting this light fixture hung.

You: Well, I'll definitely get that done for you right away. As a matter of fact, if you've got any other projects you need me to do while I'm here, I can take care of those for you too.

Rich: Well, I just need prices, then I'll decide whether to go forward.

Rich then runs you around the house making a list of projects to price out without you knowing whether he is actually going to get any of the work done at all. To get Rich to commit to doing the work, you need to make your services scarce and create some dissonance in the process. Now let's try injecting scarcity into the previous situation by indicating to Rich that he might not even need you to do the job.

You: So, Rich, what are we here to do today?

Rich: I need a price on getting this light fixture hung.

You: The other one looks good. What's wrong with that one?

Rich: It's not aesthetically pleasing to me. I want something that matches the decor of the kitchen.

You: You're a capable guy. You probably could do it yourself.

Rich: I leave that stuff to the professionals. I'm not really that good.

You: Have you hired an electrician before?

Rich: Yes.

You: So you understand that it's not going to be as cheap as doing it yourself, right?

Rich: I am not interested in doing it myself. Please just help me out with this.

Who's begging who to do this job right now?

In the first example, you were begging him for more work, right? In the second example, you were trying to talk him out of it until he convinced you he needed your services.

What was the difference? Scarcity.

For every objection we put forth, we create more desire in the customer to get the work done. The truth is you don't need to sell your services. You need to make your services scarcer. When you make them scarcer, it increases their value in the eyes of the client.

TIME SCARCITY

The next thing you can make scarce is your time.

The first clue that you need to invoke time scarcity is when a customer says, "I'm busy." Usually these are clients who are unenthusiastic or even negative, who act like they don't care about air-conditioning, electrical work, or plumbing, and, by extension, probably don't care about you or your time. (You'll learn all about the different buyer types and how to handle them in chapter 18.)

The words "I'm too busy, I don't have time for this," are a big, blinking yellow light and a sign to stop the call right now. If they are too busy, you will not be able to do the Pure Motive Service process that is in their best interest. If they are too busy, they won't want to chat with you so you won't be able to identify their buying code. And they certainly won't take the time to allow you to do a presentation of the options. They may even say, "Just do the work and leave the bill on the table. I'll send you a check." (How many of us have fallen for that one?)

So, when you hear those words, the very next thing you should say is, "I'm busy too. Let's just cancel the call and I'll come back at a time when we're both less busy."

That's your rule. It's like autopilot; you don't have to think about it. You make your time scarce. Here's what that might sound like:

Bill: Hi. Glad you're here. I'm busy. I have a meeting. Can we get this call done really quick?

You: I'm busy today, too, Bill. So why don't we schedule a more appropriate time? I can call my office and reschedule to a day that works better for both of us.

Then pick up your phone and start dialing the office. When you say, "I'm busy too," you're making your time scarce. The value of your time goes up, and almost always the call will turn around immediately. If I were to keep going and beg this guy for the call, I would get "handled." He would realize I'm a kind person and shuffle me around like a deck of cards. Don't get handled. If somebody says they're too busy, you should say, "That's OK. I'm really busy too. Let's reschedule it."

When you do that, 99.9 percent of the time the client will say, "Wait a second. I really need this work done today. I'll cancel my meeting."

Remember, by being too busy to talk with you the client is hoping that you'll do the work and leave it up to them when or whether they ever pay you for it. Make your time scarce.

INFORMATION SCARCITY

Getting a job is like a highway, and the destination is getting the work done. People are always trying to get you to take an exit ramp to Think-it-overville, some place that has nothing to do with getting the job done. The dog is barking and won't leave you alone, the kids are jumping around and doing cartwheels in the living room, the television is blaring as loud as it can. And among that chaos you're struggling to provide information about the system's problem and solution to the client.

Rather than try to present in an environment where the client won't be able to focus, withhold the information until you have their undivided attention. To get their attention, you can use a technique called stop or continue. Here's what that sounds like: "Hey, Amy. First of all, thanks for inviting me to your house. I really appreciate all the effort you're making to help everybody and then trying to get the air-conditioning working as well. Right now seems like it's not a good time for you. You look like you've got your hands full. Why don't we stop the call and I'll come back when you have more time to focus? Or we could go out to the garage and discuss this where it's quieter. What should we do?"

The stop-or-continue technique is also useful when a client wants to dictate how you will do the call. They could say something like, "I don't want you looking at the ductwork in the attic."

You are the professional, so the client cannot dictate your diagnostic process. You could say, "That's OK. But if you're not comfortable with us looking at the ductwork to make sure the sizing is right and it's not leaking fiberglass into the house, we'll have to stop the call because we don't want to misdiagnose the system. On the other hand, if you want to know whether the system that's in place is working properly, we can continue, but we will have to look in the attic. So, what should we do?"

Offering to stop the call and make yourself and your information scarce when you aren't able to clearly communicate or properly diagnose a system will get people's attention. It almost always gets the call back on track.

Scarcity has a little brother, and his name is dissonance. Almost always they work as a team. Think about it—when you create scarcity, you are also creating dissonance because you are taking something away from the client.

Scarcity creates value. Dissonance creates action. And as you'll see in the next chapter about the convince-me step, you will need both to get the customer to convince you to do the service.

— UNCLE JOE'S RULE 19 —
Only provide service for people who want it.

The Law of Dissonance

The law of dissonance says that if I create dissonance and provide a path or paths to harmony, the customer and I will then search for that harmony together.

In 1957, scientist Leon Festinger conducted a study based on his theory that inconsistency among beliefs or behaviors causes an uncomfortable psychological tension. The term he used for that tension is *cognitive dissonance*, or dissonance for short.

Dissonance is the opposite of harmony. Most of us think our job is to create harmony on service calls. There's a time and place for that—it's called a magic moment! The problem with focusing only on harmony is that it cannot create action. Only dissonance can do that. Think about it this way. If you and I had a disagreement, but I showed you a way out of it that saved your ego, you probably would latch onto that, right?

Let's look at the example from earlier in the chapter again and notice how I create scarcity by telling the client he doesn't need the service and dissonance by encouraging him to do the work himself.

You: So, Rich, what are we here to do today?

Rich: I need a price on getting this light fixture hung.

You: The other one looks good. What's wrong with that one?

Rich: It's not aesthetically pleasing to me. I want something that matches the decor of the kitchen.

You: You're a capable guy. You probably could do it yourself.

Rich: I leave that stuff to the professionals. I'm not really that good.

You: Have you hired an electrician before?

Rich: Yes.

You: So you understand that it's not going to be as cheap as doing it yourself, right?

Rich: I am not interested in doing it myself. Please just help me out with this.

The law of dissonance is the engine that creates action.

Have you ever had a client who didn't make a purchase or it seemed like it was going really well but then they decided not to do anything? That means there was too much harmony and not enough dissonance. It means you were being too nice.

This can be a problem for some of us. We've all been taught that a service provider is always nice. But to assist your client in taking action, you need to be willing to disagree or say something dissonant. You can do it in a nice way, but it has to be done because it's in the client's best interest to assist them in making a decision one way or another.

Remember, as a Pure Motive Service provider, you aren't attached to what option the client chooses or whether they buy from you at all. Dissonance is the trouble you cause by telling people the problems. However, every time you bring up a problem, you must also bring up a solution because dissonance is only relieved when the client selects a solution.

When a call goes well but the client still decides not to do anything that means there was too much harmony and not enough dissonance.

PROBLEMS MUST HAVE SOLUTIONS

Whenever you create dissonance, you've got to create solutions right away. There should be no time delay. If you say, "You've got a [insert problem] fault in the refrigeration system," and they say, "What's it going to take to fix it?" and then you say, "I don't know. I have to go out to my truck and get some prices for you," you just lost the job. When you come back in, it will be like you're speaking to a different person. Before you left, they were friendly and happy. You come back with the prices after 90 seconds and they say, "Thanks, you can put them on the counter."

What happened? What went wrong?

Dissonance boiled over, and they started searching somewhere else. They probably made a phone call to their uncle Eddie, or somebody else who does air-conditioning. Why? Because you didn't immediately offer a solution. Dissonance is the trouble you cause by bringing people problems, and solutions are giving them prices to fix the problems. Fair enough. So offer your solution and offer it soon because time is your enemy. Create a problem, but then create a solution right away. If there's no dissonance, there's no action. The solution is the client's path to action. If you create dissonance without offering a way out, the client will look to someone else who will provide that relief.

— UNCLE JOE'S RULE 20 —
Clients have to want solutions more than you want to provide them.

Scarcity and dissonance go hand in hand. The risk of you not doing the work after the client has waited around for you to arrive creates action. Instead of you selling them, the client is selling you on staying to do the work.

In the next chapter, you'll learn about the convince-me step and how to use it to connect scarcity and dissonance to get the work.

 **BULLSEYES**

- Scarcity is a huge purchase trigger in American culture.
- Creating scarcity with your services creates value, urgency, and desire, as well as an obligation to get the job done.

- There are three things you can make scarce: service, time, and information.

- Scarcity and dissonance go hand in hand. The risk of you not doing the work after the client has waited for you to arrive creates action.

- Whenever you create dissonance, you've got to create solutions right away or the client will look for someone who will provide that relief.

Chapter 15
THE CONVINCE-ME STEP

In a seminal research study cited in a 2016 *Harvard Business Review* article titled "To Increase Sales, Get Customers to Commit a Little at a Time" by Frank V. Cespedes and David Hoffeld, researchers posing as volunteers canvassed a neighborhood asking homeowners to put a large "Drive Carefully" billboard in their front yards. Nearly all of them declined because they said the signs would block the view of their homes from the street. The "volunteers" then moved to a nearby neighborhood, but this time they asked residents to display a smaller sign that read "Be a Safe Driver." Nearly all the residents the researchers spoke to agreed to display the signs.

A few weeks later, researchers returned to the second group of homeowners and asked them to put the larger "Drive Carefully" billboards in their front yards. The result was more than 75 percent of them agreed to do it. This technique works by creating a connection between the person asking for a request and the person who is being asked. If a smaller request is granted, then the person who is agreeing feels like they are obligated to keep agreeing to larger requests to stay consistent with the original decision of agreeing.

The convince-me step is an adaptation of this technique. Instead of a small commitment followed by a larger commitment, we aim to secure two equal, voluntary commitments to action from the client before we move forward.

The way to apply the convince-me step varies slightly depending on which type of call you're on—repair, maintenance, or opportunity—and what type of commitment you need for each. In all cases, the convince-me step is in play throughout the entire call.

Repair Calls

On a repair call, the first time you use the convince-me step is to confirm the mission of the call and get two commitments from the client about what they want to accomplish by the end of it.

First, you need to determine if you are fixing the problem today or just looking at it. If you're just looking at it, you know you're not going to sell anything on this call. The client just saved you time and energy you would have spent giving a presentation to the wrong person at the wrong time.

Once in a while, the customer will come out with it and say, "Yes, we need to fix this today," and then you can proceed. But if they say something like, "Can you just take a look at it? It seems like it's not working right," then you have to do something to create dissonance in order to get them to commit. It might sound something like this:

You: Hey Dustin, what inspired you to have us out here today?

Dustin: My air-conditioning is not working. I was hoping you could take a look at it.

You: OK, so we're not doing any actual work today. We're just looking at it to determine the problem. Is that right?

Dustin: No, we've got to fix it today.

Notice that Dustin was completely free to say, "Yes, that's right, we're just looking at it." But that's not what he did. He disagreed and voluntarily made a commitment that he wanted to get it fixed today.

You're not done yet though. Why? Because you need *two* commitments before action can take place.

You: OK, Dustin, so what do you want to accomplish today?

Dustin: I need this thing fixed. Can you fix it?

You: Well, I haven't seen it yet. Let's go take a look and see.

If you had said you could fix it, you'd be the one making the commitment before you've even seen the system. Now who's going to have dissonance if the customer doesn't like your price?

Once you get your two voluntary commitments, you can move into finding out about the client and their family and creating a magic moment.

There are two common situations you may run into during this process. One is that the client is either too distracted to focus on what you are saying, much less make the commitments required to advance the call. The other is they are so price-focused they try to make the commitment conditional on whether or not they like the price. Here's how to handle both of those events.

THE DISTRACTED CLIENT

Let's say you've diagnosed the system and are ready to present the problems and solutions to the client. But their kids are running all over, the television is blaring, and you don't think there's any way the client will be able to focus on your presentation. Do not just plow ahead in this situation. Instead, use the convince-me step to get the client to convince you that this is the right time to present.

You could say something like, "Jane, it's looking like you guys are really busy, and it's not a good time right now. Why don't we go ahead and reschedule this call? I'll come back at a different time when you're ready."

Either she'll perceive that you are doing her a favor and you really can come back when she will be more open to listening to you, or she will say something like, "I'm sorry, let's go into the garage where it's quiet so I can focus on what you have to say." At which point, you will ask again in a slightly different way, so you can get the second commitment.

One of those two things is going to happen. You'll get the commitment to come back later or the client will commit to making time to listen to you now.

THE PRICE-FOCUSED CLIENT

Sometimes people make the commitment conditional. They'll say something like, "I mean, if the price is right and we can find out what the problem is, I'd like to get it fixed." The response to a conditional commitment is, "So if I can find the problem and we can make it affordable, what would happen then?"

Usually they'll say, "Yes, then I want to fix it."

Then you should say, "OK, just to confirm, what should we do?" And what you want to hear is that second commitment from them: "Let's fix it."

Here's the rule of the convince-me step. Either you use it on the client to assist them in committing to action, or they will use it on you. How many times have you made a presentation of services when you were convinced it wasn't going anywhere, but you still made the presentation anyway? You were saying to yourself, "This person is not buying anything." And the presentation sucked because you and the client both knew no one was going to do anything.

Either you use the convince-me step on the client to assist them in committing to action, or they will use it on you.

To make a good presentation, you have to feel convinced you can make a difference today, and that can't happen unless the client convinces you—with two voluntary commitments—that they want to get the work done today.

If you can't make a difference today, then any presentation you give won't be valid later. Prices are going to increase. Equipment changes. Somebody else might come in and sell the job instead of you. All kinds of things can happen unless you do what is needed to move the work forward today.

— UNCLE JOE'S RULE 21 —
Getting two commitments from the client exponentially increases your success.

Maintenance Calls

Historically, HVAC is where maintenance calls originated, but electricians, plumbers, and other trades are getting into what they're calling home inspections, which is where they perform an annual evaluation of a home system. It usually takes the form of a planned service agreement with prepaid calls that you sell while on a scheduled repair.

Now you're out there six months or a year later to inspect the entire system. The customer is not expecting anything to be broken. That means the convince-me step on maintenance calls is a little more complicated. In this case, the first thing you're after is for them to convince you they want to hear about any problem you may find. Here's what that sounds like:

You: Hey, Dustin, what inspired you to have us out here today?

WHAT SHOULD WE DO?

Dustin: It's the annual trip to get our air-conditioning unit cleaned up and checked out.

You: So we're just here for the maintenance call, right?

Dustin: Yes, just get it all cleaned up and make sure it's working.

You: OK, so all we're doing is the maintenance call today. To confirm, if I were to find anything else, I should not tell you, and we'll deal with it in the summertime, right?

Dustin: Well, no, if you find something, I need to hear about it.

You: Oh, you do? OK. I probably won't find anything, but if I do, what should we do?

Dustin: You should let me know about it.

You: OK. Let me go take a look and see what I find out.

So now we move forward. That's it.

Before I even started the call, I got two commitments from him that he wanted to hear about it if I found a problem. That's all I'm looking to get from him.

For maintenance calls, you need the client to convince you they want to hear about any problem you may find.

The other thing to take note of is how I positioned my question. There are three question types: leading, neutral, and contrary. There's a time and place to use each type, and we'll go into detail about that in chapter 18, but here's what you need to know right now.

A leading question is one that's "salesy" and leads the client to answer the way you want them to answer. Let's say you want to sell a humidifier. An example of a leading question would be, "If I could show you a way to buy a humidifier today, would you be interested?" They know you want them to say yes. (Spoiler alert: Don't ask leading questions.)

An example of a neutral question would be a request for the client's opinion. You could say, "John, what's your opinion of the humidity level in this house?"

A contrary question is always the ridiculous opposite of what you would normally ask.

FIND OUT THE TRUTH

Remember, the first question I asked Dustin was, "So we're just here for the maintenance call, right? To confirm, if I were to find anything else, I should not tell you, and we'll deal with it in the summertime, right?"

I'm betting that is pretty contrary to how you normally respond. You'd probably just assume that if you found something the client would want you to fix it today. But what happens if you do find something and you haven't done this convince-me step? Let's look at an electrical inspection as an example.

You: Hi, Sharon, so what are we out here to do today?

Sharon: This is part of our maintenance agreement.

You: So, we're doing the electrical maintenance inspection today?

Sharon: Yes.

You: OK, so we're only doing the inspection today. If I do find something during the inspection, I'll make a note of it for your files, but I'm not going to tell you about it. We'll just deal with it at a later time. Is that right?

Sharon: No, I do want to know about any problems you find.

You: You do? OK, so if I find a problem, what should we do then?

Sharon: You should let me know so we can discuss a solution.

You: OK. Let's go take a look. Can you show me where the electrical panel is?

The most important part of a maintenance call is to find out what kind of call it really is:

■ Is it a routine maintenance call on modern equipment that you just put in last year?

■ Are you inheriting old equipment that you're now going to do the maintenance on every year? It's probably time to upgrade, so you want to provide the client with an option to buy a newer piece of equipment and a newer system.

■ Is it a repair in sheep's clothing? Sometimes people ask for a maintenance call when they realize something (e.g., their air-conditioning) isn't working right to see if you can figure it out. They don't want to refer to it as a repair call. They just want to figure out what's wrong now in May instead of in the middle of June or July.

Use the convince-me step in your maintenance calls to create a desire for your presentation should you discover issues not already covered in a previously sold top option.

— UNCLE JOE'S RULE 22 —
When a client is uncommitted, the answer will be no!

Opportunity Calls

The reason I use the phrase *opportunity call* rather than *estimate* is because it is an opportunity for you to compete with other contractors and go head-to-head with your competition.

It's your job to not spend too much time on these kinds of exploratory calls. You also need to accept that it will likely turn into two calls, not just one. On the first call, you're just trying to find out what is going on.

YES, NO, OR I'LL TELL YOU NO

The convince-me step on opportunity calls is really simple. Here's what it sounds like on a replacement call. In this case, the client told you they are going to buy an air-conditioning unit, and you're the first part of the process of getting bids from contractors.

You: Hey, Toni, how are you doing?

Toni: Well, you can tell it's kind of hot, and we want to get this air-conditioning replaced.

You: Not today, though? You're not planning on making the decision today, right?

Toni: We had another guy out here already. We're getting a couple more prices. But we do want to get it taken care of. If we like your price, then we're going to get this done today.

You: Well, Toni, I'm going to have several different prices. If I gave you six different price options and you found one you liked, what would happen then?

Toni: We'd get it done.

You: OK. And if I showed you the six prices and you didn't like any of them, what would you tell me then?

Toni: I would tell you I'm going to get another opinion.

You: OK. I'll tell you what, if I show you six different prices and you tell me you're still not sure what to do, I'm going to disqualify myself. Because that means I've confused you, and I would never want to sell something to someone who is confused or unsure. So you'll tell me yes or no, or I'll tell you it's over if you don't like the options at that point, right?

Toni: OK.

That's it. One of those three things is going to happen. Yes, no, or I'll tell you no. If the client is confused and saying things like, "I'm still not sure what to do," or "I need to talk to my wife," I'm going to pull the plug.

The same goes for upgrades. Let's say during your maintenance inspection you noticed that the furnace did not have a humidifier. You could say, "Toni, let me ask you a question. How come you never chose to get a humidifier?" This is important. The question should be, "Why did you *choose not* to do [insert action]?"

During the convince-me step on opportunity calls and upgrades, one of three things is going to happen: the client will say yes, no, or you'll say no.

Let's say you want to offer Toni carbon-monoxide alarms. You could say, "Toni, can I ask you a question? I noticed there is no life-safety protection system down there. How come you never chose to get one of those?" Did you notice how I verbally packaged that? Do I mention carbon monoxide? No. I'm not trying to scare people. It's called a life-safety protection system. Toni will likely ask what a life-safety protection system is, and then you can offer to explain it. Once she commits to hearing about it, you're free to give a presentation while being mindful of how you approach the client.

Before you give any presentation, however, you first have to eliminate anything or anyone that could potentially interfere and derail the opportunity by running what I call the danger line. And that's what the next chapter is all about.

🎯 BULLSEYES

- The convince-me step is an adaptation of a proven sales technique where you aim to secure two equal, voluntary commitments to action from the client before you move forward.

- It works by creating a connection between you and the client where it's easier for them to make a second commitment that is consistent with the first one.

- On a repair call, the first time you use the convince-me step is to confirm the mission of the call and get two commitments from the client about what they want to accomplish by the end of it.

- The most important part of a maintenance call is to find out what kind of call it really is: a routine maintenance call on modern equipment that you just put in, old equipment that you're inheriting and are now expected to maintain, or a maintenance call that is actually a repair.

- On opportunity calls, it's important to use a contrary question, such as, "You're not planning on making the decision today, right?" when seeking the first commitment.

Chapter 16
THE DANGER LINE

I was working for a heating and air-conditioning company in northern Illinois and was dispatched to a call for no heat. When I got there, the client, George, said he was in the middle of a remodeling project. The company he had hired for the heating and air-conditioning portion had started the project but never finished it.

I followed George down to the basement to take a look at the system. In the middle of the room was a pile of materials that had never been put together or installed. And that was probably a good thing because the ductwork on-site was too small and would have damaged the furnace if connected.

"What would you like me to accomplish on today's call?" I asked. George said that it was getting colder and he needed to get the ductwork completed and connected to the furnace so his family would be warm and comfortable in the coming months.

I called my dispatcher and told her I would need more time on the call so I could design a new air-duct system. I also said I'd need another tech to come out later to help me get the heat on. She cleared my schedule, and for the next 90 minutes I sat in my truck and meticulously designed a new, properly sized air-duct system for the client. I also made a materials list. I did all this work because I assumed that making this effort would result in me getting the job.

New plan in hand, I sat down at the kitchen table with George and his wife, Avery. I explained what the problem was with the current ductwork design. I did a walkthrough of where we would put the new registers and went with them down to the basement to explain where all the ducts would run. George and Avery agreed with my design and were delighted that I had a game plan.

All those good feelings evaporated, however, when I showed them the prices to do the work. I could tell they were shocked. Avery told me my price was twice as much money as the other HVAC contractor had quoted them, and he was doing the ductwork, the furnace, and the air-conditioning.

Avery asked if I could give her the diagram so she and her husband could think about it. I said it was fine to think about it, but why would she need the ductwork diagram? She said she wanted to show it to the other HVAC contractor so he could do the job that they had already paid him to do. (At least she was honest.) Then she told me the other HVAC company was owned by her brother, who was mainly a service tech and didn't really know much about how to run ductwork. So after 90 minutes of designing a system and creating a materials list to get the job done, plus another

90 minutes spent explaining what we were going to do, I was the one with the shocked look on my face.

Since I was inexperienced and had not been trained on what to do, I went ahead and gave Avery and George the diagram and materials list, along with my business card, and said to call me if they needed my services. (Did they ever call? Of course not.)

I left that job discouraged, angry, and frustrated. On top of it, my boss was (understandably) mad that I had not only wasted three hours when I could have been servicing other clients but also spent that time designing ductwork for another company.

All was not lost, however, because that was also the day the concept of the danger line was born. From that day forward, I made sure to test each and every opportunity to see if there was a third party lurking in the background who could mess with the call. And I would only create a solution when I was sure there would be no third-party interference.

I also began to ask every client what they had heard about my company. I wanted to make sure they could see a clear difference between my company and my competitors. Then they could decide who they wanted to complete the project before I invested my time to create custom solutions for them.

The Danger Line

The danger line is literally a line that separates you from the thing that could tank the call.

Your mission is to find out what the client thinks about each side of the line. First, you want to learn who has previously been involved in fixing the house. You want to understand how they failed. Why? Because if they had succeeded, you wouldn't be here right now. Ask the client what they liked about that company, what they didn't like, and why they didn't call them this time.

Second, you need to find out why they called you instead. What do they like about you so far, and what's their perception of your company at this point?

Why is it so important to find this information out?

Well, it's a lot easier to learn from other people's mistakes than to make the same mistakes yourself. You want to learn what other people did to fail so you can skip the failure part and learn how to succeed with them instead.

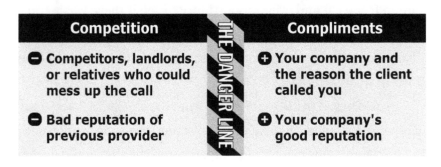

Competition	THE DANGER LINE	Compliments
⊖ Competitors, landlords, or relatives who could mess up the call		⊕ Your company and the reason the client called you
⊖ Bad reputation of previous provider		⊕ Your company's good reputation

The Left Side of the Danger Line

Have you ever been on a call where it started out kind of bad and then continued to get worse? No matter what you do, it seems like the call is doomed.

A phenomenon I call "bad service gravity momentum" occurs when clients have had so many bad experiences with contractors that they start expecting bad service. And then you end up sucked

WHAT SHOULD WE DO?

into their negative mindset, which results in you giving them what they expect (bad service), which continues the cycle.

The good news is there's a way to not only make sure that bad service gravity momentum never takes place but also use it to your advantage when working the left side of the danger line. The left side of the danger line is all about finding out how the competition failed and then letting gravity and momentum do their work until the client eventually says something like, "We're not using that guy anymore. But we're not going to fix it ourselves."

The great part about the left side of the danger line is that it really plays into the natural tendencies of the client. Clients love to talk about their home-improvement disasters. If they've ever had a problem with a contractor, they just love to tell everybody how crappy that service was.

But here's the dangerous part of the danger line. You want to find out how other people failed, but you never want to become part of the failure story yourself.

NEVER BASH THE COMPETITION

Never bash your competition. It's not ethical for you to step in and say, "Yeah, I've heard some really bad things about those guys." You don't need to add anything to the client's narrative. If that contractor is so subpar, there's likely enough negativity about them already out there.

Also, when you pile on to the client's complaints, at some point they will start thinking, "Wait a minute. Why am I listening to this guy? I can see what he's doing. He's just trying to make the other guy look bad so he looks better."

So, what questions do you need to ask that will get people to say they're not going to use another company? It's simple. As you're in motion, walking to the problem, just ask the client about the experience they've had with other contractors. You could say something like, "So, John, let me ask you a question. Who do you usually use for maintenance?"

BE IN MOTION

The reason you want to be in motion as you ask the client these questions is because their mind is focused on showing you where to go. They are saying, "Follow me. Watch your head on that beam over there. Let me turn the lights on." All these things are occupying their mind when you're asking these questions so they're not in a defensive posture.

If you stand at the front door and ask these questions, people are going to get their defenses up and say, "Why are we standing here talking about the competition right now? We should be looking at the problem." That's why you want to go look at the problem while you're asking about who has worked there in the past. That sounds something like this:

You: Who normally does your maintenance?

John: You guys do it.

You: Have we always done your maintenance?

John: Well, no, we just started with you guys.

You: Who'd you use before that?

John: Well, we used to use Acme.

You: I heard Acme is a good company. What happened? Why'd you decide to switch to us instead?

John: Yeah, they're pretty good.

You: Well, John, if you like Acme, why don't you just go back to them? Why are you calling us? I don't want to step on their toes. If you already have a relationship with Acme, I don't want to get in the middle of that.

John: No, Joe, we switched to you guys for a reason.

You: Well, what happened?

John: I don't like talking bad about other people.

Never bash the competition. Sticking up for them actually buries them faster!

The client is probably going to want to keep their cards close to the vest at first. They won't want to tell you what happened. The good news is there are three magic words that will get them to spill the tea. Those words are "off the record."

GO OFF THE RECORD

When a journalist interviews someone for a news story, the subject of the interview might ask if they can disclose something "off the record." The journalist can agree or refuse, but if they agree, the expectation is that the journalist will not report or even repeat what they were told. In this case, you are offering your client the assurance that you will not repeat whatever they tell you.

You: Well, listen, I don't want to cause any problems here, but off the record I've got to know what happened because if I don't know what the guy did wrong, I might make the same mistake he did.

John: I don't think so. You would never do what this guy did.

You: What did he do? I really want to make sure I don't repeat his mistake.

Once the customer tells you what the competition did wrong, your next step should be disbelief.

You: Come on. He really did that? He sat on a bucket and read *Playboy* in front of the furnace? He brought pornography into your home? I can't believe he did that to you. You've got small children, don't you? That's crazy!

Next, you should ask if he called the person's manager. Sometimes people do. Sometimes they don't. They might say, "Yeah, this guy kind of seemed like a psychopath. I didn't want him to get upset with me. So I didn't tell the manager." Then you should ask if he called the owner. The client might say, "No, I didn't want this guy to come after me later on, so I just didn't tell the owner about it." Now here's how you end it:

You: Well, listen, John, if you've got a relationship with these guys, the last thing I want to do is step on their toes. So are you sure you're not in the middle of a contract or an agreement with Acme? I don't want to get in the middle of any legal problems here.

John: No, no, we're done with those guys. We're never using them again.

By going off the record, you are offering your client the assurance that you will not repeat whatever they tell you.

Once you have those two commitments, immediately go into the right side of the danger line and get them to feel the love for your company. Don't wait. The next words out of your mouth should be, "Well, what have you heard about our company?"

THE BAD SIDE OF THE LEFT SIDE

I will warn you now—you will hear a lot of ugly stuff on the left side of the danger line, ranging from the mildly inconsiderate to the outright criminal. One client searched their contractor's ID on the internet and found the guy registered on the local county website as a child molester. Another said a contractor hit on his 15-year-old daughter and tried to get her to meet him at a coffee shop later that evening. Yet another had a contractor hit their dog on the head with a pipe wrench because it was sniffing his tools. You can't make this stuff up.

You'll also hear about a lot of little reasons somebody doesn't get called back. The contractor tracked in a bunch of dirt that got ground into the carpet. They scratched the heck out of the client's linoleum in the laundry room. They scuffed up the newly painted walls while moving equipment in. I'm not saying this stuff happens on every call, but when somebody loses a client, there's usually a reason for it.

The danger line exists on every call. Maybe you've lost some customers and you don't even know it. They just didn't call you back, and you don't know why. You might be on the wrong side of the danger line with them right now.

If you discover the client still loves the other company, then you have to ask yourself, "What am I doing here? If he loves that other company so much, why didn't he just call them?" That's a great time to do a technique called stop or continue. We'll talk more about stop or continue in chapter 18, but here is how it would work in this situation. You could say, "Listen I want to go ahead and disqualify myself here, John. If you think that company is better than I am, then you should probably use those guys. I don't want to step on their toes." That's the exact language you want to use. So if somebody tells you that your competition is better than you, try to stop the call.

When you do that, guess what you're going to hear? The real truth. "Yeah, they are good," they might say. "But here's what

WHAT SHOULD WE DO?

happened." Sticking up for the competition is always going to turn things against the competition. Once you clear that up, you are free to continue the call.

I'm not here to create bad feelings between homeowners and contractors, but I am here for *you* because this call is about you and this customer. I can't worry about the global picture. If people are doing bad service out there, I think it's important that the bad service gets exposed.

The industry might think, "Here's Joe out there exposing the crappy stuff that happens to customers on every single call," but it doesn't happen on every single call. It only happens every now and then—just often enough to lose the customer.

INDIRECT COMPETITORS

The threat is not always a direct competitor. It could be the client's uncle or new brother-in-law. It could even be the spouse who's not there. They might say something like, "My husband usually does all this kind of work. He's very mechanical. He's an auto mechanic, and he even does air-conditioning on cars."

And now guess who's on the danger line? That's right—the client's husband!

So you have to say, "Well, Mary, if your husband is a mechanic, he could probably charge this system too. Why don't we give him a chance? I don't want him to think I'm stepping on his toes."

Make sure you explore all the possible dangerous scenarios that are out there. It's not always just the direct competition. It could be friends of the family or even someone in the family.

— UNCLE JOE'S RULE 23 —

Learn from the mistakes of others, or learn by making the same mistakes yourself.

The Right Side of the Danger Line

At this point, the competition is gone. You've got the customer to say that they're not going to use another company. The next step is to go to the right side of the danger line immediately. Why? Because the client is experiencing a lot of dissonance now. You just discussed a pretty negative situation about the competition. Of course, *you* didn't do it. You just learned about what the other person did to fail. It's time to turn the conversation back to something more positive, which is what the client has heard about your company and the reason they called you.

The goal of the right side of the danger line is to relieve the dissonance by getting the client to feel the love for your company. To do that, you want to give the client the opportunity to make statements like these:

- "We've heard a lot of great things about you guys."
- "We've heard that you're the best company."
- "We've heard that you're more expensive, but you're worth it."

To get started, we just need to ask the client a couple of simple questions.

As soon as you've eliminated the competition, immediately move on to getting the client to feel the love for your company.

FEEL THE LOVE

John has assured you that he's done with the competition and he's never using them again. Great. Nothing more needs to be said about the left side. It's done. Go right to working the right side by asking what he's heard about your company. It might sound something like this:

You: OK. So, let me ask you a question. What'd you hear about us? How'd you get our company's name?

It's that quick.

John: Well, I called my neighbor.

You: You did? What was her name?

John: Mary Johnson.

You: What'd Mary say about us?

John: She said the service work was exceptional and you guys had a decent price.

You: Really? What else did she say?

John: I don't know. That was about it. She was really impressed with your company.

Always remember to ask the name of the person who made the referral. Then you can say something like, "What else did she say?" to get even more love. The more good things the client says about your company, the easier it will be for them to persuade themselves to use you later on. Don't skip this part.

ALWAYS THANK THE REFERRER

At the end of the danger-line sequence, always thank the client who is saying the kind comments, and then make a plan to thank the person who first said them too. Tell the client, "I'm going to have to write a note to Mary," or "I'll tell my boss to give her a call." Then, make sure you follow through. For example, you could say, "That's so nice of Mary to say that. John, I want to say thank you for saying those kind comments. And I'm also going to stop by and say hello to Mary and let her know how much it meant to me that she said those kind things about us."

Wouldn't it be nice if your company actually did follow through? What does it cost? If you had to run a blind ad, you'd probably spend $500 to get a customer to call you. A few minutes on the phone to say thank you is very well worth it. You could say, "Mary, thanks for referring us. John told us some nice things that you said about us. That's very nice that you did that for us." That's all you need to do.

Always thank the client who is saying the kind comments, and then make a plan to thank the person who first said them too.

USE THE RIGHT SIDE FOR CUSTOMER OBJECTIONS

The danger-line information will come in very handy when it's time to handle the client's objections after you've done your presentation. We'll go into handling client objections in detail in chapters 27 and 28, but here is an example so you can see how your knowledge of both sides comes into play.

In this scenario, you've given your presentation and the client, John, says he wants to get some other opinions. In this case, you want to leverage the right side of the danger line, where the client has already said some nice things about your company.

John: Thank you, but we have to get some other prices.

You: John, what did Mary say about us?

John: She said you guys were more money, but you're better.

You: OK, so what should we do?

John: Let's look at the third option again.

The other thing that is in play here is the law of social validation, which states that people follow the crowd. They like to do things that people have done before them. Reminding John what Mary said about your company allows him to give up on the idea of getting other prices and instead shop inside of your proposal for the option that's right for him and his family.

Loyal Customers

Let's say you go to a call where there is no danger from the other side of the fence. They've used your company for years. In fact, they've never used anyone else. You might think you're safe, but you're actually just sitting at a neutral point on the danger line.

The competition is just to the left. When you first get to the call, you're probably a little bit to the right side because the client has high hopes for you based on their previous experience. All you can do in that situation is do what you can to move your company even more to the right side. That's why you still have to do this step.

As you and the client are walking to the unit, start asking questions. Here's what that might sound like:

You: Tom, let me ask you a question. I know you have used us for years. Have you ever been tempted to use another company?

Tom: Oh no, we just love you guys. I went to high school with your dad, and we've known your family forever. We wouldn't dream of using anybody else.

You: Well, I'm glad to hear that, Tom. You are a loyal customer. I looked at some of the records, and we do go back a couple of generations. What is it exactly that you guys like so much about our company?

Tom: Well, you and your coworkers are always very polite and respectful and clean, and you always get the job done.

You: What's your experience like when you call the office?

Tom: Oh, Cathy at the office? It sounds like my wife is on the phone with her best friend when she calls. We just love her.

You: Well, thanks so much for those kind comments. It means a lot to me, and it helps me learn and make my services better too. Would you please let me know if you see anything that I could improve on today?

Tom: Oh, sure.

You: Thank you very much, Tom. I appreciate it.

There's really no negativity in that exchange, so there's nothing to explore at that point. With customers where there's no negativity, you don't need to turn it into dissonance.

Instead, you want to create more praise for your company. When customers say kind words about the company out loud, they will buy into them even more. They're completely on board. And you're much less likely to get a price objection because they already told you they'd never dream of looking somewhere else. So if you get them to say how much they love you, you're not going to lose that customer.

If by some chance you have a loyal customer but he's telling you, "We're going to think about it," or "We're going to hold off on this right now," don't leave until you work something out. You could say something like, "Tom, listen, you've been a loyal customer for a long time. It's not going to be on my watch that we lose your business. Let's just sit here and figure out what we can do to get this thing working for you."

Maybe it's financing. Maybe you go with one of the lower price options. If they have a long-term relationship with your company, you have a lot of equity in that relationship. Now's the time to spend some of it.

You can't afford to lose a loyal customer. Always work something out. To get a stranger to call you will cost you at least $500. It's like ripping up a check for thousands of future dollars if you leave that call without a sale of some sort.

Don't lose a loyal customer. Spend some of the equity you have in that relationship and work something out.

New Customers

In the case of a new customer, you'll want to focus on the initial experience they had with your company, which was likely a call with a customer service representative.

You: Before we head downstairs, let me ask you a question, Jane. How did you hear about our company?

Jane: Well, we'd actually never heard of you. We just got your name off the internet.

You: Well, I appreciate you giving us a call. That's great that you found our name. But let me ask you something. When you made the phone call to our office, how did our customer service team do?

Jane: Wonderful. I talked to Wendy, and she was fantastic.

You: Oh yeah? What'd you guys talk about?

Jane: Well, we talked about our families. And she got me scheduled for this call right away.

You: That sounds great. I'm going to have to tell Wendy you said those kind things about her. It makes me feel good to work for a place that is worthy of those comments.

Jane: Well, you're welcome.

You: Let's go take a look at the problem.

That's the danger line—a proven way to ensure there's nothing lurking in the background that could tank your call after you've done the work to identify the problems and come up with solutions. It allows you to tactfully neutralize the competition by either eliminating their potential interference or disqualifying yourself, and it reinforces the reasons the client called you in the first place by surfacing the nice things they have heard about you, which you can use to both reward the person who said the nice things and overcome future client objections.

— UNCLE JOE'S RULE 24 —

Most companies don't win new clients. The other company lost them.

In the next section about the fourth Pure Motive Service principle—being ethical—we will cover how to use what you've learned in accordance with the five Pure Motive Service values: enhancing quality and reliability, protecting the client's safety and health, providing customer-service choices, customized relevant solutions, and honesty (even when it's not popular).

BULLSEYES

- Bad service gravity momentum occurs when clients have had so many bad experiences with contractors that you end up sucked into their negative mindset, which results in you giving them what they expect (bad service), which continues the cycle.

- The left side of the danger line is all about finding out how the competition failed and then letting gravity and momentum do their work until the client eventually says something like, "We're not using that guy anymore. But we're not going to fix it ourselves."

- The right side of the danger line is about reminding clients about the nice things they've said about your company so they give up on the idea of getting other prices and instead shop inside of your proposal for the option that's right for them and their family.

WHAT SHOULD WE DO?

- When working the danger line with loyal customers, your goal is to do what you can to move your company even more to the right side so that if something comes up you have the opportunity to work something out.

- For new customers, the danger line is about focusing on the initial experience they had with your company, which was likely a call with a customer service representative.

TOOLS FOR YOUR SUCCESS

servicemvp.com/tools

SERVICE MVP.

* **TOTAL IMMERSION BENCHMARK WORKSHEET**
From on-site arrival to affirming your client's choice, use this outline of the sales process to hit every benchmark and measure your performance after a call.

* **QUOTES AND FIGURES**
Get all the memorable quotes and figures featured in this book. Help yourself and your team remember the fundamental principles of Pure Motive Service!

Scan to download your tools

BE
ETHICAL

Chapter 17
BE ETHICAL—OVERVIEW

To be ethical is to subscribe to a set of principles that govern our behavior or the conduct of an activity. In this case, our conduct is governed by the five Pure Motive Service values you learned in chapter 2: enhancing quality and reliability; protecting the client's safety and health; providing customer-service choices; customized relevant solutions; and honesty (even when it's not popular).

The Five Pure Motive Service Values

Let's take a deeper look at each of these values so we can connect them to the Pure Motive Service principle of being ethical.

ENHANCING QUALITY AND RELIABILITY

Growing up as the son of a plumber in the 1970s led me to believe it was a badge of honor to do things as cheaply as possible for clients. So when I got into the service business, I used to pride myself in my ability to "MacGyver" a solution to the client's problem to make the job cheaper. (Angus "Mac" MacGyver was the title character in the 1985 television series, and to "MacGyver" something has come to mean devising an inventive solution to a problem using existing resources.)

One day I had a client ask me, "Joe, why are you always trying to save me money? Why not just show me the best way to get the job done right the first time?"

I told the client that my number one goal was to save her money. She said, "Do you want to save me money in the long run or just today? Because if I have to take off work again to have your company come back to do it a second time, it'll end up being *more* expensive than if you just charge me for what it will take to do what really needs to be done today."

This was the first time someone ever shot straight with me, and it changed the arc of my career.

Once we are in a client's home, we take responsibility for the entire system, not just the problematic component. That is why we always diagnose the entire system and don't stop our process when we find the problem we were called out for. We believe in providing quality, permanent solutions and an update of all systems that are in need of renovation or repair.

We also become responsible for educating the customer on the entire range of quality and reliability solutions available to them. We do that because we want to empower them to make an informed decision about which option is right for them and their family. We believe clients should have the opportunity to live their lives free of worry and lifestyle interruptions by deteriorating systems in need of constant repair.

Once we are in a client's home, we take responsibility for the entire system, not just the problematic component.

PROTECTING THE CLIENT'S SAFETY AND HEALTH

I was doing a ride along with a service professional named Ricky when we got a call about a garage door that wouldn't open. We rang the doorbell, and a young woman answered and invited us into the home. We introduced ourselves and asked to see the problem. As the homeowner, whose name was Stacy, led us through the house to the door that led out to the garage, I noticed there were two small children in the family room watching *Peppa Pig* on the television. I also saw all kinds of child-safety devices, including electrical outlet protection and cabinet locks. I praised Stacy's effort to make the house as safe as possible for her young kids.

We looked at the garage door system and put together our options. After Ricky presented our most premium option, Stacy began questioning the price. Ricky pointed out that there were less expensive options, but Stacy said she wanted the top option but thought it was too expensive. Ricky calmly responded, "The top option has the highest level of safety and health for your family. What price can you put on that?"

After taking a moment to process Ricky's response, Stacy replied, "You can't, that's priceless."

As Pure Motive Service providers, our higher purpose is to ensure a safe and healthy living environment for our customers and community. That's why we help our clients connect their levels of safety and health to what may or may not be happening in their home and to their existing or desired system.

PROVIDING CUSTOMER-SERVICE CHOICES

After purchasing our first premium custom-built home in 1999, my wife Julie and I decided we wanted a new leather sofa for the living room. We shopped first at a few chain furniture stores but didn't find anything we liked. The last place on our list was a small furniture store in Wauconda, Illinois, called Angelo's. The owner, Angelo, greeted us at the door. I said, "We're looking for a leather sofa to go in our living room in our new house." I'll never forget what he said next.

"If you're just looking for a sofa, I'd recommend going to Sears or Sam's Club," he said. "But if you're looking for someone to make sure your home's furniture matches the way you live, you've come to the right place."

About $58,000 later, every room in our house was filled with beautiful new furniture that perfectly matched our taste and lifestyle. When we put the house on the market in 2005, everyone who offered to purchase it wanted the furniture too, and it sold for nearly $100,000 more than any other home in that neighborhood.

Pure Motive Service providers believe offering great service means anticipating the needs of your client. The client's role is reduced to choosing a solution and enjoying the result. The burden of communicating, providing solutions, and performing the work is done by you and your company. A commitment to great customer service also means refusing to participate in bad service, especially when requested by the customer.

Every client is unique in their lifestyles, routines, and challenges. As a student of your client, it's your duty to only provide custom solutions that are relevant to each family's unique situation.

CUSTOMIZED RELEVANT SOLUTIONS

After my grandpa's Ford Fairlane finally died, I bought a used 1971 Ford Pinto. It was so cheap that it only had an AM radio. I needed a better system, so I went to Kmart and bought a cheap stereo cassette deck. But I was afraid of ripping up the dashboard if I tried to install it myself, so I went to a car audio place in Highland Park, Illinois, called Sound on Wheels to see what it would cost for them to do it for me.

I went into the shop, budget tape deck in hand, and asked the guy at the counter how much it would cost to install it. He pointed at the unit I'd brought in and asked me how much I paid for it. I said, "$34.97."

"Before I give you a price on installing this in your car," he said, "I want you to listen to an equivalent system we have for sale and then go ahead and listen to some of the other systems we have as well." I said OK, and he handed me a set of headphones.

After listening to all the stereo systems, he asked me which one was my favorite. I told him it was the Pioneer stereo. It had a deep booming bass and crystal-clear highs, and it was *awesome.*

He said, "Guess what? That sound system is only $38 per month." I decided having a great stereo in my car was well worth paying $38 per month for a while. Soon I was able to listen to all of my favorite (now classic) rock tunes through this amazing system, all because the salesman allowed me to discover what I really wanted in a car stereo experience and then offered me a way to pay for it that worked for me.

Every client is unique in their lifestyles, routines, and challenges. When you practice Pure Motive Service, you are a student of each individual client and will only provide custom solutions that are relevant to each family's unique situation without an upselling pitch. Each problem and solution should be communicated in a way that is relevant to your client and their family members.

HONESTY (EVEN WHEN IT'S NOT POPULAR)

Shortly after I started offering premium, midrange, and economy options, I went on a drain-cleaning call and discovered the client's sewer pipe had cracked and the drain system had collapsed.

I wasn't looking forward to telling him that the pipe had a fracture and had collapsed, but he deserved to know the truth. I gave him the bad news and showed him a video. Then I showed him the premium, midrange, and economy solutions I'd created.

Imagine my surprise when the client said, "Yeah, I knew the pipe was fractured. I've had three different plumbers tell me that." I asked him why he didn't purchase a solution from one of those other plumbers.

"I didn't go with any of them because they promised to send me a price but never followed through," he said. "To be honest, I think they were afraid of telling me how much it would cost."

He ended up purchasing my top option, which included a new drain system, along with all new plumbing fixtures for almost $29,000.

In the course of diagnosing problems, other unseen issues with a system are often found. A Pure Motive Service provider believes that all clients have a right to know any issues that affect the quality, safety, and reliability of their systems and also to be aware of any solutions available to update or fix them. It may not be popular, but you will inform clients of all the possible problems, solutions, and upgrades.

Honesty is also about admitting when you are not the right fit for a job and then helping clients find the right solution—even if it's not you. It's also about refusing to sell a product or service that is not needed or wanted. (Remember, we first provide our unconditional friendship regardless of whether the client buys from us or not.)

— UNCLE JOE'S RULE 25 —
All clients have a right to know about any issues that affect the quality, safety, and reliability of their systems.

Money Is Not My Master

You've no doubt heard of techs or salespeople talking about a client with a Mercedes in the garage and how that influenced them to offer more premium solutions. On the other hand, there are times when a client seemed to be struggling, so the technician offered them the cheapest possible solution.

This practice is called profiling. It is the enemy of great service, and it is considered unethical based on the five values that are supposed to be guiding us. We are by definition equal-opportunity solution creators.

As you work with this system, you will encounter many people you perceive to be rich who pick the cheapest option and many people you perceive to be poor who choose the premium one. Why? Because clients purchase for their reasons, not yours.

My personal motto is, "Money is not my master. Finding the right solution for you and your family is what I live for." What I mean by that is, rich or poor, everyone deserves to at least see what a premium, high-end solution would look like. It means you don't let money stand in the way of showing a client how they could head off a flooded basement by putting in two sump pumps and a standby generator for groundwater removal, or showing them what a new Grohe faucet would cost to replace their builder-grade Moen faucet with the bad cartridge.

Money is not your master. Create the options, and then price them accordingly. Tell the client you don't expect anything other than them making the right choice for their family. Just show them the possible solutions and ask, "What should we do?" Then stand back and let the client take their time to decide.

— UNCLE JOE'S RULE 26 —

No profiling. Clients deserve to hear all the solutions available regardless of what you perceive their financial status to be.

With Great Knowledge Comes Great Responsibility

This section contains a lot of information about how the human mind works. My intent is to raise your awareness of how we humans think so you can use that information to ethically assist your clients in buying the solution that is right for them. You will be learning things like the sciences of persuasion and pricing and the laws of association and contrast, along with the diagnostic process and how to create the right proposal.

All of this information needs to be used responsibly. You may recognize some places where the information could be abused if it wasn't used in service of ensuring your client's health, wellness, safety, and comfort. Remember, our job is to offer our unconditional friendship first, and we must honor that friendship by staying true not only to our values but also to ourselves.

 **BULLSEYES**

- To be ethical is to subscribe to a set of principles that govern our behavior or the conduct of an activity. Our conduct as Pure Motive Service providers is governed by the five Pure Motive Service values.

- The five Pure Motive Service values are enhancing quality and reliability, protecting the client's safety and health, providing customer-service choices, customized relevant solutions, and honesty (even when it's not popular).

- Doing things the cheapest way can end up being *more* expensive for the client than if you just charged them for what it would take to do what really needed to be done today.

- Money is not your master. Rich or poor, everyone deserves to at least see what a premium, high-end solution would look like.

- All of this information needs to be used responsibly. We offer our unconditional friendship to the client first, and we honor that friendship by staying true to our values and ourselves.

WHAT SHOULD WE DO?

Chapter 18
THE HIERARCHY OF PERSUASION

Persuasion is the act of presenting arguments to move, motivate, or change your client. In the Pure Motive Service model, persuasion is used to guide the client through the decision-making process. We are not invested in which option they choose. All we care about is that they purchase the one that is right for them because our goal is to create friendships that turn into long-term relationships.

The Five Levels of Persuasion

There are five levels of persuasion: control, coercion, compliance, cooperation, and commitment. You need to understand all five levels because you want to avoid using the first four and only use the fifth one—commitment.

CONTROL

The lowest form of persuasion is control. Control is obtained by using fear, force, or threats. Control doesn't work if you are trying to cultivate a long-term relationship. It sounds something like, "If you don't buy this option, you're going to get electrocuted." It's always a disaster scenario to scare a person into buying something.

COERCION

The next rung up is coercion. Coercion implies a threat. It sounds something like, "John, I'm not saying you're going to die, but what do you think happens when your house holds carbon monoxide? Did you hear about that family on the south side that died from carbon-monoxide poisoning last week?" Again, it might work once, but it's not a winning strategy for building long-term relationships.

COMPLIANCE

Next up is compliance. Compliance is about offering incentives, benefits, and rewards. It sounds something like, "I can give you $100 off if you buy a humidifier from me today." This extends to the salesperson too. A boss might say, "Become a better salesperson, and we'll give you 10 percent of whatever you sell." Neither of these work to establish the trust and connection required to maintain a long-term relationship.

COOPERATION

Cooperation is the second-highest form of persuasion. Cooperation is an effort to get someone to do something by providing evidence to show the client that you're capable of handling the project. In this case, you would be encouraging cooperation by explaining why the client should hire you. It sounds something like, "Hey, I have 20 years of experience, everything I need is on my truck, and I can get it done today, so I can definitely take care of this issue right now." This is the form of persuasion most contractors use before they learn the Pure Motive Service system.

COMMITMENT

The last and highest form of persuasion is commitment. Commitment is selling from a place of respect, honor, and trust. Clients don't buy because of you. They buy because they want to buy, and because they trust you. They buy because you listened to them and gave them six good options. The options make sense to them because they are on code. They feel confident in selecting one of those options because you've been there with them facilitating the decision every step of the way. They are accountable for the choice they make, not you or your company. As you may have noticed, commitment is a big part of the Pure Motive Service system. Now you know why!

— UNCLE JOE'S RULE 27 —

Earning the respect, honor, and trust of your client is the highest form of commitment.

The Three Types of Questions

The ability to ask the right kinds of questions at the right time is a big part of this system because it allows the client to tell you the truth about the impact the problem is having on their life. You learned a little bit about the three question types—leading, contrary, and neutral—in chapter 15. Let's dive in a little deeper.

LEADING QUESTIONS

Leading questions are associated primarily with the compliance type of persuasion and are not very effective. When you ask a leading question, people see it coming. They know you're trying to sell them something, so their defenses are up. Leading questions sound something like:

- "If I could show you a way to buy a new hot water heater, would you be interested?"
- "If you feel that our service is top-notch, would you use our company again?"
- "A lot of people are installing green solutions in their homes. How do you feel about that?"
- "Our service satisfactorily met your needs, didn't it?"

You're always going to get turned down with leading questions because people can see the sales pitch coming. Plus, the fact that you are attempting to "lead" them anywhere does not align with the Pure Motive Service values, which say our job is to provide options so the client can pick the one they feel is best for their family.

The best types of questions to ask are contrary or neutral questions. They will help you create interest and desire for all the components that will appear in your top option. They are in alignment with the commitment form of persuasion because they are designed to assist the client in telling you the true impact the problem is having on their life.

Contrary and neutral questions can also help you navigate certain issues that tend to arise when working with the three different buyer types, which you'll learn about later in this chapter.

CONTRARY QUESTIONS

"John, when was the last time you cleaned the drains in this house? Do you normally get them cleaned every year?" is a good example of a contrary question.

Now, you and I know that nobody gets drain cleaning done every year. And that's the key to the contrary question—you already know the answer is going to be no. You should never ask a contrary question unless you already know what the answer is going to be.

Remember, a contrary question is always the ridiculous opposite of what you would normally ask.

Let's say you're going to an air-conditioning call and you see a four-ton unit with a 20-by-8-inch return drop going into the furnace. You do your calculations and realize that they are essentially trying to cool a four-ton house with two-and-a-half tons of airflow. You're thinking that it must get pretty hot upstairs in the summertime. They really should add a mini-split. You could ask a leading question, right?

You: I'll bet it's hot upstairs, huh?

The problem is that the client sees the pitch coming a mile away, so he tells you a fib to avoid dealing with it.

Mike: Not really. It's OK. We just open the windows. I don't really like air-conditioning.

To get around this outcome, you should ask the exact opposite question.

You: I'll bet it's too cold up there in the primary bedroom during the summer, right?

Trust me, Mike's not expecting you to say *that*.

Mike: Are you kidding? We're sweltering up there. You must be absolutely insane.

At this point, you could introduce the upgrade you're thinking of with a contrary question. As a warning, be careful not to propose anything specific during this process. You are just getting people interested and creating desire. Here's what the rest of the exchange might sound like:

You: Mike, how come you chose not to get a mini-split up there?

Mike: I never thought about it.

You: Is it important for your family to be able to sleep well?

Mike: Yes, definitely.

The next thing you do is try to shut down the conversation.

You: Well, anyway, I'm just here for maintenance on the air-conditioning unit today. I won't worry about the second floor.

If the client is sufficiently interested, they will indicate that.

Mike: Actually, if we could solve that problem, my wife would be really happy.

You: Should I give you some solution options on that?

Mike: Yes, give me some options.

This is the first commitment.

You: Are you sure? I don't want to pressure you.

Mike: Yes, I definitely want to hear about it.

This is the second commitment.

You: OK. I'll go ahead and create some options for you.

You created curiosity and desire, and now you can use that to build your top option. That's how you sell upgrades—through contrary questions.

The key to a contrary question is that you already know the answer is going to be no. You should never ask a contrary question unless you already know what the answer is going to be.

NEUTRAL QUESTIONS

Neutral questions are not the most persuasive type of questions, but they are safe territory and have their place.

A neutral question is asking someone for their opinion on something. Let's say you want to sell an air purifier. You could say, "Well, John, what's your opinion of the air quality in this house?" Or if you want to sell a humidifier, you could say, "John, what's your opinion of the humidity level in this house?"

John: It's OK right now, but it gets pretty dry in the winter.

You'd then follow up with a question about how that impacts him and his family.

You: I bet. What's that like?

John: I like it dry, but it's not great for the houseplants.

The impact of the lack of humidity on his houseplants then becomes a card you can play when you present the humidifier portion of your top option. You could say, "I added this humidifier because I want to make sure your houseplants can thrive throughout the winter." (We'll talk more about presenting on-code solutions in chapter 25.)

In addition, if you are working with a buyer who is excited and running you all over the place, it's easy to get caught up in that energy and start skipping steps. Asking a series of neutral questions will keep them from rushing you through your process, which is better for them—and better for you too. Identifying and managing an enthusiastic buyer is really important because if they are enthusiastic enough, a whole lot can go wrong, as you'll see in the next section.

An enthusiastic buyer is only one type of buyer you will encounter on your calls, though, so let's discuss these buyer types in more detail.

Asking neutral questions can slow down an enthusiastic buyer whose behavior is making it difficult or impossible for you to methodically work through the Pure Motive Service system.

The Three Buyer Types

There are three different types of buyers that you're going to face. The first is an enthusiastic buyer who wants your services and is glad to tell you so. The second is a negative buyer. This is someone you'll sense negativity from, or maybe they try to use negativity to negotiate with you early in the call. The third is a neutral buyer, who's not even sure why you're there.

ENTHUSIASTIC BUYERS

We've already talked a little bit about enthusiastic buyers, but here's a story that will show you the type of disaster that can happen if you're not paying attention. One time I was out with a plumber named George doing a call at a big mansion on a horse farm in suburban Philadelphia. We knocked on the door, and the client, Karen, answered.

Karen: Oh, thank God you're here. I've got a big wedding coming up. I'm going to have guests in all eight bedrooms of this house. We have to get this stuff fixed.

That's the first commitment. Great! I didn't even have to ask. Now for the second commitment.

Joe: OK, what are you hoping to accomplish today?

Karen: We need to get these things fixed.

That's commitment number two. So far I'm on board with the Pure Motive Service system.

Karen: Come with me, and I'll show you what I need.

Joe: OK, let's go. Come on, George. Karen, have you used any other plumbers?

She didn't answer me. We went into the first bathroom, and she waved her hand at the tub, toilet, and faucets and said, "We've got to replace all of this. We've also got to get a new water heater. Ours is not big enough. We have a lot of guests coming, and I want to make sure we have enough hot water for them."

We followed her all over the house taking notes about the things she wanted us to do. I was so busy writing the list that I forgot to follow the system. I thought it would be OK because she was so enthusiastic about getting the work done. That is, until I gave her the prices. Then she was a lot less enthusiastic.

Karen: Are you out of your mind? You're just a plumber. You're going to charge me more than $20,000? That's outrageous!

She said it like we were dirt. George and I just looked at each other, stunned, while she continued her rant.

Karen: I wouldn't even pay $10,000 for everything you're talking about. My husband's a general contractor, and we have a plumber who can do the whole thing for $5,000.

Joe: Well, why did you call us then?

She said her husband's plumber couldn't make it there for a couple of weeks so she was shopping around. I slunk out of there, tail between my legs. I couldn't handle that objection because I didn't see it coming. I was so convinced we were going to sell this one that when I got an objection, I lost my way. I didn't have the information from the Pure Motive Service system to fall back on.

If I can get so caught up in the dynamic of an enthusiastic customer that I forego working my own system, so can you. Always work the system methodically so you don't end up getting worked over by an enthusiastic client like I did.

Let's analyze what happened here a little more.

Karen said three or four times, "I have a wedding coming up, and I have guests coming." But I allowed her to rush us around so I didn't have a chance to ask about her and her family, much less create a magic moment. How was I going to be on code with my presentation?

I did get my convince-me steps in. Karen gave me two commitments without me asking her for anything. The problem is those commitments only mean something if they go along with the other parts of the system.

I really blew it with the danger line. I could have saved us all a ton of time by finding out another plumber had already been out there and provided pricing. It also would have been helpful to learn about his relationship with Karen's husband. At the very least, I should have set the rules and said, "Before we start looking at things, I need to ask you a few questions." I could have insisted we stop and slow things down a little bit.

When you encounter an enthusiastic buyer, you need to double down on working the Pure Motive Service system and slow the buyer down so you can get everything you need and respond effectively. Remember, Event + Response = Outcome. You have to be especially careful with your questions when you are dealing with an enthusiastic buyer. Negative, leading, or contrary questions might get them a little too amped up because they are already excited about getting the problem fixed quickly.

Here's another example. Note the client's response.

You: So what made you decide to call us today?

Amy: Well, the air-conditioning is not working, so I've got to get it fixed. I've got people coming in from out of town.

You: To be clear, you just want us to take a look at it and see what is going on?

Amy: No, you've got to get it fixed today. Are you crazy? I just told you I had to get it fixed!

You: OK, well let's see what we can do.

What's going on here? "You just want us to take a look at it and see what is going on?" is an example of a leading question. You're putting words in the client's mouth. "You're not looking to get the work done today, are you?" is an example of a contrary question. When it comes to enthusiastic buyers, you want to keep the questions neutral. You could say something like, "Just to be clear, what are we hoping to accomplish today?"

NEGATIVE OR NEUTRAL BUYERS

The way to deal with negative or neutral buyers is the same.

A negative buyer wears their heart on their sleeve, and they can be challenging to deal with. They are agitated or irritated about something, and they're taking it out on you. That said, since people mostly buy with emotion and only a little bit with logic, if you know how to channel that emotion correctly, a negative buyer is sometimes the easiest person to sell.

To me, the hardest customer to deal with is a neutral one who has no emotion at all. They may not even care enough to be there to let you in, and that's pretty negative. They leave their keys with a neighbor or their kid and let them receive the call. Neutral buyers are basically negative buyers who have some sort of issue or complaint that may or may not be with you.

So you are dealing with somebody who is cranky or someone who is indifferent. How can you make a presentation with prices to these people when you haven't been able to connect with them to find out what their needs and priorities are? The short answer is you can't. The way to deal with negative or neutral buyers is to do a technique called stop or continue.

Neutral buyers are basically negative buyers who have some sort of issue or complaint that may or may not be with you.

Stop or Continue

The key to the stop-or-continue technique is the phrase, "Why don't we go ahead and cancel the call?" You're not saying you *want* the client to cancel the call, but if you try to do so and leave, the real truth will come out.

You: Jerry, you seem like you're very upset right now, and the last thing I want to do is come in and disrupt your life even more because I'm going to have to go over the whole air-conditioning system. So why don't we just go ahead and cancel this call and put it off for a while?

That's stop or continue. You're not saying they should cancel it for good. You're just giving them the option to put the call off until later.

Sometimes the client is legitimately negative as a result of something you did, like being late. You can't present to them while they are in that mindset.

Jerry: It's about time you showed up. I've been waiting all day for you guys. I could have gone to work today.

You: Jerry, I'm sorry about that. It's really not a good way to do business. And I can sense that you're very upset. If you're too upset to continue, we can just cancel the call and come back at a different time because I don't want to proceed with somebody who is angry at the company. I don't think that's going to be a very productive way of going forward. What should we do?

Here's what Jerry is likely going to say because he doesn't want to take another day off work.

Jerry: No, no, no. I'm not that angry. I do want to get the work done. It's not your fault. I'm sure it's busy out there.

He will start making excuses for you! Think about all those years you've been trying to justify your prices and beg for business. You don't have to do that anymore. Just do the stop-or-continue technique, and the whole thing will turn around.

Since people mostly buy with emotion and only a little bit with logic, if you know how to channel that emotion correctly, a negative buyer is sometimes the easiest person to sell.

Recognize Yellow Lights

The key to identifying negative buyers is to watch for those yellow lights. What is the client saying to you right now (or in the middle of the call) that could hint at the fact that this call might suck? Here are some of the greatest hits:

- "The last company that was out here couldn't get it working either."
- "My brother (or uncle, or cousin, or neighbor) is in the business."
- "I usually do my own electrical work, but I figured I'd have you out this time because I'm too busy."
- "I'm really busy. I hope this isn't going to take too long."
- "It's just a small job."
- "I hope you guys don't charge me as much as you did last time."
- "Don't try to sell me something extra this time because the last couple of times you guys hit me pretty hard. Please take it easy on me."
- "I'm on a fixed income and don't have much money."

Let's walk through a couple of these examples so you can see how to handle them. Let's discuss money problems first.

MONEY

If the client brings up that they have money problems before you've had a chance to fully diagnose the system, the thing to do is to express respect for their situation and offer them the option to stop the call.

Terry: I hope this doesn't cost very much. I'm on a fixed income right now.

You: Well, Terry, listen, I'm not sure how much it's going to cost. I haven't even examined the system yet. At this point, we could either stop or continue the call. What should we do? I don't want to be a burden to your family. You guys are going through some tough times, and the last thing I want to do is add to that kind of burden.

Terry: But we really need to get it fixed.

You: I don't want to add to your family's stress.

Terry: Well, why don't you stay here and we'll just see what it's going to cost?

You: Are you sure?

Terry: Yes, please.

You: So you're not going to be mad at me when I show you the prices, right?

Terry: No, no, no.

You: All right. I'll go ahead and look at the system.

Terry already told you she doesn't have much money, so you know chances are good that she's going to be upset when you show her the prices. So you get right in front of that by saying, "You're not going to be mad at me, are you?" And she needs to agree, or you should end the call right there.

TIME

Whenever the client pressures you about the time it will take to do the job, go directly to the stop-or-continue technique.

Tom: I'm kind of busy. I hope this isn't going to take too long.

You: Well, Tom, we're awfully busy too. Here's what we could do. We could cancel this call, and I could come back later when you and I both have more time. Would that be better for you?

Tom: No, I've got to get it done today.

You: So what should we do if you don't have the time?

Tom: Oh, we need to get it fixed, so I'll make the time.

You: Are you sure? Because I can come back tomorrow or some other time next week. (Bear in mind, Tom likely has already waited for you to get there and won't want to wait longer.)

Tom: No, we're busy next week. Let's get it done now.

You: OK, then I'll go ahead and take a look at the system.

OTHER PEOPLE

And last but not least, every contractor's favorite is the client who has a relative in the business. It's time to work the left side of the danger line!

Tom: I have a brother-in-law who does electrical work.

You: Oh, why call me then? Why didn't you call him? Listen, I'm not going to take bread out of your brother-in-law's mouth.

Tom: No, let's go ahead and do it. It's hard to get him over here.

You: But he's your brother-in-law!

Tom: You know what? You're here. Let's get this done.

You: My greatest fear, Tom, is I'm going to show you the prices, then your brother-in-law is going to say he could do it a lot cheaper and you'll end up going with him. Is that going to happen?

Tom: No, no. Let's just get it done.

You: OK, let's go take a look at the system.

When you encounter yellow lights and negative things start happening, deal with them right away by doing stop or continue. How to move forward will become much clearer.

In the next chapter, we will cover the technical part of the call, which is the diagnostic process.

BULLSEYES

- There are five levels of persuasion. As contractors, we always want to use the highest form of persuasion, which is commitment.

- There are three types of questions: leading, contrary, and neutral. Avoid leading questions.

- There are three buyer types: enthusiastic, negative, and neutral. When dealing with an enthusiastic buyer, double down on the Pure Motive Service process and stick to neutral questions.

- If you are dealing with a buyer who is cranky (negative) or indifferent (neutral), and you can't connect with them to find out their needs and priorities, you may need to do the stop-or-continue technique.

- Negative buyers often trigger yellow lights. Common subjects are money, time, and other people.

WHAT SHOULD WE DO?

Chapter 19
THE DIAGNOSTIC PROCESS

I was working with a company in Minnesota who sent me out with a technician named John who had more than 20 years of experience. We were in the truck heading toward the client's house. John told me he already knew what he was doing, so I should just watch and maybe I'd learn something. I said maybe he could learn something from me, too, but I knew he didn't think so. I agreed to watch and said we'd see what happened. We arrived at the client's house, and John rang the bell. A woman answered the door, and here's how it went:

John: Hey, are you Ann?

Ann: Yes.

John: I'm here to fix the furnace.

Ann: OK, it's right downstairs.

And that was the only conversation we had with her. John headed down to the basement. I was walking behind him, and Ann was walking behind me. He looked at the furnace and removed a component. This took all of two minutes. He showed the component to Ann.

John: I found the problem. Look, there's a fracture in this part right here.

Ann: Oh, OK, so it's just that little part right there?

John: Yeah, that's the one.

Ann: Well, how much is that going to cost?

John: You're looking at $345.

Ann: $345? I'll bet I can find that part online for like $15.

Actually, if she knew where to look, she could have found it for $12. I was just watching this whole thing between John and Ann unfold.

John: You're not going to find it online. It's made specifically for the manufacturer.

Ann: Well, how long is it going to take to put the part in?

John: I have that part on my truck, so probably about 10 minutes.

Ann: What? That's ridiculous. You're charging me $345 for 10 minutes of work?

He tried to justify it by talking about the company's overhead, and it went downhill from there.

Ann: I just want you guys to leave.

John: Wait, I need to collect the $89 fee for the diagnosis.

Ann: What? You didn't even do anything. The heat's still not working. I'm not paying $89.

At that point, Ann walked us to the door, and once we were out, she shut it behind us.

Once we got back in the truck, I turned to him.

Joe: So, John, how do you think that call went?

John: That lady is just cheap. Nobody could do anything about that. That's just the way she is.

Joe: I agree she was concerned about the financial part of it. Can you think of anything you might have done to get a better result?

John: Hey, I got in there and found the problem really fast, Joe. I'm telling you, she is just cheap.

Joe: Well, why not let me run the next call?

John: Sure, if you want to do it your way, go ahead and show me.

Joe: I'm not here to show you up, John. I'm just here to try to take you to the next level. Let's go to the next call and see what happens.

So we went to the next call, which was across town. Again, a woman answered the door.

Joe: Hi, who do I have the pleasure of speaking with?

Jennifer: My name is Jennifer.

Joe: Hey, Jennifer, my name is Joe, and this is John. We're with Acme. What are we here to accomplish today?

Jennifer: Well, we've got to get the furnace working. It's 55 degrees in here.

Joe: Jennifer, first of all, thank you for inviting us into your house and allowing us to be here today. Thanks for the opportunity. I really appreciate that.

Jennifer: That's nice of you, Joe. Come on in.

Joe: Jennifer, just to be clear, what would you like to accomplish on today's call?

Jennifer: I want to get the furnace fixed. We have no heat.

Joe: OK, I'll take a look at that. Can I just say something? Your family's so lucky to have someone like you who's making the effort to stay home and get this thing done. So thank you so much for that.

Jennifer: That's nice of you. Here, I'll show you where the furnace is.

We all went downstairs to look at the system. John was eager to get into the unit to find out what was wrong, but I reminded him he was going to assist me on this call. The first thing we did was look at the house. We walked off the length and width. Then we looked at the ductwork and discovered it was undersized by 42 percent.

Joe: John, look at the size of the ductwork. Do you think that's the right size for this equipment? And is the equipment even the right size for the house?

John: What difference does it make? The problem is they don't have any heat right now.

Joe: John, just bear with me. This house is only 1,400 square feet and the furnace is 100,000 BTUs.

John: Yeah, that's way too big.

Joe: So what do you think that would do to a system?

John: It probably overrecycles and goes very fast.

Joe: And how would that impact the parts?

John just looked at me.

Joe: How about the ductwork being undersized?

John: Oh, shoot.

In addition to the house and the ductwork, we also looked at the control system. The wiring was a mess and posed a legitimate fire hazard. The furnace filter was also packed with dust. At some point, Jennifer came downstairs and asked what we were finding.

Joe: We'll get to that shortly. We just want to make sure we do a thorough system analysis so we don't have any callbacks and you don't need any other repairs for this issue in the future.

Jennifer: Oh, good. I definitely want to make sure we don't have any other problems. I can't keep taking time off work.

Joe: That's our goal too. I can't wait to help you with that.

Jennifer went back upstairs, and I finished writing down all of the options.

John: Joe, why are you writing all this stuff down? Can't we just tell her the problem?

Joe: We need to make sure we write down all the possible solutions before we share the problem.

John: All right, but I can tell she's just like the last lady. She's going to be too cheap.

Joe: Well, let's just see what happens, OK?

We went back upstairs, and after coaching John a bit more on his word choices, we sat down at the kitchen table with Jennifer.

Joe: John, go ahead and tell Jennifer what the problem is.

John: You've got a fracture fault in the ignition system.

I jumped in.

Joe: Can I share something more, Jennifer?

Jennifer: What's that?

Joe: Well, the way the system is designed is actually making some of your components go bad. I noticed a bunch of old parts boxes next to the equipment. How many repairs have you already had on this thing?

Jennifer: About five. It's been an issue ever since we moved in here four years ago.

Joe: Well, here's why that's happening. First, the furnace is oversized for the house. It's cycling too fast, and it's wearing out all the components. Second, the system that distributes the air is restricted by 42 percent. I bet the second floor gets too cool in the summertime, right?

Note the contrary question.

Jennifer: Ha, no, it's super hot upstairs when it gets warmer than 85 degrees outside.

Joe: That's because the ductwork also restricts the air-conditioning, and that impacts those components as well.

Jennifer: Oh my goodness, how can we fix all this stuff?

Joe: John can fix the immediate problem. The premium option would be to do a temporary fix to get the heat back on and then replace the entire system, which is 22 years old. We've also provided you with five other options so you can pick the one that is best for you.

Jennifer: I think I just want to replace it. It's old, and it sounds like it's just going to keep breaking.

Joe: Well, you have that option, as well as some other options to consider. What should we do?

Jennifer got her husband on the phone and he came home from work to look at the options. Next thing you know, we were writing up a ticket for an $18,000 system that fully addressed the exact same problem we had on the first call.

What is the lesson I want you to take from this story?

We have to diagnose a system like we're medical professionals. If you go to the dentist for a toothache, the first thing they do is take X-rays. That's because the dentist wants to be able to zoom out and look at the condition of the whole system—your teeth, gums, and jaw. Only after they've looked at your whole dental system do they diagnose the reason for your toothache and tell you what your options are.

It's the same with a doctor. Let's say your knee hurts. All you want is some pain medication, but your doctor is not a drug dealer. They have protocols to follow to make sure they make an accurate diagnosis. They are going to collect some general information from you first, maybe run a few tests, and once they have all that information, they will diagnose the problem and offer you some options, which may include pain medication.

So when we're diagnosing a system, we have to do the same thing. No matter what the patient says they want to do, we have to zoom out and look at the whole system before we can tell them what the problem and solution options are.

The client decides if they want to invite us into their house. They also decide which solution they want and when they want the job done. How we go about diagnosing their system is our decision, not theirs.

Think like a medical professional. Diagnose the entire system first before you reveal the problem and propose any solutions.

Diagnosis Game Plan

You've arrived at the client's home and you are getting ready to get out of the truck and walk up to the door. What should you bring with you? The answer is, at most, a screwdriver and flashlight. Leave your tools in the truck for now.

If you go in with your tools, it indicates that you're ready to work. But you don't know yet whether it's a good time to work. Does the client want the problem fixed today? Or do they want you to just look at it? You have to know that and a few other things before you get your tools.

So here's the game plan. You should go to the door with the goal of offering your unconditional friendship. That starts with finding out about the client and listening for clues about their unique buying code. You should create a magic moment. You should do the convince-me step and work the danger line. By now you should also know what type of buyer you're dealing with (enthusiastic, negative, or neutral).

Then, and only then, do you go look at the equipment. Tell the client that you're going to go get your tools, then come back and do some diagnosing. Also remember to bring your iPad or whatever you need to fill out your presentation worksheet and access your price book.

Then, start making up the solutions *while* you are diagnosing the system. Don't wait. You don't want to spend a lot of time diagnosing the system and then disappear into your truck for another 20 minutes to put together the proposal. That will break the flow of the call. Do it as you go along.

Start making up the solutions while you are diagnosing the system; otherwise you'll break the flow of the call.

The Six Factors

The diagnosis starts with your observations of six factors: the system's age, neglect, design, installation, client impact, and the immediate problem.

You want to formulate solutions based on all six of these factors because you need to do more than just solve the immediate problem. You need to come up with a long-term solution to address any issues the client may have with that system for the next several years.

The first two things to look at are age and neglect.

AGE

You're going to look at the age of the system to see if the current problem is indicative of a more serious problem. If you have a circuit breaker on an electrical panel that has failed, well, how old is the system? For example, if it's an old Federal Pacific breaker, you already know it's obsolete.

NEGLECT

Age and neglect are usually related. So, again, if you're an electrical contractor, and you find that old Federal Pacific breaker from 1976, you're going to write down "main electrical system, 47 years old, no maintenance done on the system." It has been neglected.

In electrical and plumbing, neglect is built into the situation. Include an offer in your premium option to come and do a follow-up visit, especially after you've done major surgery, to ensure things are fixed for good. With HVAC, maintenance is expected, so you want to get in there at least annually to make sure everything continues to work as promised.

DESIGN

People make all kinds of design mistakes. If you were diagnosing a heating problem, and you had the manual for the furnace in front of you, would the pipes coming out of the sidewall and the termination kit be perfect? Maybe. Maybe not. I see design mistakes all the time, and you will, too, once you start looking for them.

INSTALLATION

Design and installation are often related. While examining the design, you might discover an installation fault. Maybe somebody installed the unit the wrong way, or screws are missing on the flue pipe, or the gas pressure or temperature on the equipment is incorrect, or the air-conditioning unit is not properly charged.

CLIENT IMPACT

Now you want to find out if the client is aware of what else they *could* have. In the following scenario, Jill just moved into a new home and she calls you, a plumber, to unclog the kitchen sink.

You: Hey Jill, can I ask you a question? Did you choose this faucet when you moved into this house?

Jill: No, it just came with the house.

You: Would you select it again if you had the choice?

Jill: No. My last house had this loop-type faucet where the faucet wouldn't hit the pots. I have to get one of those again someday.

Well, guess what? Someday just might be today. You're going to offer this customer that kind of faucet.

You: Jill, I also noticed you have no garbage disposal. How come?

Jill: The house didn't come with one.

You: Did your last house have it?

Jill: Oh yeah. It had that too.

Guess what else you're going to put in your proposal? A garbage disposal. Then you notice a big box of different teas on the counter.

You: I see you have a lot of tea over here. Are you a big fan of tea?

Jill: Oh yeah, I love having a cup of tea in the afternoon. It's tea time at 2:00 p.m. in our house.

And now you know you're going to offer her an Instahot water heater at the faucet, which means that she can have a cup of hot water instantly.

These are all examples of the importance of being on code with the customer. Right now, Jill has a drain clog, but while you're there, why not offer her everything you have available? She can say no to it. She can just fix the drain clog if she wants to, right? The bottom option is simply unclogging the drain. Don't worry; you're not going to take that option away from her. But the top option is going to address not only the drain clog in the kitchen sink but also every other drain in the house, as well as anything else that impacts the client.

You: Jill, when was the last time the drains were cleaned in this house?

Jill: I honestly don't know.

You: Well, the house is 20 years old. Can you imagine what's inside the pipes after 20 years?

Jill: Oh, it must be nasty.

Am I justified in offering a whole house drain cleaning? Sure, why not? Just offer it. It's not the only option you've got, but it is certainly a valid choice. Will somebody actually buy the whole house drain cleaning from me? Who knows? But as hockey player Wayne Gretzky once said, you miss 100 percent of the shots you don't take.

How much justification do you have to have to sell an Instahot water heater? You see the teabags on the counter, and she told you she has tea at 2:00 p.m. every day. Offering her something that could make life more convenient for her is just good service.

You could also offer other items you think the client could benefit from, like improvements in air quality, safety, or service maintenance. As an example, you could offer air filtration or a life-safety protection system with carbon-monoxide alarms. You're always justified in offering to bring things back to their safest condition. As another example, if a client has purchased maintenance every year for the past five years, you could offer them a five-year plan going forward instead of just one year. These things alone are valuable, but there are even more options. Be observant. Always think about what might benefit the client.

THE IMMEDIATE PROBLEM

We've covered age, neglect, design, installation, and client impact, so now it's time to address the immediate problem, which is the thing that's currently wrong with the system. Jill's drain is clogged. Most technicians zero in on the problem, and that's as far as they go.

As an expert technician, you have to filter through age, neglect, design, installation, and client impact before you even *look* at the problem. Do you need to find what the problem is right now? No, you don't. You just need to find out what the problem is in general, not where it exists exactly. Then you need to go and write up a solution where you can clear out the drain, along with whatever else the client decides they want you to do.

— UNCLE JOE'S RULE 28 —

Zoom out! Diagnose in a way that will solve the client's problems permanently.

Now that you've completed your diagnosis, it's time to roll your options up into the right proposal. We'll cover that in detail in chapter 22, but first you need to understand the science of pricing, how people buy, and the laws of association and contrast—and that's what the next two chapters are all about.

 BULLSEYES

- As a reminder, talking about parts rather than components and systems does not allow the client to understand the true value of your services.

- The diagnostic process has six factors: the system's age, neglect, design, installation, client impact, and the immediate problem.

- Age and neglect are usually related problems, as are design and installation faults.

- Be observant and provide the client with any additional options you think would make their lives easier or more enjoyable—for example, offering an Instahot faucet to a daily tea drinker.

- As an expert technician, you have to filter through age, neglect, design, installation, and client impact before you even *look* at the immediate problem.

Chapter 20
THE SCIENCE OF PRICING

In 1991, I had just gone through a divorce and was deeply in debt. One day, I was doing a job at a longtime client's house. His name was Dave Muller. He was a pharmaceutical salesman who was doing pretty well. We were doing our usual back-and-forth banter when he asked me this question:

Dave: So, how's business going, Joe?

Joe: It's going good, Dave.

Dave: Is it really? Because I noticed your shop has 17 trucks parked in front of it, and they never seem to move. Your trucks used to move all the time, Joe. What happened?

Joe: Well, some of my employees left. And I went through a divorce, and the economy sucks.

Dave: Joe, the problem is not the economy, or your ex-wife, or your employees. It's you.

Joe: What do you mean it's me?

Dave: You're always trying to save people money, so you're not offering them enough service.

Joe: OK. You have my attention. Tell me more.

Dave told me there had been a lot of recent academic studies on the science of pricing, which is also known as tiered pricing. He showed me the basics of how to select the price points and arrange them, then told me where I could find more information. (Israeli-American economist Dan Ariely has also written great stuff about the science of pricing and options.)

It is not an exaggeration to say this conversation with Dave saved my business. The way it was going, it would have taken me 200 years to get out of the debt I was in. Instead, I was debt-free by 1994. Dave passed away in 2008, but not before I was able to thank him numerous times for caring enough to intervene. I owe him an eternal debt of gratitude that cannot be repaid, except through teaching others.

When I started teaching the science of pricing to the trades in 2001, people thought I was crazy. But I kept at it because I knew how drastically it had changed my life. Finally, by about 2005, more people started adopting tiered pricing because they discovered how much better it works than flat-rate pricing.

Since then, the practice of providing premium, midrange, and economy options has become a lot more mainstream, and there are also a lot more tools available now to help. ServiceTitan now lets you create estimated pricing bundles, and many programs have premium, midrange, and economy models built right into them. And that's a great thing.

If you do nothing else as a result of reading or listening to this book other than provide your clients with at least three options, your sales will get better. It really is a science.

Now that you know where this concept came from and why I'm so passionate about it, let's talk about some different pricing approaches and their implications.

Options, Not Ultimatums

Pure Motive Service is about providing options, not ultimatums. That's why we always provide the client with six options: two premium, two midrange, and two economy. Many of you may still be offering just one or, at most, three options. My goal in this chapter is to change your mind by showing you the *massive* difference that offering options can make in your revenue based on just 100 closed calls. Ready? Let's go.

FLAT-RATE PRICING

Flat-rate pricing, which was introduced to the plumbing industry around 1990 by the legendary contractor Frank Blau Jr., allowed contractors to begin charging what it actually cost to be in business instead of being hostage to the idea that their price had to align with "what the market would bear." The good news for contractors was that the new flat rate was often two to three times what plumbers were charging before. The bad news was that if the client didn't like the flat-rate price, their only option was to shop the competition in hopes of finding someone who was less enlightened and thus less expensive.

Let's say the average "what the market will bear" price for a call averages out to $75 an hour, and the flat-rate price calls for $200 an hour. No question, that's better for the contractor. Assuming for the purpose of demonstration that each call takes only one hour, if you closed 100 calls, you would earn $20,000 instead of $7,500.

But there's a problem. To close 100 calls using this model, you actually need to do 400 calls because the conversion ratio with a single option is only 25 percent.

GOOD-BETTER-BEST PRICING

Another approach is to offer three prices—good, better, and best. This is an upselling model, where you start with the lowest option and work your way up to the highest.

Let's throw in some conservative estimates based on my experience with good-better-best pricing and our client type and see what happens. Let's assume the $200 service you've been providing is good, $400 is better, and $600 is best. Here's how it typically plays out:

■ 60 percent of customers purchase the "good" offering at $200
■ 20 percent of customers purchase the "better" offering at $400

- 20 percent of customers purchase the "best" offering at $600

In this case, 100 closed calls would bring in a total of $32,000. And because you're providing the client with options, you likely will need a lot fewer calls to get there. You can clearly see the difference between providing the client with just one option versus providing three options in the chart below.

THE SCIENCE OF PRICING

1 Option	3 Options
$200 – 100% x 100 Calls = **$20,000**	$200 – 60% $400 – 20% $600 – 20% x 100 Calls = **$32,000**

That's a 60 percent increase in revenue on 100 closed calls, and the only thing you did was provide three options instead of just one.

But there's an even better way, and that is to present the options in descending order of price.

Research published in the *Journal of Marketing Research* in 2012 found that displaying a menu of beer prices from highest to lowest made it more likely that customers would choose a more expensive beer. According to the authors, this is likely due to what we call FOMO, or "fear of missing out." When presented with the most expensive options first, customers felt they would lose out on quality the farther down the list they went, which would never have occurred to them had the prices been listed lowest to highest.

For contractors, that means presenting the best or most premium option first increases the chances the client will choose a higher option.

PREMIUM-MIDRANGE-ECONOMY PRICING

In this model, the premium or "best" option is shown first. This completely flips the conversion rate. Again, based on my personal experience over many decades of pricing this way, the spread looks like this:

- 30 percent of customers purchase the premium option at $600
- 50 percent of customers purchase the midrange option at $400
- 20 percent of customers purchase the economy option at $200

So, in this case, 100 closed calls nets you a total of $42,000. That's more than double the revenue than if you only offered one economy option. Also interesting is that when presented with premium-midrange-economy pricing, 80 percent of clients will select either the premium or midrange option versus only 40 percent choosing those options when presented with good-better-best pricing. Take a look at the chart at the top of the next page.

WHAT SHOULD WE DO?

START WITH PREMIUM

Good-Better-Best Upselling Model (Show economy option first)	Premium-Midrange-Economy Model (Show premium option first)
$200 – 60% $400 – 20% $600 – 20% ⎤–40% x 100 Calls = **$32,000**	$600 – 30% $400 – 50% ⎤–80% $200 – 20% x 100 Calls = **$42,000**

THE SIX-OPTION DIFFERENCE

But I'm not done yet. According to a 1994 study at the University of Notre Dame, if you offer six options—two premium, two midrange, and two economy—the conversion rate is 77 percent higher than it is when clients are offered just three options.

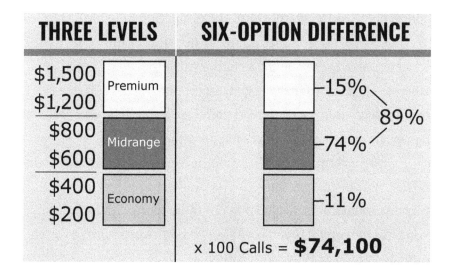

THREE LEVELS · SIX-OPTION DIFFERENCE

$1,500 Premium
$1,200
$800 Midrange
$600
$400 Economy
$200

–15%
–74%   89%
–11%

x 100 Calls = **$74,100**

- 7 percent of customers purchase the premium plus option at $1,500
- 8 percent of customers purchase the premium option at $1,200
- 28 percent of customers purchase the midrange plus option at $800
- 46 percent of customers purchase the midrange option at $600
- 9 percent of customers purchase the economy plus option at $400
- 2 percent of customers purchase the economy option at $200

That's $74,100 for 100 closed calls.

The average person makes a choice in 2.7 seconds. If you are only offering one choice, when you say, "What should we do?" there's a 75 percent chance the client is going to say, "Let me get some more prices and get back to you."

When you offer three choices, if the client is a midrange buyer, the question becomes which one they want. The question is no longer yes or no; it's which one they prefer. Now they're shopping in-house and not with the competition.

Offering six options, priced at the correct intervals, makes it even easier for the client to find a price they like. Even people who are cheaper will usually go with economy plus. Offering more options increases the likelihood that the client will be able to make a decision they—and you—are happy with.

Your premium plus option is designed to change the infrastructure to last longer. That means fewer callbacks and higher revenue. It is designed to put more money in the coffers so you have the capital to improve your own infrastructure so you can offer even more service to your clients.

It also helps you identify your customer base because the people who pay more are going to get more service. People who pay less will also get what they want, which is less service.

I want to give you a word of warning about toxic customers, though. There's always going to be someone who will complain even about the price of your cheapest option. Your company is like a family, and clients become part of that family too. If you let a toxic customer into your company, your name will be associated with it.

Let's say a certain client has a reputation within your company for being a problem. You decide to go out there anyway and do your best, but the client is having a bad day so she leaves a negative review on Yelp. And when that happens to a small company, your whole life stops. In the long run, it's much cheaper to filter out toxic clients and let someone else deal with them.

If you are only offering one choice, when you say, "What should we do?" there's a 75 percent chance the client is going to say, "Let me get some more prices and get back to you."

The Triad of Decision-Making

Clients are influenced by three things when making a decision about which option is right for them: price, title, and warranty and service. Let's discuss each factor in more detail.

PRICE

When it comes to offering six options, each price should be different and better than the one below it so the client can easily understand why it costs more. It's very important to get the spacing right because the science of pricing fails when two or more options are too similar to one another. In this example, the top option is about six times the price of the bottom option.

- Platinum No Stress for Joe and Julie Complete Repair...$3,497
- Gold System Repair..............................$2,613
- Silver System Repair............................$1,878
- Bronze Partial System Repair $1,345
- Economy Plus Repair $820
- Economy Repair $571

TITLE

When offering six choices, your highest-priced option should appear first and be personalized based on the client's buying code. The following offerings have titles that reflect their value in descending order, in this case, platinum, gold, silver, bronze, economy plus, and economy. There's no hard-and-fast rule about these titles.

Platinum No Stress for Joe and Julie Complete Repair
- Complete heavy-duty system repair
- Wi-Fi-enabled smartphone control
- Family safety-alert system
- 10-year complete system warranty
- Investment: $3,497

Gold System Repair

- Complete heavy-duty system repair
- Wi-Fi-enabled smartphone control
- Seven-year warranty
- Investment: $2,613

Silver System Repair

- Complete heavy-duty system repair
- Five-year warranty
- Investment: $1,878

Bronze Partial System Repair

- Partial standard-duty system repair
- Three-year warranty
- Investment: $1,345

Economy Plus Repair

- Single component repair
- One-year warranty
- Investment: $820

Economy Repair

- Single component repair
- 30-day warranty
- Investment: $571

— UNCLE JOE'S RULE 29 —

*If you really believe you're a premium service provider,
show it by starting with your premium option first.*

WARRANTY AND SERVICE

Warranties and service are the most powerful and profitable things you can sell as a service professional. When structured the right way, warranty and service agreements will add between 35 and 42 percent more revenue to the company at 80 percent gross profit.

The enemy of warranties and service agreements is when all six of the options have the same level of service. Why would somebody purchase your premium option when they can get the same warranty on the bottom option?

Worse, since warranty and service agreements are the most profitable part of your company, you'll be stealing from your company's future if you offer these options incorrectly or not at all. Warranties and service agreements are what will make your business both recession-proof and weatherproof.

There are two different types of warranties: repair warranties and renovation warranties. A repair warranty is when we are fixing something inside of the current system, and a renovation warranty is when we are replacing the whole system. There are different rules for each.

Repair Warranties: The rule for repair options is that the warranty and service have a hard cap of five years, starting with the top repair option and ratcheting down one year for each following option, all the way to 60 days at the bottom. The warranties offered for each option are based on the number of tasks and the level of service membership that the client buys on a yearly basis. If the client already bought a service agreement from you, then the bottom two options would be one year and not 60 days because the warranty tasks are the way we're going to build this system.

Obviously, giving your client a five-year warranty on their repair sounds great, but how are you going to pay for it to make sure the company doesn't suffer financially? Here's how to think about it.

A service membership should cost the client about $250 a year. You are going to charge the client for that on a yearly (not monthly) basis. That makes the lifetime value of a five-year warranty $1,250.

A five-year warranty should have five tasks and five years of service membership. Each task involves travel time, paperwork, talking to the customer, diagnosing the system, creating the options, doing the work, and walking the customer through the repair at the end of it. Now all that time is built into each task.

Here's the great thing. Only about 18 percent of the people will ever use the repair warranty. But for those who do, your visits can result in additional opportunities as opposed to a cost.

When the levels of service are aligned with the options you've created, warranties and service agreements are the most powerful and profitable things you can sell as a service professional.

Renovation Warranties: Renovation warranties are slightly different because they are no longer dependent on the number of tasks. In this case, there is a minimum 12-year warranty on the top option.

The options start at 12 years, then 10 years, then seven, then five, then three, until the bottom option of one year. When there is a renovation top option, one year is the lowest warranty and service to offer.

The way we fund a renovation warranty is by doubling the amount of the service agreement and then multiplying that number by the length of the warranty offered. If the service membership is $250 per year, you would double that amount, which would be $500 per year. So for a 12-year warranty, you would multiply $500 by 12, which would give you $6,000 to fund the warranty.

The years of warranty and service must match at every level. You can't do a 12-year warranty with a one-year service membership. It has to be a 12-year warranty and a 12-year service membership, or a 10-year warranty and 10-year service membership. You get the idea. (Do not mention the manufacturer's warranty since you are now superseding it.)

For these longer warranties, you'll want to offer the client the option of a bridge loan where they can pay over time to make sure you give people the gift of affordability.

OK, that's it for the science of pricing. In the next chapter, you'll learn about the laws of association and contrast, which will inform what you call your options and how to position them with the client.

 **BULLSEYES**

- There are four types of pricing: flat-rate pricing, good-better-best pricing, premium-midrange-economy pricing, and the six-option approach, which offers two premium, two midrange, and two economy options, where the lowest option is just fixing the immediate problem.

- Presenting the best or most premium option first increases the chances the client will choose a higher option.

- When offering six choices, your highest-priced option should appear first and be personalized based on the client's buying code.

- Make sure that all warranty types are aligned with the service level of the option they accompany.

- If you do nothing else as a result of reading or listening to this book other than provide your clients with at least three options, your sales will improve. It really is a science.

Chapter 21
THE LAWS OF ASSOCIATION AND CONTRAST

Back in the day, if you got coffee outside the home, it was probably at a diner. You'd order bacon and eggs, and the coffee was included for free. That's just how it was. Two eggs, bacon, and toast used to be cheap. I remember seeing signs in the window advertising a $2.49 breakfast with free coffee. Now you go into a greasy spoon and the cup of coffee alone costs that much. What happened? Who changed the rules?

Starbucks.

Starbucks said, what if we just sell coffee and charge customers $2.35 a cup?

I love Starbucks because it's living proof that if you do it properly, you can charge more for a product and make it more popular. When you put a higher price on something, it raises its value in people's minds.

Are you really buying coffee when you buy Starbucks? No. You're buying the experience, a feeling of self-worth, and the ability to choose freely. When you go to Starbucks, do you ever order a plain black coffee? Or do you order a venti half-caf soy-milk latte with 10 pumps of sugar-free vanilla? Starbucks will make anything you want. People have actually had contests to see who can order the most expensive drink. Starbucks is all about options, and it is not afraid to offer you the opportunity to purchase a venti pumpkin spice Frappuccino for $5.95.

The upside for the traditional diner owner is that the premium-pricing model of Starbucks allows the diner to use the law of association to raise its own prices and make more profit.

The Law of Association

The law of association is when you borrow the meaning from a brand or other cultural reference to indicate the level of quality or other characteristics of your package. It can also borrow meaning from the client's buying code. For example, the diner is borrowing meaning from Starbucks, which has reset the expectation that a plain cup of coffee is now worth $2.35 per cup.

Let's say in the process of finding a client's buying code, I learn that he is a district manager of McDonald's. And he's complaining about how inconsistent his services from other companies have been, and how he has had nothing but guys who didn't show up on time. Nobody stands by their products. Nobody does what they say they're going to do. So when presenting my top option, I'm going to say, "This is our McDonald's package, John. You know all about McDonald's and how consistently it delivers its product." In that situation, would I be on code with that buyer? You bet. I'd be hitting it right out of the park.

On the other hand, if at another client's house I noticed Whole Foods bags and organic cookbooks on the kitchen counter, would it be on code to present a top option called the McDonald's package? No! The client would think, "This guy does not get what I'm trying to accomplish here," and your connection would be broken. So when you name your options or packages, use the law of association to indicate where they are on the pricing spectrum, ranging from premium to economy.

Here's a little exercise. I'm going to give you a word, and you say what you think its value is. Don't overthink it. Just say the first thing that comes to your mind. For example, if I say "premium plus," most people will say high value. OK, your turn:

■ When I say Band-Aid, you think the value is _____.
■ When I say economical, you think the value is _____.
■ When I say standard, you think the value is _____.
■ When I say Rolls-Royce, you think the value is _____.

If I say it's a Rolls-Royce package, it better be a luxurious package. It better have a steam shower with a dozen showerheads. It better include a smart toilet with ambient color lighting, a built-in audio speaker system, and a heated seat with hands-free opening and closing, plus an emergency flush capability for power outages. (This toilet actually exists! Google "Numi 2.0.")

To that end, when it comes to equipment, I suggest you find a product you like and look into creating your own signature series around it (sometimes called "white label"). That way the customer won't be comparing your service with other services that offer the same name brands, which means you're free to establish the value based on the service you are going to provide around it. You're the one standing behind it, so all the client cares about is whether they trust you.

When you're coming up with titles for your packages, make the top options the best and the bottom options the worst. And then use the law of association to indicate every level of quality.

Creating your own signature series of equipment frees you to establish the value based on the service you are going to provide around it.

The Law of Contrast

The law of contrast is the most powerful tool you have in your persuasion toolbox. You can use it to create value and diminish price concerns with your clients. The law of contrast says if you offer an option with a price that seems unreasonable at first, followed by an option that is more reasonably priced, the price of that second offering will seem way more reasonable than it did originally.

Remember the Numi toilet I just described? It retails for about $8,600. Would you buy it? Probably not. Most people wouldn't. Then why does it exist? Because someone is buying it, and the fact that it exists gives contractors like you the ability to employ the law of contrast even more effectively.

The way we price the six options is all about the law of contrast. If you show somebody your first option, which is $2,500, and then your bottom option, which is $500, does $500 seem unreasonable? No, it seems positively cheap. If you want to increase the value of something you want to sell for $500, just multiply it by five and offer something for that price first. Then you will make that $500 thing seem unbelievably cheap.

— UNCLE JOE'S RULE 30 —
Make yourself a hero by showing your highest price first and then save the day by showing your lower prices after that.

Now that you know about the law of contrast, you will start seeing it in play everywhere. Next time you go to a nice restaurant, take a look at the menu. The Kobe beef filet is $150, the porterhouse is $95, the chicken parmesan is $32, and the fettuccine alfredo at the very bottom is $19. If the menu had listed the fettuccine alfredo first, you'd think, $19 for noodles? It would seem like too much.

That's the law of contrast. Ask for something more, and settle for something less.

There's one more thing you need to learn before we move on to the actual presentation process, and that is to create the right proposal. That information and more awaits you in the next chapter.

BULLSEYES

- ○ The law of association is when you borrow the meaning from a brand or other cultural reference to indicate the level of quality or other characteristics of your package.

- ○ When you name your options or packages, use the law of association to indicate where they are on the pricing spectrum, ranging from premium to economy.

- ○ The law of contrast says if you offer an option with a price that seems unreasonable at first, followed by an option that is more reasonably priced, the price of that second offering will seem way more reasonable than it did originally.

- ○ If you want to increase the value of something you want to sell, just multiply it by five and offer something for that price first.

- ○ Now that you know about the law of contrast, you will start seeing it in play everywhere—especially at restaurants.

➤➤

Chapter 22
CREATING THE RIGHT PROPOSAL

Dave Muller, who you met back in chapter 20, certainly saved my business by introducing me to the science of pricing. What I didn't mention then was that he was also the one who insisted I offer clients multiple options—two premium, two midrange, and two economy—so they could see everything I had to offer.

After I completed his repair, Dave invited me to sit down at his kitchen table so he could show me how to create what would become my first option sheet. He gave me a blank piece of paper and had me divide it into six sections. Then he told me to label each section: premium plus, premium, pro, standard, economy plus, and economy (two options for premium, two for midrange, and two for economy). Here's what happened next.

Dave: So, Joe, tell me something that commonly goes wrong on a furnace.

Joe: How about a faulty gas valve?

Dave: OK, so in the premium plus box, write out everything you would want the customer to fix if money were no object.

I wrote down replace the entire ignition system, burners, gas valve, ignitor, and safety switches, and include a five-year warranty and service plan.

Joe: How much should I charge for that?

Dave: A better question is how much is your bottom option, which is just fixing the gas valve, no warranty included?

Joe: I don't know. $250?

Dave: That seems low. Make it $330. What's 330 times six?

Joe: $1,980.

Dave: Make it $1,979.

I wrote down $1,979 for the top option.

Dave: Now work on the second option.

I made the premium option include everything listed above except for the burners, took a year off the warranty and service plan, and priced it at $1,497.

We continued to work our way down the option sheet. The pro option was for the gas valve, ignitor, and flame sensor with a three-year warranty and service plan for $1,249. The standard option was for the gas valve and ignitor with a two-year warranty and service plan for $797. The economy plus option was just the gas valve with a one-year warranty and service plan for $519. Finally, the bottom economy option was the gas valve with no warranty for $330.

Dave nodded his head in approval. Then he said, "From now on, you want to start at the top and show the customer the most premium option first, then work your way down the list."

I thanked Dave for investing his time to teach me and promised I would try it out on the next similar customer and let him know what happened. What I didn't tell him was I hoped that it would be a while before I got another gas valve repair so Dave would have time to forget about it. I was charging $1,597 for a whole new furnace at that time. Why would a customer want to pay $1,979 for a renovation?

I continued doing my cheap repairs until I got a call from a woman named Linda, who had—you guessed it—a bad gas valve.

I thought about the pile of overdue bills sitting on the passenger seat of my truck. I knew I had to do something different if I was ever going to get out of the mess I was in. So I pulled the option sheet that Dave and I had made out of my binder.

I then proceeded to make the worst presentation in the world. I said, "Linda, I got this price sheet from one of my crazy customers named Dave. He told me to offer you premium, midrange, and economy options for fixing your furnace. You're not going to want the top one because it costs more than the entire furnace, but here are the prices."

Dead silence. I was starting to sweat. After about three minutes Linda looked up and said, "No way am I doing the top option. It costs more than the entire furnace." Ugh, I knew it.

But then she said, "Can we go ahead and do the one for $1,249? That's the one I want."

I was stunned. I said, "Are you sure? I've got cheaper options down below. You didn't even look at those."

Linda said, "I'm sure. I want the third option. Write it up."

No one could talk her out of the one she wanted once she was given all the choices at the same time. It was not only the first time I had ever sold more than the rock-bottom repair in this situation but also the first time I had ever sold a package that cost nearly four times the amount of my cheapest option.

I called Dave and told him what had happened. I said I was now a believer. Every call I did going forward had these premium, midrange, and economy options. Did I always sell the most premium option? Of course not. All I knew was my jobs were now selling for three to 10 times more than they were during the previous era of uninformed pricing ignorance.

Here's the bottom line:

- In January 1991, I was $471,000 in debt and teetering on the edge of bankruptcy.
- By December 1994, I was debt-free and building resources.

And this was all because I was willing to do something different by applying the new pricing concept I learned from Dave. It has saved my financial life and may save yours, too, if you're willing to follow the Pure Motive Service program.

Start at the top and show the customer the most premium option first, then work your way down the list.

Note that the actual price intervals between your six options will depend on your costs and your desired profit. What I want you to take away from this is that you need to space out the costs of the options so the client has six distinct price points to choose from.

Here are some other things I've learned over the years about creating the right proposal.

No Such Thing as a Verbal Proposal

A proposal is a piece of paper or a form displayed on a tablet. There is no such thing as a verbal proposal. The prices have to be delivered on some kind of tangible object. Why?

Well, you're going to tell the client what the problem is and then describe the top option in detail. But there are also five other options to keep track of. Let's say the client picks the third one but then says, "What was that fifth one again?" You're not going to remember what it is, and then what happens? You lose credibility.

The other problem is if you're giving a price verbally and the client says it's too high, where did that price come from? You! So now there's an association, and not only is the price a problem, you're a problem too.

If we're going to handle objections or talk about difficulties, let the difficulty be between the client and the piece of paper. You and the client are on the same page. You both want to fix the problem. The only thing that's preventing it is this piece of paper with multiple options. To be able to move forward, something has to change and a decision must be made. What should we do?

There is no such thing as a verbal proposal. The prices have to be delivered on some kind of tangible object so you and the client are united against what's on the page.

Solution Pick List

As I said to John back in chapter 19 about the diagnostic process, you've got to record your observations and start creating the options as you are doing the diagnosis. If you disappear into your truck for 20 minutes to put your presentation together, it's going to break the rhythm of the call. A good tool for this process is what I call a solution pick list.

A solution pick list is a form that allows you to collect the following information in one place. There are five categories in two columns—one for the category and one for the price. You'll want to code the prices in some way, so if the customer happens to be looking over your shoulder the amounts will stay secure. For instance, if the price is $595, you could note #7600595 next to the task so it looks like a SKU number. You simply make up the leading numbers and put "595" at the end of the code so you know the price. Depending on your client's needs, there may be more than one item to list in each category.

There are five categories to include in your proposal: main repair or equipment solution, additional system enhancements, warranty options, service memberships, and consumables.

MAIN REPAIR OR EQUIPMENT SOLUTION

This is the minimum solution and its heavy-duty or commercial alternatives.

ADDITIONAL SYSTEM ENHANCEMENTS

Start with the system with the broken component and then look for ways to improve the system's quality and reliability, as well as features you could add that would enhance the safety and health of the people living in the home.

For quality and reliability, you could expand the scope of the solution to replace components that are old but have not yet broken. Another option is to offer the client heavier-duty solutions that will make the system even more reliable. Safety and health enhancements could include replacing all of the smoke detectors in the house or installing carbon-monoxide detectors.

WARRANTY OPTIONS

Warranties are an important differentiator. Remember, since you are selling the benefits of the system and not the equipment, parts, or brand, whatever warranty you decide to offer will supersede the manufacturer's warranty. Deciding on warranty terms depends on whether the job is a repair or renovation.

The warranty for a top option repair should be five years max, decreasing one year until you hit the bottom option, which is 60 days.

The warranty for a top option renovation should be a minimum of 12 years, decreasing two or three years until you hit the bottom option, which is one year.

SERVICE MEMBERSHIPS

This refers to scheduled or on-demand system maintenance and future services needed. These are multiyear service memberships that not only cover the client for maintenance calls but also may confer VIP status, where they move to the front of the line if they do need interim service. If you've done a top option replacement, and you're doing regular maintenance, there should be few if any issues you ever have to deal with—and that's the whole goal.

Service memberships start at five years for repairs (top option) and decrease by one year until the bottom option, which is 60 days. For renovations and replacements, they start at 12 years and decrease by two to three years until the bottom option, which is one year. The length of the warranty and service plan should always be the same.

CONSUMABLES

Note any consumables, such as furnace filters or salt for a water softener, and include an option for the client to have you supply those things when you come and do your annual or semiannual service calls.

I often add the words "can't write a check" to the warranty and service descriptions. That lets the client know there will be no extra charges for the warranty and service as described once they select and pay for their desired option.

The next step is to take the notes you've made in the five categories on your solution pick list and use that information to create your proposal.

Since you are selling the benefits of the system and not the parts, whatever warranty you decide to offer will supersede the manufacturer's warranty.

Meet Your Client: Jane Smith

So you can follow the process from creating the right proposal through presenting the on-code solutions, I thought it would be useful to spend the next few chapters with just one client. Her name is Jane Smith. She is married to Marc and has two young kids, Aaron and Jennifer. They both travel for work, so Jane's mom comes and stays with the kids when they are away.

Jane called you out because she discovered there was no power in the primary bedroom. She is upset because her phone, which was plugged in to charge, died in the middle of the night so her alarm did not go off. This caused her to miss an important meeting at work and take the kids to school two hours late. She said she never thought she'd have electrical problems in a house that was only five years old.

YOUR DIAGNOSIS

Because you took the time to diagnose Jane as a client first, you know you will be presenting to her alone because her husband, Marc, is out of town. She assures you (with two commitments) that she is the right person to present to, i.e., the one who will make the decision. You then diagnose the entire system using all six factors: age, neglect, design, installation, client impact, and the immediate problem.

In this case, your system diagnosis reveals several issues. While diagnosing for age and neglect, you note that the electrical panel is only five years old and confirm it was installed when the house was built. You check all the breakers to ensure they are sized appropriately and note they are not clearly marked on the panel door so the homeowner is not able to identify what each switch controls. In terms of design and installation, you confirm there are 220 volts coming into the electrical panel, which you note is the smallest one the builder could legally install. You anticipate that once you go upstairs and look at the outlets and what is plugged into them, it will already be overloaded.

You test the outlets and switches in the primary bedroom and confirm no power is getting to them, which means there is a fracture or disconnection of the conductors somewhere between the panel and the outlets and switches. Additionally, you notice

WHAT SHOULD WE DO?

that whoever installed them failed to secure the wires properly, and in some outlets the poles were reversed, which creates a shock and fire hazard.

You check the primary bathroom and notice there is a GFCI outlet next to the sink, but it isn't getting power either. You notice there's a light bulb out in the fixture over the vanity. You also check the outlets in the rest of the house and make note of the ones that have similar issues to the bedroom. While doing that, you notice a pile of wires around the television, which poses a choking hazard for kids.

Creating the Right Proposal

When creating a proposal, the law of verbal packaging comes into play right away. Clients are looking for you to provide them with options and solutions, so the title of your proposal should be something like "client option sheet" or "client solution sheet." (No one is looking for a proposal!)

There should be a place at the top of the page for the job number, the client's name, and the technician's name. Don't use a service ticket for this; it's too busy.

Now, you're going to fill out the client option sheet. (Don't worry; you'll see a graphic of what it looks like all filled out on page 302 after I finish explaining all of the necessary elements.)

SYSTEM OBSERVATIONS

The first section of the client option sheet is called system observations. This is where you will summarize the problems you found during your diagnosis and note the main emotional reason for the call, which is then referenced in the title of the top option.

Although you zoom out when you diagnose a system, you must reverse the order and zoom in when you explain these observations to your client. Since you always want to address the main reason why you were called out first, here is the order in which you should explain your diagnosis:

- The main problem
- The impact of the problem on the client and their family
- Design and installation faults (related to quality, reliability, safety, and health)
- The impact of age and neglect (in this case the panel is newer but undersized, which is a design fault)

Here's what those system observations should sound like when properly verbally packaged for the client option sheet:

- Fracture fault in the conductors going to the primary bedroom
- Jane and her husband, Marc, work long hours; Jane stressed about her cell phone going dead; worried about the kids' safety; kids are sometimes home alone after school and are heavy users of electronics and appliances
- Fracture fault in the conductors going to the primary bathroom
- Design fault in the electrical-distribution system; capacity doesn't match what's needed to power today's electronics and appliances
- Installation faults in most outlets and switches, as well as in the electrical-distribution system

WHAT SHOULD WE DO?

Each one of the faults mentioned above should inspire you to think of all the possible solutions to offset them. For example, here you have a system that is only five years old, but its design doesn't match the needs of a busy family with multiple devices and appliances. You were called out for a repair, but you know there is a chance the client may ask you how much it would cost to do a whole system renovation instead.

In this situation, you or someone from your company will want to create an option that includes renovating the entire electrical system as well as the immediate repair needed. This is called a "lead turnover." A lead turnover in this situation would be offering a choice between a series of options that would repair the situation versus a series of options that would completely renovate the electrical system in the entire home, not just the primary bedroom.

This way, if your client asks, "How much would it be to just replace the entire electrical system including the panel?" you can say, "I'm glad you brought that up. If I told you I had both a repair option as well as an option to renovate the entire system, what would happen then?" Since the cost to renovate the system will be a lot higher than the cost to do a repair, when it comes time to reveal the price you can always show them the monthly cost if they finance it rather than the full five-figure amount.

Remember, world-class service is going above and beyond, and that means anticipating the client's needs and being ready to address them whenever possible.

CUSTOMER OPTIONS

Since you're just learning this system, we're going to focus on the repair example rather than confuse you by trying to talk through both the repair and renovation options at the same time. Just know that you should be prepared if you think the client will ask you for a larger solution, and both repair and renovation proposals should always feature six options: two premium, two midrange, and two economy.

Let's continue.

All six repair options should list the problem that you were called out for first. For each option, you're going to create what I call a solution sandwich. The top slice of bread is always the title of the option. Next, you have the solution to the problem you were called out to fix, followed by any other renovations, repairs, or upgrades you are proposing. The bottom slice of bread is the warranty and service options. The more service you're proposing, the thicker the sandwich will be.

Let's take a look at the top option on the customer option sheet prepared for Jane Smith on page 302. The title is the Premium Plus Jane and Marc's Worry-Free Primary Bed and Bath Electrical Conductor Repair, which aligns with what we wrote in our system observations section. It indicates the solution to the problem we were called out to fix, which is a fracture fault in the conductors going to the primary bedroom, and is followed by options to improve whatever else is relevant. Following are different parts of the premium plus solution we will be proposing:

- Replace conductors from panel to bedroom
- Replace conductors in the primary bedroom and bathroom wing
- Renovate all bed and bath outlet terminals and voltage-control switches
- Install child-safety outlet terminals and power surge protection
- Update electrocution-prevention system in primary bathroom
- Five-year "can't-write-a-check" warranty and service plan

Notice I'm using bullet points to call out the parts of each solution. Don't write a big wall of text. Even though you will be walking the client through this proposal verbally, you still want the text on the sheet to be clear and clean in case you have to use it to discuss the different options.

The consumables attached to this system, such as light bulbs and smoke detector batteries, will be included in the warranty and service plan. Warranties and service plans are always equal in length. Don't offer a warranty unless you have service going along with it. You aren't an insurance salesperson. You'll let the client know that the warranty and service plan includes consumables during your verbal presentation. The sheet is just there to prompt you on what each option consists of.

Once you have determined the top option, figuring out the rest of them is a matter of reducing the amount of service in each option until you get to the bottom, which is always just the repair of the broken component. On the next page, you will see what that form looks like filled out.

SERVICE MVP.

Electrical Repair Option Sheet

Job # _____ Client: _____ Tech: _____

System Observations

☐ Fracture fault in the conductors going to the primary bedroom

☐ Jane and her husband, Marc, work long hours; Jane stressed about her cell phone going dead; worried about the kids' safety; kids are sometimes home alone after school and are heavy users of electronics and appliances

☐ Fracture fault in the conductors going to the primary bathroom

☐ Design fault in the electrical-distribution system; capacity doesn't match what's needed to power today's electronics and appliances

☐ Installation faults in most outlets and switches, as well as in the electrical distribution system

Customer Options

Premium Plus Jane and Marc's Worry-Free Primary Bed and Bath Electrical Conductor Repair

☐ Replace conductors from panel to bedroom

☐ Replace conductors in the primary bedroom and bathroom wing

☐ Renovate bed and bath outlet terminals and voltage-control switches

☐ Install child-safety outlet terminals and power surge protection

☐ Update electrocution-prevention system in primary bathroom

☐ Five-year "can't-write-a-check" warranty and service plan | **Investment: $4,792**

Premium Electrical Conductor Repair

☐ Replace conductors from panel to bedroom

☐ Replace conductors in the primary bedroom and bathroom wing

☐ Renovate bed and bath outlet terminals and voltage-control switches

☐ Four-year "can't-write-a-check" warranty and service plan | **Investment: $3,619**

Pro Electrical Conductor Repair

☐ Replace conductors from panel to bedroom

☐ Rebuild existing outlet terminals and control switches

☐ Three-year "can't-write-a-check" warranty and service plan | **Investment: $2,577**

Standard Electrical Conductor Repair

☐ Find fractured conductor and replace fractured section

☐ Rebuild existing outlet terminals and control switches

☐ Two-year "can't-write-a-check" warranty and service plan | **Investment: $1,467**

Economy Plus Electrical Conductor Repair

☐ Find fracture and reconnect conductor

☐ One-year "can't-write-a-check" warranty and service plan | **Investment: $975**

Economy Electrical Conductor Repair

☐ Attempt to find fracture and reconnect conductor

☐ 60-day workmanship warranty | **Investment: $577**

World-class service is going above and beyond, and that means anticipating the client's needs and being ready to address them whenever possible.

If it's easier, you can also start with the bottom repair option and work your way up to the top as you price everything, but always remember to present the options to the client in descending order. You already know the bottom option is just the repair you were called out to fix. The top option is always a complete system repair. In terms of pricing, remember to space out the price points to provide the client with distinct choices.

The same methodology applies to building a renovation option sheet. The only difference is that the renovation will be a whole house solution that eliminates the problem completely by replacing everything, not just addressing the problem the client is having right now. So, if you started with the bottom renovation solution, it would actually be more all-inclusive than the top repair option!

By the way, creating a renovation option before the client asks you for it is the reason the top service professionals in the country do such amazing numbers. They are rewarded for anticipating what a client may ask when faced with a very expensive repair on a system that's only five years old.

— UNCLE JOE'S RULE 31 —

Pure Motive Service allows you to stop worrying about selling so you can focus on providing clients with a range of options so they can choose the one that's right for them.

Don't Worry about Selling

The top option and its high investment may make you feel uncomfortable at first. If so, that's your cue to send your mother back to the truck. Remember, you're not selling anything. You are just providing clients with a range of options so they can choose the one that's right for them.

Plus, you're going to let your customer off the hook for that top option right away by saying, "You may not want this one because it's too expensive." (That's called the money warning, and you'll learn more about it in chapter 24.)

The reality is that the client is going to say no to five of your options every time you give a presentation because they can only pick one. So you shouldn't care about getting a no. All you should care about is getting one yes, and it doesn't matter which option they pick. If the client buys the cheapest option, that's just a seed you're planting for the next time something breaks. Maybe then they will be open to buying a more premium option.

Do you want to reduce callbacks in your company? Offer six options that include packages that solve the entire problem. That said, every callback is just an opportunity to sell what the client should have had to begin with. Imagine yourself going on a callback for a client who was offered six options and they bought the Band-Aid one. You could say something like, "Well, Ted, last year, we did offer you some better options. So I can fix the same thing that just failed for free, or I can upgrade it so it doesn't happen again in the future. What should we do?" Ted will likely say, "Let's just fix it. Let's go with that third option."

If you want to reduce callbacks in your company, offer six options that include packages that solve the entire problem.

In this section about being ethical, you've learned a lot about persuasion, the diagnostic process, the science of pricing, the laws of association and contrast, and how to create the right proposal. The next thing you need to learn is how to successfully present the proposal to the client, and that's what the next section about being determined covers.

 **BULLSEYES**

- A solution pick list is a form you can use to collect information about five different categories: main repair or equipment solution, additional system enhancements, warranty options, service memberships, and consumables.

º There is no such thing as a verbal proposal. Proposals must be written down and presented on a tangible object.

º World-class service is going above and beyond, and that means anticipating the client's needs and being ready to address them whenever possible.

º Warranties and service plans are always equal in length. Don't offer warranties unless you have service going along with it.

º When you focus on providing clients with a range of options, they're able to sell themselves on the one that's right for them.

TOOLS FOR YOUR SUCCESS

SERVICE MVP

servicemvp.com/tools

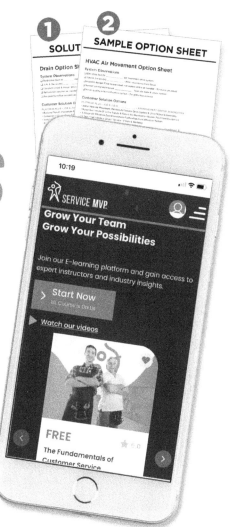

✳ SOLUTION PICK LIST
Record your observations and bundle tasks into six client options during your diagnosis. This tool maintains the rhythm of the call, collects the information in one place, and builds your credibility.

✳ SAMPLE OPTION SHEET
Use this sample to build your finished product. You'll present premium, midrange, and economy options for your client.

Scan to download your tools

BE
DETERMINED

Chapter 23
BE DETERMINED—OVERVIEW

I was doing some ride-along training with the now-famous $12 million sales producer Rick Picard for the company he was working for in Providence, Rhode Island. The company was in the process of moving from doing mostly new construction HVAC to being more of a service-based company, and I was there to help the technicians learn to sell to the end consumer, which most of them had never done before.

One day, Rick's boss called us into the office to brief us on a special client he wanted us to go visit. The boss said, "I want you to go visit a general contractor friend of mine. He's from a business referral group I belong to, and he wants us to bid on a new construction home. I told him we're getting out of new construction, but he's insisting that we give him a price."

Rick asked, "If we're supposed to be getting out of new construction, why go out there?"

The boss said, "I know, but I have to see this guy at our meetings. I can't just ignore him."

He reached across his desk and handed a roll of blueprints to Rick. "Guys, just do me a favor, look at these prints, go see the builder, and shoot him a really high price so he goes away."

Rick said, "OK, boss. Whatever you want." Rick and I found an empty conference room, spread out the plans, and reviewed them. We knew that the fees Rick's company charged this builder in the past for this kind of work had ranged between $16,000 and $30,000. Since the assignment was to get rid of this low-margin job so we could focus all our resources on building the higher-margin service business, Rick and I decided to come back with a series of options with prices that were so high even the economy option would seem ridiculous.

We came up with six options, where the highest one was $349,000 and the economy one was $98,000—more than three times the amount of our top fee in the past. Confident he'd never go for any of it, we grabbed the proposal and prints and headed to the builder's office to lose ourselves a job.

The general contractor, Bill, met us at the door and led us to a conference room. After some small talk, Rick said, "Bill, we have to be honest with you. Our company is now focused on service-generated installations, and as a result our new profit structure has increased our prices dramatically."

Bill seemed unfazed. He said, "I understand. You have to make a profit, right? I'm not asking for a discount. I've used your company for 15 years, and I love your service. Can you show me the new prices?"

"We want to give you a heads-up," Rick said. "It's like 10 times more than you're used to."

The expression on Bill's weathered face did not change. "Show me what you've got!" he said.

Rick handed Bill the sheet of paper showing the six options and said, "Here you go. The top option is $349,000 for the finest system we have. What should we do?"

We braced ourselves for his reaction.

Bill laughed. Rick and I looked at each other. That was a good sign. Bill then let out a huge sigh and said, "OK. When can you start?"

Rick answered, "Wait. Which option are we talking about?"

After studying the proposal for a minute more, Bill answered, "I'll take the gold option for $269,000."

Rick said, "Are you sure?"

Bill interrupted. "The homeowner wants the best, and he's willing to pay for it. When can your crew start?"

Rick and I looked at each other in disbelief. We had failed miserably in our attempt to scare Bill away, and he actually seemed attracted to the new price structure.

In a last-ditch attempt to lose the job, Rick said, "We have also changed our payment terms. We need a retainer for 100 percent of the purchase price up front. So we'll need $269,000 to schedule this work. What should we do?"

Bill took out a business checkbook from his briefcase, wrote a $269,000 check to the company, and handed it to Rick. "Here you go," he said. I was dumbstruck. Rick somehow managed to say, "Great, thanks. Uh, we'll get back to you about scheduling." We walked back to the truck in a daze and drove in silence back to the office as we tried to process what had just happened.

Back at the office, Rick's boss was waiting for us. He said, "First, thanks for taking one for the team. Second, how did Bill take the bad news?"

Rick said, "Technically, we failed." Then he handed him the $269,000 check and explained what we had done and what had happened.

The boss said, "You did what?" And then he laughed, saying, "Well, if we have to do one last new construction project, at least this one will be profitable!"

Probably true. The real lesson, however, was this: when you act like you don't need the job, people will want you to do it more than ever.

What Should We Do?

The truth is you probably don't need to try to lose a job. It happens all by itself because you get nervous or intimidated and you throw in the towel when you are just a few minutes away from selling the job. The sad thing is you have no idea how close you are to getting the business, especially during the final phase, when objections are trickling in. Here's the thing: even if you're bad at handling objections, if you add the question "What should we do?" at the end of your response, you will increase your chances of selling the job a hundredfold.

When you're with me in person at a seminar, during the role-play sessions, you might see me gesture like I've got a hammer in my hand and I'm getting ready to hit a nail. When I do that, you know I'm trying to get you to "drop the hammer," which is to say the words, "What should we do?"

If a client says, "The price is too high," you should say, "Jane, I know it's a high investment. So, what should we do?" Adding the question, "What should we do?" creates an expectation that the client should take action. If you fail to say these words after you handle an objection, you are not going to get the job.

It's the same when you give the presentation. When you show your prices to someone, those four magic words must happen right away. At every phase of the sales process where action is required, you should say, "What should we do?" Say the words, and then sit there and wait. You don't have to be smiling and happy, but don't look angry or confused. Just look neutral. Like you expect to get moving forward. You expect to get this job.

If somebody says, "What do you mean, 'What should we do?'" you could say, "Well, Andy there are six options. What should we do?" Just repeat it again. If someone says, "Well, it is a lot to think about," you could say, "Definitely. It's a lot to think about, Andy. So, what should we do?"

At every phase of the sales process where action is required, you should say, "What should we do?"

Be Mentally Tough

If someone says, "Your prices are expensive," is that an objection? No. It's just a statement. All you need to do is acknowledge what they said. Say, "I know it's a high investment, Andy. So, what should we do?" If someone says, "I've got to think about it," say, "Go ahead, Andy, take your time. I can wait. So, what should we do?" And don't say anything else until they respond.

You may feel nervous because you don't know how they are going to respond. It may be with another statement, or they may rephrase the statement into an actual objection such as, "It's too expensive." Either way, by the time you get done with this book, you will have all the tools you need to respond effectively to almost any situation.

What you don't want to do is cave to your own internal pressure and end the call because you're afraid the client is going to get mad at you for being persistent and show you the door first. That's probably not going to happen. In fact, out of 16,000 calls as a heating and cooling contractor, it has only happened to me once, and I can count on one hand the number of times I've heard of it happening to a student.

"It's expensive" is just a statement. "It's too expensive" is an objection.

Hang in There

Let me ask you a question: How many calls have you decided to leave even though no one specifically told you to go? After you voluntarily left that call, the clients, Jerry and Clara, were sitting at the kitchen table saying, "Did you see the look on that guy's face? Yeah, he knew he was too expensive." They tested you, and you did not pass. Looking for the door immediately tells the client that you also believe you're too expensive. You don't believe in your prices. You don't believe what you're offering is worth it. Because if you did believe in it, you'd still be there talking to them about it.

If the going is getting tough in a negotiation, what do you think is going to happen when the going gets tough up in the attic, down in the basement, at the electrical panel, or by the municipal entry system? In this situation, the client hasn't said no. They've said they need to think about it, or it's a lot of money, or they have to ask their spouse. They've said all kinds of things, but they haven't yet said that you're not getting the job. So keep your poise, your quiet, and your calm. You have to hang in there, be tough mentally, and be ready for objections.

Remember: you have a passion for your job. You can make this happen. Be determined.

— UNCLE JOE'S RULE 32 —
Working through challenges is the effort needed to make us grow stronger.

In this last section, you'll learn my step-by-step process for effectively presenting the problems you discovered and the solutions you created, as well as how to use my ultimate closing technique to guide the client to the decision that's right for them. You'll also learn how to effectively deal with client objections, how to eliminate buyer's remorse so the deal stays done, and how to get great referrals and outstanding reviews—every time.

Ready? Take a deep breath. Here we go.

 **BULLSEYES**

○ Even if you're bad at handling objections, if you add the question "What should we do?" at the end of your presentation, you will increase your chances of selling the job.

○ Be mentally tough. Don't cave to your own internal pressure and end the call because you're afraid the client is going to get mad at you for being persistent.

○ Hang in there. If you leave before the client has said you're not getting the job, they will assume you don't believe in your prices or you don't think what you're offering is worth it.

WHAT SHOULD WE DO?

Chapter 24
THE MONEY WARNING

You've created your options and bundled everything up into a presentation. Now you're ready to go meet the customer and tell them all about your solutions, right? Not so fast!

The first thing you need to do is make sure the client has time to talk to you. Say something like, "Hey, Jane, is this a good time to talk about what's going on with your system?"

You should have your tablet with the solutions in hand, but you're not going to talk about the solutions or prices yet. At this point you want to focus the client on the problems and concerns and then warn them that the premium option will be a high investment, hence the title "money warning."

The money warning uses the law of dissonance. Remember, the law of dissonance says if you create dissonance but provide a path to harmony, you and the customer will then search for that harmony together.

There are five parts to the money warning:

- **Get Their Attention:** Start by saying, "I don't like what I'm seeing, but I have some solutions." The client will ask what is going on. If they don't, go ahead and state the problems.
- **State the Problems:** State the problems as faults, not parts. Then immediately say you have some solutions without revealing what they are.
- **Express Your Concern:** Say, "My greatest fear is . . ." and connect that concern to something related to your client's buying code.
- **Offer the Money Warning:** Warn them that the premium option will be a high investment and may have too much service so they might not want it.
- **Ask Them to Choose the Option That Is Best for Their Family:** Ask the client to listen to all of the options first, then choose the one that's best for their family.

Let's discuss each of these steps in more detail.

Get Their Attention

Always start by saying, "I don't like what I'm seeing. But don't worry, I have some solutions." Then the money warning draws the client into your presentation. So when Jane looks at the option sheet, she's taking it seriously. She is thinking, "I better get my glasses. I better go shut the TV off. I need to listen because it sounds like he's got some serious stuff to discuss."

How many times have you made a presentation where the client wasn't paying attention? When you tell a client you don't like what you're seeing—which sounds like a serious problem—they will give you their undivided attention. Once you have it, make sure to let them know right away that you have some solutions. Remember, any time you create dissonance you must relieve that tension immediately by saying you have solutions.

State the Problems

In the second step, you state the problems as faults and tell the client you have several solutions ranging from premium to economy. This is where you will go through your system observations. Here's an example of what steps one and two sound like together:

You: Jane, I don't like what I'm seeing here, but I have some solutions for you. Let me take you through what I found.

We have a fracture fault in the conductor from the panel to the primary bedroom. I checked the power in the panel, and there are 220 volts going into it, but there is no power in the bedroom and that fracture is what is interrupting it. While I was at it, I checked the outlet in the bathroom, and it doesn't have any power either, so there's a fracture there as well.

In addition, the outlets and switches are installed incorrectly. See how the wires are just pushed through the back of the device? They should be secured around the screw so they maintain 100 percent contact without any arcing or burning. I also noticed that several of the outlets are wired incorrectly.

On top of that, based on all of the devices and appliances you currently have, you are already at capacity.

Express Your Concern

The next step is to express your concern about the personal impact the problem is having on the client and their family.

You: My greatest fear is that because of the many design and installation faults, this problem will keep recurring in the future. Jane, what did you say it was like when you didn't wake up in time to make your meeting this morning because your phone hadn't charged overnight?

Jane: I was obviously frustrated and stressed because I couldn't get the kids to school and I had to call my client and apologize. It was a nightmare.

You: Look at this panel. You see what's going on here? We're catching small electrical shorts inside the panel around the primary bedroom and bathroom breakers. What did you say before about assuming that you and your family would have reliable power in this home?

Jane: Yes, that is part of the reason we built a new house. I never thought we'd have electrical problems in a house that was only five years old. I don't ever want to go through another morning like the one we had today.

Remember, whenever you hear about a victory or a challenge, that's a great time to create a magic moment.

You: Jane, may I say something? Your kids are lucky to have a mom like you who makes the effort to ensure they get to school on time. It makes me feel good to see someone who cares as much about their family as you do. Thank you for sharing that.

That's the whole presentation on the problems. You started with the immediate problem, followed by the issues around age, neglect, design, and installation, with a magic moment added in for good measure. That's how quickly it can go.

Express your concern about the personal impact the problem is having on the client and their family.

There's one more thing you need to do before you give Jane the actual money warning, and that is make sure you will be presenting to the right people.

In this case, you would ask Jane if she would like to include her spouse, Marc, in the presentation to make sure they both have equal access to the information. To keep things simple, let's assume that Jane has assured you (twice) that she will be the one making the decision because Marc is out of town.

Now it's time to give Jane the actual money warning.

Offer the Money Warning

You should say, "The top option you're probably not going to like. It might be too premium with too much service, but I have other solutions that are a little bit more economical and are probably more like what you expected."

This statement is designed to get a commitment from the buyer to not get mad when they see the prices of your options. You're also creating scarcity by verbally taking the premium plus option away by telling them you know they probably won't be buying it anyway.

If you have also created a whole home renovation option sheet, now is the time to introduce it. You could say, "With all these faults in mind, my greatest fear is that the system is only five years old and it's already at capacity. I've actually got two ways to fix this problem. One way is to repair the part of the old system that goes to the primary bedroom and bathroom, and the other way is to replace the entire electrical system in the home—the lighting, conductors, panel, everything. What should we do?"

For the sake of this exercise we are focusing on the repair option. Just know that the client may end up asking you about the total home renovation option, and you should have something ready to show them.

Ask Them to Choose the Option That Is Best for Their Family

This is just a quick reminder that you are simply reporting what you found via your thorough examination of their entire system, as well as requesting their commitment to look at all of the options. All you want is for them to pick the one they like best.

If you do the money warning before you show the client the prices, will they commit to looking at all of the options? Yes. Because they want to see what you have.

The money warning also raises the client's perception of the value of your service because you're taking their problem seriously now. Before, you were all happy-go-lucky, talking about their kids and Little League and what vacations they were going to take. All of a sudden, you're like a different person. The client thinks, "Man, this guy thinks I'm going to get upset. This must be a lot of money. He's not taking this lightly."

How does the client get out of the dissonance created by the money warning? By picking a solution. Then we're back to harmony. If you go in without this dissonance, there's no harmony to search for, and the client is busy trying to figure out how to get rid of you.

It's important to note that the money warning takes a bit of a different shape on repair calls versus maintenance calls or opportunity calls, where you are doing estimates for new equipment. The big difference is that you've got to make sure the timing is right. On a repair call, something is broken, so the time frame is right now. There's less urgency on maintenance and opportunity calls, so you have to make sure you are presenting at the right time and to the right people. They should be excited to hear your presentation. If they aren't, you need to wait until a different time.

Once you get the commitment from the client to look at all of the options without getting too upset, you should immediately begin the presentation by saying the title of your top option.

— UNCLE JOE'S RULE 33 —
If you explain the problem so it's relevant to the family, then clients will sell themselves on the solution.

There's more to this step, but these are the basics of how to set yourself up for success as you proceed through the presentation.

Now it's time to present your on-code solutions to the client—and that's what the next chapter is all about.

 **BULLSEYES**

- The money warning uses the law of dissonance, which says if you create dissonance but then provide a path to harmony, you and the customer will then search for that harmony together.

- The five parts of the money warning are get their attention, state the problems, express your concern, offer the money warning, and ask them to choose the option that is best for their family.

- The first three parts of the money warning are when you talk about the problems and connect them to the impact on the family.

- The last two parts of the money warning are about getting a commitment from the buyer to not get mad when they see your prices, which also creates the desire to see what the prices are.

- Once you get the commitment from the client to look at all of your options without getting upset, you should immediately begin the presentation by saying the title of your top option.

Chapter 25
PRESENTING ON-CODE SOLUTIONS

You've done the money warning, and your client, Jane, is a little uncomfortable right now. You've created dissonance by saying you don't like what you're seeing, and you've let her know the top option is going to be expensive. Remember that you've also given Jane the choice between a repair or a renovation and she chose to stay with the repair. Once you've made her promise to pick the option that is right for her family, bring back harmony by immediately telling her about the top option—without revealing the price.

Only Describe the Top Option

At first, you're only going to describe the top option, even though you've got six written down. (You'll let the client review the rest on their own.) I'm going to walk you through the process. Here is the description of the top option again for reference:

- Replace conductors from panel to bedroom
- Replace conductors in the primary bedroom and bathroom wing
- Renovate all bed and bath outlet terminals and voltage-control switches
- Install child-safety outlet terminals and power surge protection
- Update electrocution-prevention system in primary bathroom
- Five-year "can't-write-a-check" warranty and service plan

You should say, "The top option is called the Premium Plus Jane and Marc's Worry-Free Primary Bed and Bath Electrical Conductor Repair."

The premium solution must always have the client's name in it and refer to their buying code, which in this case is Jane's worry about the electrical in the primary bedroom.

Then, you're going to pause for a few seconds before you go into your explanation of what the premium option contains. Why? If you've ever watched a TED Talk on YouTube, have you noticed there's usually a healthy pause that takes place between the words? That pause wakes people up and creates a more compelling presentation. It adds more drama.

The prices should still be covered up right now. If they're on a tablet, you can move the screen to the side so they're out of sight. If they're on a piece of paper, use another piece of paper to cover up the right side of the proposal where the prices appear. You are not ready to reveal the cost of any of the options just yet.

The Power of Because

Every task you explain has to have the word *because* after it. The structure of your explanation should be: "[Describe the task], and I did this for you, [client name], *because* [buying code you've learned from them] and [what the solution allows you to do for them]." You're going to use this formula to explain each task within the top option.

Let's continue.

MAIN REPAIR OR EQUIPMENT SOLUTION

Remember, this is the minimum solution and its heavy-duty or commercial alternatives.

Say, "Jane, the first thing we're going to do is replace the conductors from the panel to the primary bedroom and the bathroom. I did this for you, Jane, *because* you said you and Marc work long hours and you're worried about your kids' safety when they're home alone after school and using the gaming console. You also need to make sure your phone reliably charges when you plug it in so your alarm goes off. Renovating these conductors will give you peace of mind."

Remember, the first thing to address in your presentation is always the issue the client called you out for.

ADDITIONAL SYSTEM ENHANCEMENTS

Here you are looking for ways to improve the system's quality and reliability, as well as features you could add that would enhance the safety and health of the people living in the home.

Say, "We're also going to replace the conductors in the primary bedroom and bathroom. I did this for you, Jane, because their capacity doesn't match what's needed to power today's electronics and appliances. Replacing these will give you peace of mind. Another thing we are going to do is renovate the bed and bath outlet terminals and voltage-control switches. I did this because I wanted to be sure that the outlets were safe for your family. Finally, we're going to install child-safety outlet terminals and power surge protection and update the electrocution-prevention system in the primary bathroom. Jane, I did this because of your family. I want this home to be a safe place for them."

WARRANTY AND SERVICE PLAN

Remember, the length of the warranty and service plans should always be the same.

Say, "Jane, this also includes a five-year 'can't-write-a-check' warranty and service plan with annual light bulb and smoke detector battery replacements. I did this for you and Marc because I want you to have time to relax while I take care of the system."

If you're not sure what the buyer's code is at this point, use a Pure Motive Service value as a fallback. As a quick review, the five values are:

- Enhancing quality and reliability
- Protecting the client's safety and health
- Providing customer-service choices
- Customized relevant solutions
- Honesty (even when it's not popular)

You could say things like, "John, I did this because I wanted to make sure the air in your home is healthy," or "April, I did this because I wanted to make sure your garage door opens and closes reliably every time," or "Andy, I did this high-quality solution because you said you wanted this system to last for a long time."

OK, back to our presentation to Jane.

You: You mentioned that you buy a planned service every year from the company that takes care of your furnace and air conditioner, right?

Jane: Yes.

You: How much does it cost for that agreement every year?

Jane: I think it's $249.

You: Well, now you're going to have five years of VIP service for your electrical system. The plan includes a free diagnostic and travel fee for the rest of the year. We'll come out once a year and replace the batteries in your smoke detectors. You can also call us to replace the light bulbs in all your fixtures, including the chandelier, and we'll climb the ladder and put them in. On demand or scheduled. If a battery beeps or a light bulb goes out, all you have to do is call because it's included with this option. Guess how much extra it's going to cost you per year?

Jane: How much?

You: With this option, it's free. And it's all-inclusive.

Jane: Wow.

— UNCLE JOE'S RULE 34 —

Saying "I did this because . . ." is an instant benefit generator. It lets the client know that your solution is personalized.

The Price-Guess Game

Remember, you still have not revealed the prices yet. The next step is to go into what I call the "price-guess game." Here's what it sounds like in context, and we'll discuss it more afterward.

Jane: So how much is it?

You: Why don't you take a guess? How much do you think we're talking about, Jane?

Jane: Let's see, you're going to replace the conductors in the primary bedroom and bathroom, and then come out to change my chandelier bulbs right before Christmas? It's got to be $6,000.

You: Jane, come on. This is the premium option.

Jane: More than $6,000?

You: Actually, you were pretty close. It's only $4,792. What should we do?

That's how the whole presentation should go right there. That's staying on code with the buyer. Now, did the client give part of the presentation too? Actually, she pretty much gave herself the entire presentation. That's the power of the law of involvement.

As a reminder, the law of involvement says that if you involve your buyer, you're going to be more on code with their solutions, and they will be more open to those solutions because they actually made them themselves.

So what is the point of the price-guess game? Why do you think we make people do that? The first reason is to get the client to participate in the presentation. The other reason is that making the client guess the price gives you immediate feedback on how you're doing when it comes to building value.

Remember, one of the Pure Motive Service principles is to be a student. You will learn from every presentation. You will learn about your ability to read your client and how to stay on code by asking them to guess the price.

What if someone doesn't want to guess? What if Jane had said, "You know, Joe, just tell me what the price is. Don't play games with me." In that case, what you do is guess for them. Here's what that might sound like:

You: That's my premium solution. So do me a favor and take a guess. What do you think we're talking about for this one?

Jane: I really don't know how to answer that.

You: If I told you the system was $6,000, would you think that price was too high?

Jane: Yeah, I think so.

You: I agree. It's only $4,792. What should we do?

If your client doesn't want to guess, throw out a high number and ask their opinion about it. Basically, you're guessing for them, and that's even better.

If people guess low, what does that tell you about what you're doing? If the client is consistently guessing $300 when the price is $2,000, you're not doing a good enough job of creating value in your presentation.

Making the client guess the price gives you immediate feedback on how you're doing when it comes to building value.

You're Not a Horse Unless You Are

My grandpa, Emil, used to own a tavern in the Chicago suburbs. I used to work at his bar, slinging beer cases in the back room and sweeping the floors. One day he stopped me and said, "Joe, I've got to tell you something. If one person tells you you're a horse, they're crazy. Because you're clearly not a horse. Now if three people tell you you're a horse, there's probably a conspiracy involved. The first guy who said you're a horse probably got to the other two guys, right? But you know what, Joe? If 10 people tell you you're a horse, it's time to buy a saddle because you probably are one."

The reason I'm telling you this story is that it's possible to have one or two customers complain about your price and say it should be cheaper. What my grandpa would say is don't let a couple of clients out of a hundred convince you that your prices are too high. Instead, look at the trends. What will the next 10 clients guess? Are they also going to guess way too low? Or are they going to guess way higher?

Keeping track of what clients are guessing over time can help you dial in your service offerings so you can deliver more value to the client and make sure your prices are the right ones.

Let's say your top option is $2,500, but people are always guessing $5,000 or $6,000. Your ability to create value is great. You could probably expand that top option to include more services. I'm not saying charge more money for the same thing you would have done cheaper yesterday—unless your costs (or profit goals) go up. But you could add more services, things you may have been afraid to offer. You could offer to repair the drywall issue that's not even yours. You could offer to put a fence in if you're doing a sewer and digging up the front yard. You could offer to add landscape packages. You now have the freedom and ability to create value.

Keeping track of what clients are guessing over time can help you dial in your service offerings so you can deliver more value to the client and make sure your prices are the right ones.

Revealing the Price

Once you reveal the price, the client's eye will go straight to it because price is the ultimate shortcut to measuring the quality of what you are offering. That's why you don't let them see it until you've built the value around the top option.

Once you reveal it, the price—along with the title, verbal packaging, and description—is what will indicate the quality of each option. It's a lot of information, so you and the client need the written proposal to be able to keep track of everything.

Let's return to our presentation to Jane. After you confirm the price of the top option is $4,792, you have to provide her with the presentation immediately.

Now, watch your client's body language. Is she holding the paper or tablet with one hand or two hands? Or does she put it back down on the table? If she puts it on the table, no matter what she says, she's probably thinking, "That's ridiculous." Whenever somebody sets the option sheet on the table, pick it back up and say the following:

You: Listen, Jane, I know the premium-plus option is a high investment. No doubt about it. I'm not going to deny that. But when I first got here, what did you say you wanted to accomplish today? You said you wanted to get this taken care of. Take a look one more time. What should we do?

Jane: Oh, well, we can get it done. But maybe we should go with one of the lower options?

You: OK, which one are you talking about?

Jane: How about the premium option?

You: Good choice. What do you like about that one? It's still a high option.

Jane: The other one was just more than I was looking for.

You: OK. So, what should we do?

Jane: I like that second option. Let's get it done.

You: OK. Check, credit card, or bridge loan?

Always be aware of the client's body language. What people do sometimes speaks louder than the words they say. If you hand the paper to Jane and she holds it with two hands, shut up. All you need to say at that point is, "What should we do?" If she's holding it with one hand, expect an objection. She could be ready to put it down if she's only holding it with one hand. If it's two hands, you've got a little time. It's not likely that she'll go from holding it with two hands to putting it down on the table.

If she's only holding it with one hand, you better get ready for an objection because it's going to happen. What's it going to be? Maybe she needs to talk to her husband. Maybe she wants you to leave the proposal and she'll call you back next week. You don't know what it's going to be, but you are sure some objection is going to happen, and you better be ready with your response.

This is your game—presenting the options. Every time your client makes a choice—any choice—you say "Good choice. What do you like about it?" to continue the opportunity. When the client doesn't like an option, say "Good choice. Let's get rid of that one."

When you get the client to admit, "I hate that top option," you should be thinking, "Yes! You hate something! Let's get rid of it and look at the other five things that you hate less."

Don't worry too much about the specifics of handling objections right now. I'll share my top techniques for effectively identifying and handling anything that comes your way in chapters 27 and 28.

Always be aware of the client's body language. What people do sometimes speaks louder than the words they say.

KEEPING A CONSISTENT PACE

If you see me do these role-playing exercises in person at a Total Immersion Summit, you will notice that my pace does not change, no matter what choice the subject makes. If it's the wrong choice for them, I just get rid of it.

Your pace shapes the client's perception of your ability. You need to be able to keep the opportunity moving smoothly forward by knowing how you are going to respond no matter what the client says so the pace remains consistent.

"You hate that one? I hate it too. Let's get rid of it."

"You like that one? Great. What do you like about it?"

So now you can see the problem with giving the client only one choice—if they don't like it, you're screwed!

WHAT SHOULD WE DO?

Don't Paint Seagulls

What if I told you there will be times when you won't even have to finish your presentation? Here's what that might sound like, this time with another client named Dustin:

You: So, Dustin, either way, do me a favor. Don't get mad. Just choose the one that's right for your family.

Dustin: I won't get mad. What do you have here?

You: My top option is called the Premium-Plus Keep Dustin Cool Complete Air-Conditioning Renovation. It's a complete renovation, so it's got a heat-absorption system . . .

Dustin: Stop. I want that one. I don't care what it costs.

You: Dustin, you didn't even consider the cheaper options. Let's look at those.

Dustin: I don't care. I just want the best one. That's the best one you've got?

You: Yes, it's the premium-plus option. Good choice. What should we do?

Dustin: Sign me up.

It does happen.

If you're thinking, "But, Joe, I haven't told him about the 12-year warranty with 12 years of service. I haven't talked about the renovation of the outdoor heat-removal system." Stop. He already bought it!

If somebody stops you in the middle of a presentation, let them. You can offer them the opportunity to look at the cheaper options, but if they say no again, you're done. The next thing out of your mouth should be, "OK. Check, credit card, or bridge loan?"

This is when you have to make sure your mother stays in the truck. If she gets out, she's going to make you say stuff like, "Are you sure you want to spend that much money on this thing? It's cheaper to do it this way."

Let me tell you a story to illustrate this point. A girl in San Francisco painted a picture of the Golden Gate Bridge to enter in an art contest. Her teacher, who meant well, wanted her to win, so she added seagulls to the landscape but never told the girl about it. The girl finished in second place. The judges' feedback was, "Seagulls out of context with painting." And the girl was like, "What seagulls?" The teacher ended up getting fired, and the school district had to pay for another scholarship for the girl to go to Stanford University, which was the first-place prize. All because of some seagulls!

Don't paint seagulls to try to help people out. Once they say they want an option, stop talking and sell it to them.

It's OK to hope for a slam dunk like this one, but in the event the client does object, you need to know what to do next. In the next chapter, you will learn the next step, which is to get your client from presentation to purchase with my ultimate closing technique.

 **BULLSEYES**

° After the money warning, immediately bring back harmony by telling the client about the top option—without revealing the price.

° Every solution must include the word *because*: "[Describe the task], and I did this for you, [client name], *because* [buying code you've learned from them] and [what the solution allows you to do for them]."

° The price-guess game gets the client to participate in the presentation. It also gives you immediate feedback on how you're doing when it comes to building value.

° Price is the ultimate measurement of the quality of what you are offering. Never let the client see the price until you've built the value around the top option.

° When a client likes an option, say, "Good choice. What do you like about that one?" If they don't like an option, say, "Good choice. Let's get rid of that one."

° Your pace shapes the client's perception of your ability. Know how you are going to respond no matter what the client says so the pace remains consistent.

° Don't paint seagulls. If a client cuts the presentation short and says they want the top option, believe them. (And don't forget to leave your mother in the truck!)

Chapter 26
ULTIMATE CLOSING TECHNIQUE

Back in the late 1990s, my wife, Julie, and I were finalizing the purchase of a new home in northern Illinois. We took another walk around the model home we were interested in with our "new home specialist," whose name was Dudley, and then we all sat down at the big table in the dining room. After some discussion, Dudley slid a piece of paper across the table to us and said, "Here's the monthly payment. It's $2,477. What are your thoughts?"

Julie looked over at me, and based on her expression I could tell she *really* wanted this house. The problem (in my mind) was that the payment was more than we were used to, so as a contractor I started thinking about how we could get the price down. In the meantime, Dudley sat quietly. After a long minute, it finally occurred to me that he was waiting for one of us to say something.

I said, "Dudley, it looks really good, but I have a buddy who can do hardwood floors. How much would the payment be if we did our own floors?"

Julie and Dudley just looked at each other like they were saying, "Is this guy crazy?"

Then Dudley said—and I'll remember these words forever— "Joe, do you want a *real* house or a *but* house?"

"Dudley, what is a *but* house?"

"A *but* house is where you move into your dream house and everything is perfect. But you decide to turn this dream into a nightmare by trying, for example, to save $13 per month by installing your own flooring."

He had a point. But . . .

I looked at Julie, and she frowned.

"OK, Dudley. You're right. We don't want a *but* house. Let's get a *real* house. Where do we sign?"

"Good choice, Joe!" Dudley said. Then he reached across the table and high-fived me.

And we lived very happily ever after in this beautiful *real* house with its stunning hardwood floors that were expertly installed by the builder.

Dudley knew how to close a deal and do it in a way where the clients felt good about it. He knew the power of silence and how to handle our questions and objections. He knew how to get the ball across the goal line—and that is the purpose of the ultimate closing technique.

The close comes right after the price-guess game, after you reveal the actual price. Let's say your client, Tom, guesses the price is about $4,000, and you reveal it is only $2,795. Naturally, you follow that with the question, "What should we do?"

What do *you* do next? Nothing. Nada. Zippo.

You wait for them to answer your question.

Be Quiet

Resist the urge to keep talking. Just be quiet and let the client think. The silence might make you uncomfortable at first—until you see how well it works. Breathe. Smile with your eyes. Think about something else. Is your baseball team going to make the playoffs? Will the fish be biting when you go out on the boat this weekend? Stay calm and quiet. If you start talking, you (and your mother) are going to talk yourself out of the job.

In some ways, it would be nice if the client just said no because there are a lot of ways to deal with objections. (For example, "It is just too much money.") But if you do the magic moments, lay out all the problems and solutions, and explain why you created each part of your top option ("I did this because . . ."), the client's initial response is probably not going to be about the price—even if it's ultimately about the price. It's going to be a stalling tactic. They will likely say something like, "I need some more time to think about this," or "Do you mind emailing that proposal to me? I'll call you back later."

Clients stall because they are feeling pressure to decide which option they want and they aren't sure which one is right yet. The law of expectation is in force ("What should we do?") and it's making them uncomfortable.

If you leave now without relieving that discomfort by helping them complete the decision-making process, they are never going to call you back. Someone who doesn't know them and their needs as well as you do will end up getting the job. Worse, if you do email the client your proposal, they are going to show it to your competitors, who will do it cheaper. The client will tell people that you're too expensive because they never got to experience the value of the service, expertise, and unconditional friendship that was rolled up into your options.

Clients stall because they aren't sure which option they want yet. Be determined to hang in there with them. Otherwise, someone who doesn't know them and their needs as well as you do will end up with the job.

This is why the Pure Motive Service principle about being determined exists. You have to be determined to do whatever it takes to assist the client in choosing the option that's right for them and their family—even if it's the bottom option. It doesn't have to be complicated. Here's what it could sound like:

Tom: I need some time to think about this. Can you email the proposal to me?

WHAT SHOULD WE DO?

You: Actually, I can do better than that. We both think the top option is too much, right? Let's get rid of that one.

Tom: But I like the top option.

You: I'll tell you a secret. I like that one too. So, what do you like about that one?

Tom: I like the warranty and service for 12 years.

You: OK, then, what should we do?

Tom: But that's more than I wanted to spend.

You: So, what should we do?

Tom: Could I get the second option with a 12-year warranty instead of a 10-year warranty?

You: If I could do that second option with the higher warranty, what would happen then?

Tom: I would do the second option.

You: So, what should we do?

Tom: Let's do the second option with the 12-year warranty.

You: OK. Check, credit card, or bridge loan?

— UNCLE JOE'S RULE 35 —

Questions continue opportunities; answers end them.

Sometimes that's really all it takes. And even if Tom turns around and says the second option is still too much money, you aren't worried because you have four other options and plenty of tools you can use to help him cross the finish line.

Be patient. This is going to get done. Stay in the moment and just do one thing at a time. If the client keeps introducing obstacles, understand that the average person is only capable of 2.3 objections. All you have to do is get through two or three of them, and after that, they will almost always make the decision.

While you're waiting in silence, you may think of something you should have covered in the presentation. Don't start talking about it now. Never answer an unasked question. Wait and see if the client needs it to make their decision, and if so, let it become part of the objection-handling process.

Handling Client Questions

At this point, the client may start asking additional questions about things like brand names, tonnage, BTUs, or SEERs. (In the heating and cooling industry, SEER is representative of how much energy and money the unit requires to operate effectively over a single year.) They might also ask for literature about the system.

This falls into the category of them asking about parts, and you don't sell parts, you sell Pure Motive Service. Getting the client back on track might sound like this:

Tom: What's the brand name of the equipment I'm getting?

You: Well, Tom, I would be hesitant to share a brand name because 100 percent of what we offer is a service. We select the brand that allows us to give you a 12-year warranty.

Tom: What's the SEER rating on that unit?

You: The SEER on the unit you're getting will translate into a savings of $16,000 to $18,000 over a 20-year period. That's why we did it.

Tom: And what's the tonnage on the unit?

You: The effectiveness of tonnage and BTUs is dependent on the air-delivery system. I'm giving you the maximum amount of tonnage and BTUs that are needed to heat this house effectively for the next 12 years. So, what should we do?

There is no need to explain, justify, or give them specifics about these kinds of questions. If you do, all it will do is reduce the value of what you've proposed back to the cost of the parts. It's the same thing if they ask for literature. You could just say, "What would you like literature on that I haven't already covered?" Send the question back to them.

— UNCLE JOE'S RULE 36 —
Never answer an unasked question.
Acknowledge the client's statement and ask
"What should we do?" Then shut up.

Trick Questions

There are also some trick questions the client may ask that you need to know how to answer. The most common one is, "When can you get the job done?"

That sounds like such an innocent question, doesn't it? It sounds like you're definitely going to get the job, right? Wrong. It's a sidetrack, and I've seen thousands of techs lose the call the moment they answer that question the wrong way.

So what's the wrong way? Telling them exactly when you can do the job. I'm serious. Here's what's going to happen:

Tom: When can you get the job done?

You: We can do it tomorrow.

Tom: All right, I'll think about it tonight. I'll give you a call back tomorrow.

You just lost that call because they will not be calling you back tomorrow. The key to answering trick questions safely is to ask a question back: "If I could do that, what would happen then?" Here's what that sounds like:

Tom: When can you get the job done?

You: That's a good question, Tom. Thank you for asking. What is the timeframe you were thinking of?

Tom: I'd like it to be done tomorrow.

You: What if I cleared my schedule right now? I could pull an engineering report on this house, take the measurements I need to get the equipment ordered, and get someone over here to take out the old equipment tonight. Then we could come back first thing tomorrow morning to finish the job and you'd have a new system by 4:00 p.m. If I could do all of that, what would happen then?

Tom: I'd say let's get it done.

You: So, what should we do?

Tom: Let's do it.

Sometimes the client is ready to move forward, but you can't get them on the schedule for a couple of weeks. In that case, you need to provide a temporary solution. In terms of HVAC, it may mean installing a temporary furnace or window air-conditioning unit that you provide. You might also put them up in a nice hotel for a few nights while you do the work. Once you explain what you could do, then ask the question, "If I could do that, what would happen then?"

You're not scrambling. You've priced the job properly so enough money to do these types of extra things is already built into your proposal.

The key to answering trick questions safely is to ask a question back: "If I could do that, what would happen then?"

What Is an Objection?

The key to successfully closing a client is the ability to tell the difference between a nonobjection, such as a statement, and a real objection. A real objection is when someone specifically tells you "no" or "not now."

For example, "Oh my goodness, that's a lot of money" is a statement, not an objection. Same with something like, "I think I'm going to have to ask you to get out of my house pretty soon." That one is just a statement of something they are thinking about.

If clients are making statements like these, they are just sorting through their options out loud. There's no need to do anything because they haven't given you a "no" or "not now" yet. Just stay quiet and give them time to think it through.

Don't get me wrong, real objections can and do happen. That's why, in the next chapter, I'm going to arm you with all the techniques you could ever need to confidently handle any objection a client may throw at you.

 **BULLSEYES**

○ The close comes after you've revealed the price of the top option and asked, "What should we do?"

○ Step one is to resist the urge to keep talking. Just be quiet and let the client think.

○ The average person is only capable of 2.3 objections. All you have to do is get through two or three of them. After that, they will almost always make the decision.

○ Answering specific questions about equipment will reduce the value of what you've proposed back to the cost of the parts. Instead, reconnect the client with the value of your service by explaining what the system you've prescribed will do for them.

○ When a client asks, "When can you get the job done?" the answer should be, "What is the timeframe you were thinking of?" followed by, "If I could do that, what would happen then?"

Chapter 27

DEALING WITH CLIENT OBJECTIONS— LEVELS 1 TO 3

In the 1980s, San Francisco 49ers football coach Bill Walsh made a game plan known as the "West Coast Offense" very popular. Part of the strategy was that he scripted all his plays in the first series. He didn't care what the defense was going to do. He said, "We're going to impose the first series of downs of the first quarter. We're going to run these plays, and we're going to work on them in practice."

Similarly, you need to practice handling objections. If you don't, there will be some clients that will knock you off your game. Maybe the dog is barking and running around, the kids are interrupting, or the spouse is not home. Or maybe the client is just determined to let the price get in the way of making a decision.

Going the extra mile and pushing through the resistance is real service, not just lip service. It's letting you know what is required to complete the call. It's working together to find a solution that is right for everyone. Remember, you and the client are working together.

To be able to respond effectively, you have to be like Joe Montana under Bill Walsh—calm, cool, and collected. You know what that first quarter is about, and you're prepared for any challenge that might come your way, especially the first objection—because you know it's coming.

The Gift of Objections

An objection is a gift your client gives you to increase your ability to understand what's in the way of getting the job done so you can resolve it. Objections are also opportunities to practice overcoming resistance and increase everyone's confidence in the value of your solutions.

The ability to effectively address objections can potentially increase your closing rate by 70 percent—from the industry average of 22 percent to about 92 percent. All of the techniques I'm about to share allow you to lock your mind on one objective: to keep going until you bring each opportunity to a conclusion.

Another benefit of mastering objection handling is that once you understand these techniques, they can be adapted and applied to resolve conflicts in other parts of your life.

My main goal here is to give you the tools you need to shift your mindset surrounding objections from fear and dread to joy and appreciation so you can see the client's objections for what they really are: the willingness to provide you with the feedback you need to help them make the best choice for their family.

I also want to take this opportunity to tell you how much I appreciate the effort you've been making to learn this system. Your clients are fortunate to have a provider like you who cares enough about them to learn Pure Motive Service at such a high level. It makes me feel good that you are investing your valuable time here, and I thank you again for your trust in me.

Now, let's get to some objection handling!

The Five Levels of Objections

In Pure Motive Service, there are five distinct levels of objections, ranging from ones that aren't really objections at all to being shown the door. The levels are:

LEVEL ONE: NONOBJECTIONS AND WEAK OBJECTIONS

Nonobjections and weak objections are client statements that don't clearly indicate a refusal. This means any statement a client makes that isn't explicitly "no" or "not now."

LEVEL TWO: SIX PACK OF OBJECTION HANDLING

When a client says no, expresses hesitation, or wants to delay the decision to another day, there are six strategies you can use to effectively address their concerns and guide the conversation to a successful outcome.

LEVEL THREE: PRICE OBJECTIONS

This approach is used when a client expresses concern or flat out asks you for a lower price. There are six techniques to choose from here too.

LEVEL FOUR: HANDLING DEEP CARDS

When a client clearly states that they don't want to get the work done, playing your "deep cards" reminds them of the commitments they made earlier in the call, as well as things they've said about the urgency and the impact of the problem on their family. Caution: the *only* time to bring these out is if you need more leverage to close the deal.

LEVEL FIVE: YOUR PASSION MOMENT

The only time to use this approach is if the client has explicitly asked you to leave. It involves expressing your passion and protectiveness of your client, someone you've taken the time to get to know and build rapport with, along with your genuine concern that no one is going to care as much about them or the quality of work as you do.

You'll be able to handle most objections with levels one, two, or three. Levels four and five are intense and should be reserved for when the call is really going south.

When it comes to handling objections, there's a lot to cover, so to keep the length of this chapter reasonable we decided to focus on levels one through three here and levels four and five in the next chapter. Ready? Let's go.

Level One: Nonobjections and Weak Objections

These are usually just statements people make to try to stall or throw you off track. "Why is it so expensive?" is the client testing you to see if you really believe in what you're saying. If you blush, stammer, or lose it, they've got you. You've just confirmed their suspicion that you don't really believe in what you're saying and you're just trying to sell them something.

"I need to think about it" is just the client buying time to process the information you've given them. In this case, all you have to do is acknowledge their request and ask again. Here's what that sounds like:

Tom: Man, this is a lot of money. I need time to think about this.

What you want to do here is agree, verbally repackage what Tom said, and then ask again.

You: Well, it's certainly a high investment. No doubt about it. So, what should we do?

Tom: I need some more time to think about it.

You: I understand, Tom, it is a big decision. Take as much time as you want. I'm here at your service for as long as you need me today. So, what should we do?

Did Tom say he needed two weeks? A day? He just said he needed more time, right? Listen to the objection. It's a weak one.

If Tom says something like, "Would you mind if we take some time to talk in private about this?" then you could say, "Sure.

Would you like me to go outside for five minutes?" Then, when you come back, say, "So, what should we do?"

"I need to think about it" is just the client buying time to process the information you've given them. Acknowledge their request and ask again.

Here are a couple more examples of weak objections you might hear:

Stacy: Wow. I'm embarrassed to say, but I didn't think it would be this much money for an electrical panel.

You: Yeah, I know. It's a high investment, Stacy. But remember, this is an investment in your family. So, what should we do?

Just like that—stay poised, calm, and ask again. They didn't say they wouldn't buy it. They're just testing to see what you think.

What if they come on stronger?

Ken: You've got to be out of your mind. What do you think, I'm made of money?

You: Well, listen, I know that in this economy everybody's suffering. Just choose the one that's right for your family. So, what should we do?

Always go back to the "What should we do?" moment. Ultimately, people know they still have to get the job done, and they will usually agree to get it over with today.

— UNCLE JOE'S RULE 37 —
Objections are the feedback you need to find the right solution for your client.

Level Two: Six Pack of Objection Handling

There are six effective ways to address any objection when a client says "no" or "not now." I call it the six pack of objection handling.

Objection handling is not about arguing with people. It's about shifting the focus away from the barrier and toward getting the job done, and any one of these six strategies will do that:

- Take away the top option.
- Determine how they normally buy.
- Ask how a third party (such as a friend or family member) would buy.
- Take responsibility (for everything).
- Identify the client's favorite choice.
- Find out which option they hate the most.

Remember: this process is always done while you are still inside the presentation.

TAKE AWAY THE TOP OPTION

This technique can be used to handle any objection. For instance, you've presented the top option, and the client's objection is, "It's too much money." Or, "Can you email those prices to me and I'll call you when I'm ready?"

What you're going to do in this case is agree with the client and immediately take away the top option.

Aaron: Can you email those prices to me and I'll call you when I'm ready?

You: Actually, I can do better than that. Let's just admit that the top one is too much money. Let's take away that top one. Take a look at the rest of the options. What should we do?

DETERMINE HOW THEY NORMALLY BUY

The second technique is used when clients act confused, tired, or incapable of making a choice.

All you need to do here is ask how the client normally purchases services in your industry. That sounds something like this:

John: I had no idea the price would be so high. I'll need to research this and get back to you later.

You: Well, John, let me ask you a question. When you purchase things for the safety and health of your family, do you normally purchase a premium, midrange, or economical solution?

John: Usually I go to the more midrange ones.

You: Like the ones in the middle?

John: Yes, the one in the middle—the third one.

You: Good choice! What do you like about that one?

John: I like that it both fixes the problem and addresses what caused it. That's all I really want.

You: So, what should we do?

ASK HOW A THIRD PARTY WOULD BUY

Sometimes clients like to bring in outsiders to support them in the decision-making process. In a perfect world, you would already have uncovered this information during the danger line and addressed this objection, but people can surprise you. Just roll with it and ask what they would pick.

Steve: I've got an uncle who is in the business.

You: Oh? What's his name?

Steve: His name is Mike.

You: Well, good. I'm glad you have a guy like that in the family. Let me ask you a question.

Steve: OK.

You: Mike would never do the top one, right? It costs way too much money.

Steve: Definitely not.

You: OK, let's get rid of the top one then. If Mike was here, which one would he choose?

Steve: Probably the economy option.

You: What would he like about that one?

Steve: The price.

You: And what would you choose if you were buying it?

Steve: One of the ones higher up than that.

You: So you would buy one better than what Mike would choose?

Steve: Yes.

You: Like which one?

Steve: The standard option.

You: Good choice! What do you like about that one?

Steve: It seems like it's right in my budget.

You: Are you sure? I've got a cheaper one, like Mike would pick.

Steve: That's all right. I didn't call Mike for a reason.

You: OK. So, what should we do?

TAKE RESPONSIBILITY

I call this one the responsibility technique. This is where you fall on your own sword and blame yourself for screwing up the presentation in some way. I would reserve this one for when the client tells you straight out that they are not going to go with you. It might sound something like this:

Bob: I like you and your company, and your presentation was very comprehensive. Obviously, you know your stuff. I wish I could afford you, but I'm going to go with another company that's a lot less expensive.

You: Can I ask you something? I'm starting to think this is my fault. Did I do a bad job of putting these options together for you?

Bob: No, you did a great job. It was a great presentation.

You: Bob, if I did such a great job, do you think we'd be leaving here without getting the job done?

Bob: No, I guess we'd get the job done.

You: So, what should we do?

Bob: Is there anything you could do closer to the price of the third option?

You: The third option? Good choice. If I told you that I could offer you 12 months same as cash, what would happen then?

Bob: If you could do that, I would do the third option.

You: OK. So, what should we do?

Bob: Let's do the third option.

— UNCLE JOE'S RULE 38 —
The word "no" is just an interesting first point in the negotiation process.

IDENTIFY THE CLIENT'S FAVORITE CHOICE

If the client is still on the fence about which option they want, and they haven't responded to your other strategies, reframe the question by saying, "Let's put the price aside. If you had to pick your favorite one, which one would it be?" It might sound something like this:

Paula: It's still a lot to think about. I think I'm going to hold off.

You: Well, Paula, regardless of the price, if you had to pick your favorite option, which one would it be?

Paula: Obviously the top one.

You: That's a good choice. What do you like about that one?

Paula: You get a 12-year warranty and service plan. You provide us with all the consumables and things like that. Nobody has ever offered me that.

You: So, what should we do?

Paula: When can we get that one done?

You: Well, if I cleared my schedule and made you my highest priority, what would happen then?

Paula: We'd get this done!

You: So, what should we do?

Paula: Let's do it!

Another way this could go is that Paula could say she doesn't like any of the options. Don't panic! A statement like this one is just confirmation that the client needs your help. When someone says they don't like any of the options, ask for feedback.

Paula: I don't think I like any of them.

You: Oh? Which one do you like the least?

Paula: The top option. It's the price.

You: Well, let me ask you a question. When was the last time you purchased something premium that was cheaper?

Paula: Never.

You: So, what should we do?

Paula: It's just a lot of money.

You: Well, there are five other options there. Let's take a look at those again.

Paula: Can we go over the middle option again?

FIND OUT WHICH OPTION THEY HATE THE MOST

When nothing else is working, you can do another kind of takeaway. You basically disqualify all of the options for them. Since scarcity creates higher value, chances are the client is going to try to prove to you that they do in fact like one of the options.

Tony: I just need more time. Give me the weekend, and I promise I'll make a decision.

You: Listen, Tony, we've been here for a while. What am I missing? I'm starting to think you hate all of these options, am I correct?

Tony: No, I like the third one.

You: What do you like about that one?

Tony: I like the warranty and service plan. (Just to prove to you he doesn't hate it.)

You: So, what should we do?

The goal of this technique is to get people to really look at the options again. Ask questions. Say, "Which part of the presentation are we talking about? We have premium, midrange, and economy options." And then start working your way through the list again.

The six pack of objection handling is done while you are still inside the presentation.

WHAT SHOULD WE DO?

Level Three: Price Objections

Here are six techniques you can go to when your client says awarding the job is a numbers game and your price is just not in their budget.

HIGHLIGHT QUALITY AND RELIABILITY

In this technique, you point out the benefit of paying more for higher quality and reliability.

Andy: I'm going to go with another company because it has a much lower price.

You: When's the last time you got the best-quality service at a restaurant or hotel and the price was the cheapest?

Andy: Never.

You: So, what should we do?

EMPHASIZE EXPERTISE AND VALUE

In this technique, you express your concern about the level of service the client might receive if their goal is only to find the cheapest price.

Marcia: I need to get more prices to see if I can find someone who can do this for less money.

You: My greatest fear is that you'd get the same level of service you got last time for a cheaper price. Is that really what you want?

Marcia: Ugh, no.

You: So, what should we do?

TURN THE TABLES

In this technique, you are getting the client to see it from your point of view. Ask them if they would take less money for their work. The approach varies a little bit based on the type of job they have.

BLUE-COLLAR ROLE REVERSAL

Avery: Can you ask your manager if he can lower his price?

You: Avery, what do you do for a living?

Avery: I'm a finish carpenter.

You: What if someone said they could do your job cheaper? What would the quality of your work be in that house?

Avery: You can't do my job for less; the quality would drop drastically.

You: That's exactly the same with our work. So, what should we do?

WHITE-COLLAR ROLE REVERSAL

Gayle: You're going to have to sharpen your pencil and lower your price.

You: Didn't you mention you were a (doctor, lawyer, accountant)?

Gayle: Yes.

You: Why would someone pay you more money for the level of quality and reliability you provide?

Gayle: Because I'll get the job done right!

You: That's exactly the same with us. So, what should we do?

EXPLAIN LOWER PRICES MEAN CUTTING CORNERS

In this technique, you explain that to lower the price you would have to dial back the quality, reliability, safety, and health aspects of the solution.

Jackie: There must be something you can do to lower the price.

You: Sure, Jackie, but we'd have to cut corners on something you can't see to do that. Should we cut corners on quality and reliability? Or on the safety and health impacts of the solution?

Jackie: No, of course not. I like it the way it is.

You: Can I tell you something? So do I. So, what should we do?

STRESS THE VALUE OF SERVICE

In this technique, when a client asks why your price is higher than your competitors, ask them why they think your service is more expensive, so the words come out of their mouth, not yours.

Sam: Why is your price so much higher than the others I've seen?

You: Only you would know, Sam. After comparing the number of choices and how personalized our solutions are, why do you think we're worth more?

Sam: Your service and level of detail are better.

You: So, what should we do?

MAKE IT PERSONAL

If the client says they are going with someone who offered them a lower price, refer to the high quality of your service and the impact it will have on them and their family.

Michael: I'm sorry, I have to go with another company with a lower price.

You: I know the quality of the service we are providing is very high. I included those options because of your daughter, Melissa. What price can you put on her comfort?

Michael: No price.

You: So, what should we do?

A further word about price objections: if a client says, "The price is too high," that is a signal that you need to clarify the value of the options you've proposed. Let me explain.

What if I told you the price for a car is $50,000? Would you say that's a high price or a low price? You don't know because I didn't specify what kind of car it is. If you're used to paying $15,000 for an older used car, $50,000 is going to seem too expensive.

If a client says, "The price is too high," that is a signal that you need to clarify the value of the options you've proposed.

But let's say I had a brand-new Rolls-Royce I wanted to sell for $50,000. (By the way, the cheapest Rolls-Royce costs $578,000.) That would be cheap, right? The point is a price by itself has no meaning. What has meaning is what you are getting for that price.

So, if somebody tells you that your price is too high and they want to hold off on everything, you need to say, "Well, Mary, which one of these six options is too high? Let's get rid of the top one. Now which one do you like?"

The ability for a client to dial into the price that is right for them is exactly why you should provide a range of six options. A client might also say something like, "You know you're five times more than everybody else, right?" In that case, you should say, "I hope so because we provide five times more service than everybody else. So, what should we do?"

I always hope people get to a price objection because I'm going to win that objection every time. Why? Because you're never going to convince me that getting a cheaper price will result in getting the work done properly.

If you're like me, you'll develop a hundred different ways to respond to an objection. After about the third time, however, the client will think, "Why am I resisting so hard? This guy knows his stuff." So, in a way, objections—if you handle them right—are an opportunity to demonstrate that you're competent enough to do the job.

These ways to handle the first three levels of objections should provide you with the tools you need to handle 95 percent of the objections you will encounter on a routine call. Every so often, however, there are those calls that require extreme measures, meaning levels four and five—handling deep cards and your passion moment. You may not have to go there often, but eventually you will be faced with a call that's going badly, and the next chapter outlines two powerful things you can do to save it.

 **BULLSEYES**

- ○ Objections—if you handle them right—are an opportunity to demonstrate that you're competent enough to do this job.

- ○ There are five levels of objections: nonobjections and weak objections, six pack of objection handling, price objections, handling deep cards, and your passion moment.

- ○ The six pack of objection handling gives you six strategies for shifting the focus away from the barrier and toward getting the job done: take away the top option, determine how they normally buy, ask how a third party would buy, take responsibility, identify the client's favorite choice, and find out which option they hate the most.

○ There are six ways to address price objections: highlight quality and reliability, emphasize expertise and value, turn the tables, explain lower prices mean cutting corners, stress the value of service, and make it personal.

Chapter 28
DEALING WITH CLIENT OBJECTIONS— LEVELS 4 AND 5

In the last chapter, you learned levels one through three of objection handling, which should allow you to handle objections on 95 percent of the calls you go on. This chapter is about what you can do when a client clearly states that they don't want to get the work done or has explicitly asked you to leave.

Levels four and five—handling deep cards and your passion moment—are intense and should be reserved for when the call is really going south.

Level Four: Handling Deep Cards

Client commitments made earlier in the call—as well as things they've said about the urgency and impact of the problem on their family—are like high-value playing cards you've been holding in the hole if needed.

If, at the end of your presentation, the client clearly states that they don't want to get the work done, it's time to play one or more of those cards.

There are three types of deep cards: family and health, client values, and emotional connection. Think of family and health like the jack of hearts, client values like the queen of hearts, and emotional connection like the king of hearts. To play a deep card, invite the client to repeat the words they said earlier. Don't say their words for them. Let them hear themselves say it again. Try to start with the lowest card, which in this case would be family and health.

Caution: the only time to ever play a deep card is when the client has stated they are not going to get the work done.

FAMILY AND HEALTH (JACK OF HEARTS)

To play this card, refer back to the family situation or health concerns discussed earlier to emphasize the urgency and importance of fixing the problem. In this scenario, Cindy called you out to look at her broken air conditioner. Here are two of her voluntary commitments from the beginning of the call:

You: So, we are just looking at the problem and not doing any work today, right?

Cindy: No, we have to get the work done today. My mother is coming to stay with us this weekend, and she has breathing issues.

You: OK, so just to be clear, what exactly do you hope to accomplish today?

Cindy: I need to get the work done.

The sentence "My mother is coming to stay with us this weekend, and she has breathing issues" is the deep card.

Now let's say you are at the end of the presentation, and Cindy tells you that she is going to hold off on making a decision about fixing the air conditioner. This is the time to play that deep card.

You: I could hold off on everything, Cindy. But what did you say about your mom coming in from out of town? What condition does she have again?

Cindy: She has COPD.

You: I just can't see her coming to this house and not being comfortable. So, what should we do?

Or you could say something like:

You: Cindy, remember, I asked at the beginning if we were just looking at the problem today and not getting any work done. What did you tell me about that?

Cindy: I said we have to get the work done today because my mom's coming to stay with us.

You: So, what should we do?

CLIENT VALUES (QUEEN OF HEARTS)

To play this deep card, align the client's objections with their previously expressed values, showing how the suggested course of action resonates with their beliefs.

In this scenario, Fred called you out to fix a leaky toilet, but now he wants to take some time to think about the plumbing work that needs to be done. In this case, you discovered one of his buying codes was that he was involved in a local water-conservation group.

You: So, we are just looking at the problem and not doing any work today, right?

Fred: No, we have to get the work done today. Clearly this toilet has been leaking for a while because my water bill is crazy. And in my water-conservation group we spend a lot of time educating the public about how much water gets wasted this way!

You: Your town is lucky to have someone like you teaching the public about how to conserve these resources. It makes me feel good to know someone like you who cares so much. So, what do we want to accomplish today?

Fred: Let's get this toilet fixed.

The sentence "We spend a lot of time educating the public about how much water gets wasted this way" is the deep card.

Now let's say you have reached the end of your presentation and are waiting for Fred's answer to the question, "What should we do?"

Fred: Let's hold off for now. I'll call you back when I'm ready.

You: I could hold off on this project, Fred. But what did you say about how much water a leaky toilet wastes and the effect it has on your community resources?

Fred: A lot. It wastes a lot of water, and people need clean water.

You: So, what should we do?

EMOTIONAL CONNECTION (KING OF HEARTS)

To play this card, bring up personal connections or emotional aspects discussed earlier in the conversation to highlight the importance of the decision.

Let's say your client, Rich, is upset because his wife and newborn baby are coming home from the hospital. It's 110 degrees in the shade outside, and the air-conditioning is barely working.

Rich: I can't believe the bad timing. My wife and new baby are coming home tomorrow, and it's so hot in here!

You: Can I share something, Rich? Your family is so fortunate to have a man like you preparing the home so it will be a safe and comfortable place for them. It just makes my day that you care so much. Thanks for inspiring me.

But then, later in the call, let's say Rich tells you he wants to hold off on getting the job done.

Rich: This is a bad time. I can't deal with this decision now. We can just turn on some fans until things calm down.

Remember that when people haven't had enough sleep or are under a lot of pressure, they aren't always thinking clearly. In this case, you are doing Rich a favor by reconnecting him to the reason he needs to let you get the work done today.

You: Rich, I understand it's overwhelming. What did you say about getting this done before your wife and new daughter come home tomorrow?

Rich: I know! We have to get this done.

You: So, what should we do?

Be aware that playing deep cards is as close as you can come to pushing the agenda, and the client might even ask you to leave. If they do, it's time to create a passion moment.

Deep cards are meant to reconnect the client with the voluntary commitments and reasons they gave you to get the work done today.

Level Five: Your Passion Moment

When the call is really falling apart and the client is getting ready to ask you to leave, it's time for what I call a passion moment. Passion moments are real. You've taken the time to get to know this client and what's important to them, and you've thoroughly diagnosed their system and created a series of options. And you've made it clear that you don't care which one they pick as long as it's the best one for them and their family.

After everything you and your client have been through together so far, your mindset should be, "I am not turning this over to somebody else because there's no one who will care about this job as much as I do or do it as well as I will. I am determined to get this done." Here's one example of what a passion moment might sound like:

June: I need to ask you to leave now.

You: I was considering that, too, but we haven't got the job done like you said you wanted. Can I ask you a question?

June: What's that?

You: After this experience with me, do you think there's anyone else who would care about this job as much as I do?

June: Probably not. But you're just too expensive.

You: I can assure you no one is going to care as much as I do. Can we just agree that the first three options are out? The fourth option would fix the problem and allow us to come back every six months to make sure we can catch any additional issues right away. So, what should we do?

Here's another example. (This one has a little more fire. Use your judgment.)

June: I think I'm going to have to ask you to leave.

You: I was just about to leave. But, can I ask you something?

June: What?

You: Do you want a real solution or a *but* solution?

June: What's a *but* solution?

You: That's where you could have got someone like me who has the passion to serve your family and get the job done right, *but* you chose someone who doesn't care as much as I do. Do you want someone who would quit in the middle of the job? Or someone like me who's passionate about getting this done right? What should we do?

To be fair, June could say, "I appreciate all that, but I still want you to leave." This rarely happens, but if it does, you know you've left it all out on the field and can go on to the next call with a clear conscience.

Your passion moment mindset should be, "I am not turning this over to somebody else because there's no one who will care about this job as much as I do or do it as well as I will. I am determined to get this done."

— UNCLE JOE'S RULE 39 —

Drop anchor and don't leave until the client tells you to.

Let's assume for a moment that June has selected the top option and is ready to give you a check. Most people would take the money and run, but not you. You first need to make sure June is happy with her choice and feels that she has made it of her own free will.

To do that, you need to do something essential that will seem very counterintuitive at first. In the next chapter, you will learn what that is and why it's critical to your success.

🎯 BULLSEYES

- Handling deep cards and your passion moment are intense and should be reserved for when the call is really going badly.

- The three keys to handling deep cards are referring to family and health (jack of hearts), aligning with client values (queen of hearts), and remembering an emotional connection (king of hearts). Use deep cards only if you absolutely need them to close the deal.

- Sharing your passion moment is a last-resort strategy, but done correctly it can strengthen your connection with the client and save the call.

Chapter 29
GIVE IT BACK

People who buy from service companies are vulnerable to buyer's remorse because they can't see or touch the bulk of what you are selling. All they can see is the equipment—the furnace, thermostat, and registers, or the faucet and toilet, or the outlets and electrical panel.

What they can't see is the expertise you use to diagnose the problem, specify the right equipment, install it properly, and make sure it's all working when you leave. They don't know what you know, and they're not going to learn it during the call.

Because the client can't see what they are buying in three dimensions, it's easy for them to get nervous and start to worry whether they actually got what they paid for or bought too much. And it's those doubts that cause buyer's remorse.

Don't Spike the Ball

One trigger of buyer's remorse can be your behavior. Have you ever watched a football game where a team that's losing by 20 points finally scores a touchdown, and then the guy spikes the ball and his teammates join in for a big dance party? Is that the behavior of a championship team? No.

When you celebrate too much about selling one of the better options, the client is going to think, "He's so excited it seems like he's never sold this type of thing before. Maybe I shouldn't have bought it."

So when a client buys a higher option, keep your excitement to yourself until you get back in the truck. You want the client to feel that you're so confident in the quality of this option that you've sold a million of them.

Post-Closing Giveback

To reduce the chances of your client experiencing buyer's remorse, you need to do what I call the post-closing giveback. Here's a scenario. You're walking through the presentation, and the client is interested in the third option.

Tim: What's that third option you have there?

You: That's a good choice. What do you like about it?

Tim: Well, it's got the warranty and service plan and everything else I want.

You: So, what should we do?

Tim: Let's go ahead and do that one.

You: Are you sure? We do have cheaper options. You didn't even look at those, just to be fair.

Make sure you always offer them the less expensive options so you can be certain they know they have that choice. This is called a giveback.

Tim: No, I don't want a cheap one. I want the better one.

You: So, what should we do?

Tim: I'll take the third one.

You: OK. Check, credit card, or bridge loan?

When a client buys a higher option, keep your excitement to yourself until you get back in the truck.

It's that quick. Once you get the final commitment on what they are buying, ask how they are paying. You've made it through all of their objections, so don't be timid about asking the client for payment at this point. You need to get paid for this job somehow. Plus, once you have their payment information, you can be convinced the job is sold.

The post-closing giveback offers the client a chance to change their mind and pick a lower option in case they were saying yes to the higher one to make you happy or to get the call over with.

Money Savers

Let's say you have a client who has talked the entire time about not having much money and needing to save money.

You presented your top option, and the client, Carol, is looking over the rest of them. Then she says she likes the second option. You're a little bit confused because the entire call all she has talked about is having no money. All of a sudden, she wants to buy the second one from the top? (*Blink, blink, blink*: this is a yellow light!)

Here's the secret of a giveback: you can't lose what you never had. You could say, "Carol, there are cheaper options. You didn't even look at those. I just want to make sure you're aware that there are some cheaper options available." You can use the word "cheaper" here (rather than "more economical") to try to repel her from those options. But don't tell her you're doing that.

Then Carol says, "Well, maybe I should go with the fourth option instead. That would probably be better for me. Let's go ahead and do that one right now."

WHAT SHOULD WE DO?

So, is it a good thing or a bad thing that she went down two levels? It's not just OK—it's better. If you don't do the giveback, here is what can happen. You write up the second option, you secure the payment, and you do the work. You get back to the office only to find out that right after you left, Carol called your boss and said you pressured her into buying the second option. She really wanted a cheaper one.

You need to make sure the client is not saying yes to a higher option just to make you happy or to get the call over with. If the initial option they selected is too much for them, let them figure it out now. It's a bad feeling to do all that work only to have people take the money back out of your bank account.

— UNCLE JOE'S RULE 40 —

You can't lose what you never had. Don't be afraid of showing people all the possible solutions.

Past Concerns Cleanup

If there are past concerns still lingering, now is the time to deal with them. Here are a couple of examples.

THE THERMOSTAT

Let's say a client called you in and said, "I want a new thermostat," and you found the real problem was that the air-conditioning unit was out of refrigerant. The client was asking you to replace a part that may or may not be a problem. Here's what that sounds like:

You: Rick, you said you wanted a new thermostat. But the actual problem is you have a fault in the refrigerant-containment system. That's why the thermostat is operating on its own. There's nothing wrong with it. But I did offer you a new one anyway in the top two options because you said you wanted one.

Rick: OK, then give me the third one, since I don't need the thermostat.

You: OK, I just want to make sure you understand that you aren't getting a new thermostat with that one. You're only going to get the refrigerant-containment system. Are you OK with that?

Rick: Yes, I'm good with that.

THE SPECIFIC BRAND

Your client, Tony, calls you in and says he wants a Binford air-conditioning system. You do your evaluation, and your top option is actually something better—a unit that is part of a custom signature series that has your company name on it. Tony likes the top option and purchases it.

Remember, Tony swore up and down that he wanted a Binford because that's what he's always had. (*Blink, blink, blink:* yellow light!) You need to address this concern at the end of the call.

You: Tony, I want to confirm something. When I first got here, you said you wanted a Binford unit. Now you've decided to go with our signature series, which I know is better than Binford, but are you OK with not getting the Binford unit?

Tony: Yes, I'm fine with it.

Don't let him off the hook yet.

You: Are you sure? What made you change your mind?

You've got to put that question out there now. And it takes a little bit of backbone. You might be thinking, "Aren't I talking myself out of a sale?" But what if you're not? You want to make sure it's actually going to happen. If the client is going to have buyer's remorse, you want it to happen while you're still there so you can sell it again. If you wait, and they do get buyer's remorse, it's going to be a mess. When you take the time to clean up any past concerns, you don't have to worry about that.

Three Blinking Yellow Lights

There are three common blinking yellow lights you may encounter during the giveback process:

- "I guess I'll do that one."
- "I've got no choice."
- Unspoken concerns, but you sense they are still there.

I GUESS I'LL DO THAT ONE

The first yellow light occurs when the client chooses an option with tentative language, such as, "I guess I'll do that one." If you hear those words, you need to address the issue right away or it will come back to bite you later. Here's what that might sound like:

Bob: I guess I'll do that one.

You: You're only guessing?

Bob: Oh, yeah, we'll do that one.

You: Are you sure? Have you looked at all of the options? Because I don't want to move forward until you're sure.

Bob: Yes, I'm sure. Let's do that one.

You: OK. How do you want to do this? Check, credit card, or bridge loan?

You have to say, "I don't want to move forward until you're sure." Give them a chance to consider the options one more time before committing.

I'VE GOT NO CHOICE

This one typically occurs when the client has selected an option that is more than they really want to spend. You just need to remind them that they do have other less expensive choices and then open the door for them to gracefully downgrade.

David: I've got no choice.

You: Well, David, I understand how you might feel some pressure right now, but actually there are six choices. Why are you choosing the third one?

David: You said you wouldn't leave until we did something.

You: So why not go with the fourth or fifth option or even the cheapest one?

David: I need to get it done. I've just got no choice.

You: But you've got six choices. Why are you choosing to go with the middle one?

David: I like stuff in the middle, and it has a better warranty.

You: OK. Well, we can only move forward when you're sure about which one you want. So, what should we do?

David: We need to save money, so let's go with the fifth one.

You: The fifth one?

David: Yes, the fifth one.

You're not done yet. Remember, you always need two commitments. Every time.

You: Just to be clear, what should we do?

David: Let's move forward with the fifth one.

You: OK. How do you want to do this? Check, credit card, or bridge loan?

Post-closing givebacks make sure you don't move forward until people have solidified their choice.

If the client is going to have buyer's remorse, you want it to happen while you're still there so you can sell it again.

UNSPOKEN CONCERNS

There also are some unspoken concerns that may occur during the process. In fact, the top unspoken concern occurs when you are selling to senior citizens.

Senior Citizens: Let's say you're about to sell a big job, like a new electrical panel that costs $12,000 or a sewer dig for $10,000, to a senior citizen named Ann.

In this case, you have to not only neutralize the client's buyer's remorse but also make sure no kids are going to pop up who will feel and express buyer's remorse on their parent's behalf—whether the parent wants it or not.

So when it comes to senior citizens, always ask about their children. That sounds something like, "Ann, can I ask you a question? Is there anybody else we need to talk to about this before we move forward? Sometimes people have kids who want to be in on a decision like this one. I don't want anyone to be mad at me."

Ann is likely going to say, "No, they're not a part of this decision," or "I don't want them sticking their nose in it." If she says that, great. The next question you ask is, "How do you want to do this? Check, credit card, or bridge loan?"

WHAT SHOULD WE DO?

Absent Spouses: Another potential for buyer's remorse is when you are selling to only one spouse. Let's say you've presented your options to Ken, and he picks the second one. His spouse, Karen, is out of town. You want to make sure you get a clear statement from Ken that Karen will be on board with his choice or assurance that he is the sole decision-maker.

You: Now, Ken, are you sure Karen will be on board with this? Are you sure we shouldn't get her on the phone and ask her what she thinks? The last thing I want is for her to be upset with us or you. Which option would she choose?

Ken: Well, she'd probably go with the cheaper one.

You: Well, maybe we should do the cheaper one then. I don't want to move forward until Karen is happy about this decision too. Could we give her a call right now?

Take the time to do this step because you don't want to go through all of this effort and put it in the win column only to have it boomerang back at you and land in the loss column.

Securing the Sale

Again, once the client has selected an option, it's time to secure the sale, meaning collect the payment for the service you're about to provide. You want to collect payment before you perform the service because payment in advance is the ultimate commitment to getting the work done.

The other reason you must secure payment before you start the work is if you don't, the chance that the client will forget how much they love you—and thus forget why they need to pay a bill for something that happened three weeks ago—increases exponentially.

All you have to do is say, "How do you want to do this today? Check, credit card, or bridge loan?"

When a client asks, "How much do you need?" just say, "We do need to secure the whole payment. We can do that with a check, credit card, or bridge loan. What should we do?"

From now on, forevermore, before you do any work, be sure to secure the payment.

FINANCING IS THE GIFT OF AFFORDABILITY

For many homeowners, the key to making essential upgrades—such as a new furnace, re-piping, electrical panel replacement, or a garage door installation—is through the power of consumer financing, which we are calling a bridge loan.

Financing is the gift of affordability. It ensures that homeowners don't have to decline or delay essential upgrades due to budget constraints and don't miss out on the opportunity to reap the many long-term benefits of a modern, fully optimized, and well-maintained system.

Home-improvement financing also takes into account the escalating costs of these solutions. If the client has to delay necessary upgrades, they might face higher bills, increased energy expenses, and higher repair costs down the road, as well as the inconvenience or even ever-increasing danger of living with a broken system.

Consumer financing offsets these future expenses by allowing the client to tackle them now and protect their future. It's a strategic financial move that bolsters the client's immediate quality of life while supporting their long-term financial well-being.

Post-Selling Interview

After you've secured the client's method of payment, there's one more step, which is the post-selling interview. Let's say our client, Debra, decided to go with the second option:

You: Hey, Debra, can I ask you a question?

Debra: What's that?

You: What was the reason you decided to go with the second option as opposed to a less expensive one? What did I say that made you want to go with that one?

Debra: Well, when you said it had a five-year warranty, I had to have that one.

The post-selling interview has two roles. First, it helps eliminate buyer's remorse by reminding the client what they liked about the option they chose. Second, it helps you learn the kind of language you're using that helps people make a decision.

The moral of the story is always do a post-closing giveback after you close every sale because you can't lose what you never had, and then follow up with a post-selling interview. Pure Motive Service results in happy, long-term clients who will love to refer you to others. In the next chapter, you will learn some strategies to engage your existing clients in helping you grow your business through referrals and five-star reviews.

 **BULLSEYES**

- People who buy from service companies are vulnerable to buyer's remorse. To avoid it, keep your excitement about selling the job to yourself and do a post-closing giveback.

- A giveback is offering the client the less expensive options again after they've selected a higher option, so you can be certain they knew they had that choice.

- If you have a client who has talked the entire time about needing to save money and then they pick a higher option, be sure to offer them another chance to change to a lower option.

- Uncertainty, resignation, and unspoken concerns that trigger your "Scooby sense" are three blinking yellow lights that call for a giveback.

- After you've received the client's check or credit card or arranged for financing, it's time to do a post-selling interview where you remind them what they liked about their choice.

Chapter 30
REFERRALS AND REVIEWS

What's the biggest challenge for any business? It's not making sales (especially if you know this system). The biggest challenge is keeping the pipeline full of potential new customers so you always have someone to sell to.

The problem is that acquiring new customers can be expensive. Even if your marketing and advertising is on point, it can cost $500 or more just to get the phone to ring one time.

The good news is there is a rich source of potential new customers right in front of you every day. You just need to know the right way to get referrals and five-star reviews from your existing clients.

Let's say you were able to bring in an average of five new clients a week. How much would just one of those clients be worth over the lifetime of your company? $15,000? $30,000? According to a 2020 study by SEO company First Page Sage, the average lifetime value (LTV) for an HVAC company is $47,200! Multiply that by five, and that's $236,000. Do that every week for 50 weeks a year and you can see how it will add up—all because you knew what to say and do to get great referrals and reviews on the spot.

The best time to get referrals and reviews is while you are still at the client's house doing the call. Let's talk about getting referrals first.

Getting Referrals

There are two great ways to start a conversation with the client about referrals. The first is to talk about how your business is going, and the second is to ask the client their opinion of how the call went. The first typically happens near the beginning of the call, and the second occurs at the end of the call when the client's problem has already been fixed and they are feeling the love. Here's how it works.

HOW'S BUSINESS?

Let's say you were supposed to be at your client Mike's house between 8:00 a.m. and noon, but you're swamped and don't get there until 12:30 p.m. Mike's not even mad about it; he's just glad you finally showed up.

Mike: How's business?

You: We're swamped. It's a good problem to have though.

Here's the issue with that response. Is Mike likely to turn his friends over to you when you could barely make it to his house on time? No! You said it yourself—you're swamped. The number one reason why people don't give your name to other customers is because they think you're too busy. They don't want to create additional competition for your service, and they also don't want to hear about how you got to their house late because you're already so busy. Let's look at that question again, this time with a different response:

Mike: How's business?

You: Well, you know, Mike, business is OK. But I was just talking to the other guys at the shop about how the biggest challenge we have is finding more great customers, people who understand the value of service like you do. If you were me, what would you do to find more customers like you?

Mike: Well, actually, I know a couple of people who need some work done.

You: Oh yeah? Who are we talking about?

Mike: My neighbor, Sally, right down the street.

You: What does she need done?

Mike: I'm not sure specifically, but I know she said she needs a ton of work done.

You: You wouldn't introduce me to her, would you? (This is a contrary question.)

Mike: Absolutely. Let me go get her number.

You: OK, thanks. I'll wait for you.

That's what it sounds like to get referrals. The other strategy you can use, if your client doesn't inquire about your business, is to ask their opinion of the work you've just performed.

The number one reason why people don't give your name to other customers is because they think you're too busy.

WHAT'S YOUR OPINION?

Let's say you've finished the call. You've collected the money. It's all working out great. The client is happy. Now, you'd love to get a referral from them. Here's what that sounds like:

You: So, Mike, can I ask you a question? What was your opinion of the way we did the call? What did you think?

Mike: You did a great job.

You: Well, thank you very much, Mike. I appreciate that. It means a lot to me, and I had a great time working with you too. Can I ask you a question?

Mike: Sure.

You: Our biggest challenge is finding more customers like you who understand the value of great service. If you were me, what would you do to find more customers like you?

WHAT SHOULD WE DO?

Mike: I'm not really sure.

You: Well, would you keep me in mind if you hear about anyone who might need any plumbing services?

Mike: Yeah, I will definitely do that.

Now the next time one of Mike's friends needs some work done, he will think of you and recommend your company.

Getting Great Reviews

The time to ask for a review is at the end of the call when the client is feeling the love. If you've provided five-star service, it's likely the client will be willing to give you a five-star review.

Uneasy about asking for reviews? Feeling hesitant is your gut telling you there's a chance the client could give you fewer than five stars, and that is a signal you probably could have done more to serve that client.

There are two ways to get reviews. The first is to leverage your outstanding service while you are still on the call. If for some reason that doesn't happen, the other way is to get it during the "happy call" that a customer service representative (CSR) should be making the day after the service. In both cases, the goal is to make the process as easy as possible for the client.

If you've provided five-star service, it's likely the client will be willing to give you a five-star review.

LEVERAGING YOUR OUTSTANDING SERVICE

If you do feel comfortable that the level of your service was outstanding and you can tell the client is feeling the love, here's an example of the best way to get them to give you an online review on the spot.

You: Janet, based on the level of service you received today, if your friends asked about our company, what would you tell them?

Janet: I'd say you did a great job.

You: Really? What else would you tell them? (If the first response was good, of course.)

Janet: I would say you were very thorough, explained the options clearly, and cleaned up after yourself.

You: I'm so glad to hear that.

There are a few places you can go from here. You could say something like:

- "So, if you were going to give us a review online, how many stars would you give us?"
- "If you were me and you wanted top-notch people like you to write an online review, what would you do?"

Once the client answers, be ready to provide the link to the review site you want them to use. Let's say Janet is willing to write a review.

You: Great. I can send you a link right now. Text or email?

You can then text or email them the link. Another great option is to use something like Popcard. (You can Google it.) It's a physical card you carry with you. The client taps it with their phone and is taken right to your review form.

Janet: Got it.

You: Great. I'll hang out here for a minute while you fill it out in case you have any questions.

Janet: All done. Thanks again.

When you've provided Pure Motive Service to a tee, getting referrals and reviews is that easy.

— UNCLE JOE'S RULE 41 —
There is no higher honor than receiving a client's personal referral or five-star review online.

If the client doesn't have time to provide a review on the spot, you can still get it later if you have your CSRs make what we call "happy calls."

MAKING HAPPY CALLS

A happy call is a phone call a CSR makes to the client the day after the service has been performed. The call follows a script that is designed to get feedback on the client's state of mind about the relationship they have with you and your company, as well as to spot-check the type of service they received (i.e., whether your tech showed them options and inquired about their level of interest in other solutions). Finally, it's a great tool for offering upgrades and getting referrals and reviews from your clients.

A CSR conducts a survey that includes many of the same elements of the Pure Motive Service system the client experienced with the technician. The call is specifically designed to surface what the client would say to their friends about their experience and then guide them through the process of saying it.

The tech should have recorded in the system whether or not they were able to get a review from the client. If they weren't able to get one, here are some questions the CSR could ask:

- "Now that you've experienced our service, how many stars would you give us?"
- "If your friends asked about our kind of service, what would you tell them about us today?"
- "If you were me and wanted premium clients like you to repeat what you just said about us in an online review, what would you do?"
- "If I said I could send you a link via email or text that will take you to the site to leave us a review, what would happen then?"

One of the most important aspects of the happy call is that it is another opportunity for the client to experience a magic moment with your company. At the very end of the call, the CSR should say something like, "We are fortunate to have a client like you who cares enough to share your feedback so we have the opportunity to improve. Not many clients would take the time, and I really appreciate that. Thank you so much for allowing us to serve you!"

I also feel fortunate to have a reader like you who cares enough about your clients and your success to have invested the time to read this book. It makes me feel good that you saw enough potential value here that you were willing to give me your attention. I hope I have many more opportunities to assist you in your journey toward mastery of the Pure Motive Service system so you can continue to leverage the information in *What Should We Do?* to win clients, double profit, and grow your home service sales for years to come.

We're not quite done yet, however. Please proceed to the conclusion, where I will reveal how you can maximize the impact of everything you've learned in this book. See you there!

 **BULLSEYES**

- The biggest challenge most service businesses face is keeping the pipeline full of potential new customers so you always have someone to sell *to*.

- The best time to get referrals and reviews is while you are still at the client's house doing the call.

- The best way to start a conversation with a client about referrals is talking about how your business is going or, once the call is done, asking them their opinion of how it went.

- Once the client says they are willing to write a five-star review, be ready to provide the link to the review site and stay with them to offer assistance in completing the review if needed.

- If you don't get a referral or review while you are there, a CSR can get one during a "happy call."

WHAT SHOULD WE DO?

TOOLS FOR YOUR SUCCESS

servicemvp.com/tools

* **HANDLING OBJECTIONS GUIDE**
Be ready to handle the six most common objections to getting the job done. When you overcome resistance, you increase everyone's confidence in the value of your solutions—and can increase your closing rate by 70 percent!

* **QUOTES AND FIGURES**
Get all the memorable quotes and figures featured in this book. You and your team will remember the fundamental principles of the Pure Motive Service approach!

Scan to download your tools

CONCLUSION

You probably picked up this book because you wanted to get better at sales, but I hope that by now you realize that the magic happens when you make meaningful connections with your clients first and then provide them with options so they can sell themselves on the solution that is right for them.

Pure Motive Service is about creating a relationship first so the client comes to know, like, and trust you and your company so much that they will stay customers for life.

Remember: if the *only* change you make as a result of reading this book is to let your clients know about all the solutions available to them and then ask the question, "What should we do?" you will automatically become more successful than you are now.

If you follow the entire system in this book, and if you're like most of my students, you will become successful beyond your wildest imagination.

Before we wrap this up, let me acknowledge the significant effort you've made in reading this book. Your clients and your company are lucky to have someone like you who is willing to invest the time to learn this system. It makes me feel good that you found enough value in these pages to make it to the end.

In this way, you are already working the first Pure Motive Service principle—be a student. You are someone who is willing to learn about their clients, new ways of thinking, and new techniques.

Hopefully you have already started to look at things differently and are fearlessly challenging any beliefs that may be keeping you stuck. The keys you need to free yourself from your own inner-belief prison are in your hands. Stay humble, and remember Uncle Joe's Rule 3: your ego is *not* your amigo!

Remember, no matter what your beliefs are, you have the power to change them. In particular, you can release the belief that it's a badge of honor to buy and sell cheap. You can love your mother but still leave her in the truck while you serve your client. No longer will you profile clients or sell the way you would buy.

I especially hope you embrace the principles in chapter 6 about the goal party. The application of that information changed my life, and it can change yours too. Dream big and make it real for yourself. Invest time every day to imagine what it would look like, feel like, or even smell like to do, be, or have your goals, as though they've already happened.

While you're at it, aim to become the best inverse paranoid you know, choosing to believe that the majority of people you talk to about your goals will be happy to help you and will want to see you succeed.

You're still going to encounter certain events, but now you know that while you can't change them, you can influence their outcome by the way you respond. Focus on responding to each event in a way that will produce the best outcome for both you and your client. While you're at it, give up complaining, saying "I can't," being sarcastic, blaming others, and making excuses. None of those things will move you closer to your goals. Pay attention to yellow lights—the things that clients do that give you pause—and recognize them as events with outcomes you can influence by the way you respond.

Being a student is always in play. You never stop learning and growing. There's always another summit to pursue.

I also want to acknowledge your efforts to understand and embrace the second Pure Motive Service principle—be on code. You now know how to use the client's language to describe the solution to their problem in a way that resonates with them. When you find your client's unique buying code, you are no longer asking them to spend money on you. You're asking them to invest money in getting their family's life back on track.

One of the most powerful aspects of being on code is the magic moment. I like to think of magic moments as the heart of the Pure Motive Service system. They allow you to quickly establish a powerful emotional connection with another person. Praising someone's effort, sharing how you feel about it, and expressing your gratitude for that effort has the power to make them feel better about themselves—and people who feel better about themselves will feel better about you too. When you master magic moments, you will find that your calls will become much easier, and if you decide to create them outside of work, you will find that your life will become much richer as well.

Another important tool you now have in your tool kit is the law of verbal packaging. Using the right words at the right time will go a long way in helping you manage the emotions and expectations of your clients and make you more persuasive when explaining your options. Write the word *because* on a Post-it note and put it on your dashboard so you remember to use it when presenting your options. It is an instant value creator. Avoid using trade jargon at all costs because it has no meaning to the customer, and no meaning makes it easy for them to say no. Memorize the types of faults and systems for your industry and practice using that language so communicating what the system does and what the client will get from fixing or enhancing that system becomes second nature.

All of these things will help you be on code with your client and create a rapport that is so strong they may ask you if you're reading their mind.

The third Pure Motive Service principle—be skeptical—is probably the most counterintuitive of everything I teach. To make this system work, however, you have to suspend your judgment about whether or not the client really wants a solution to the problem they said they wanted you to fix.

From now on, every client must convince you that they are serious about getting the work done before you do anything. That means getting not just one but two commitments from them that they want to get the work done. The convince-me step not only protects you in many ways but also is a great service to the

WHAT SHOULD WE DO?

client because it propels them past their indecision and fear and reconnects them to why they called you out. You'll also use the convince-me step to make sure that you are presenting at the right time. In fact, the convince-me step is a technique you will use again and again on the call to keep things moving forward.

In this section, I also talked about the value of creating scarcity when it comes to your service, time, and information. Scarcity is a huge purchase trigger because it creates value, a sense of urgency, and desire. Scarcity and dissonance go hand in hand and, when used properly, can also get the client unstuck and moving forward.

Once the client has convinced you they want to do the work, I hope you'll remember to work the two sides of the danger line. On the left side, you have to find out how your competition failed and then let momentum do its thing until the client says they're not going to use that company anymore (or do it themselves). The right side is about reminding clients of the nice things they've said about your company so they will shop inside of your proposal for an option that's right for them and their family.

Being skeptical is about consistently challenging the client's commitment, which will either propel the call forward or cause it to end if it will not result in a sale. It saves both you and the client from spending time and energy pursuing a solution that will never come to fruition.

The fourth Pure Motive Service principle—be ethical—is one of the most important things to keep in mind. Remember: to be ethical is to subscribe to a set of principles that govern our behavior or the conduct of an activity.

Our conduct as Pure Motive Service providers is governed by the five Pure Motive Service values: enhancing quality and reliability, protecting the client's safety and health, providing customer-service choices, customized relevant solutions, and honesty (even when it's not popular).

Write this next statement on another Post-it note and put it on the mirror in your bathroom: "Money is not my master. Rich or poor, everyone deserves to at least see what a premium, high-end solution would look like." Be a window, not a door! All you need to do is provide the six options and then empower your client to choose the one that is right for them and their family. If you adopt this approach, your clients will sell themselves on exactly what they want.

I also want to emphasize something. The information I provided in this section is powerful, and I'm trusting you to use it for good. To that end, you learned about the five levels of persuasion, the three types of questions, and the three buyer types. This information was passed on to you for one reason—so you could better understand your client and assist them in making the decision that is right for them. We are like card dealers in Vegas. We don't have any interest in what option our client selects as long as they feel comfortable with their decision.

You also learned the Pure Motive Service diagnostic process, which is to look at the entire system first, assessing its age, neglect, design, installation, and client impact. Only after you have assessed the condition of the total system are you ready to address the immediate problem. Remember, money is not your master. If there's an additional option you could offer that you think would make your client's life easier or more enjoyable, offer it. It may end up being something they'd love to have but didn't even know was available.

When it comes to pricing, remember it really is a science. In fact, chapter 20 is one you may want to review, especially the charts. The difference that offering six options makes really is remarkable. The six options should include two premium, two midrange, and two economy, where the lowest option is just fixing the immediate problem. Remember, the highest-priced option should always appear first and be personalized based on the client's buying code.

Use the law of association when naming your options and packages. Borrowing meaning from a brand, for example, is a quick way to communicate the level of quality that you're offering. You're already using the law of contrast by putting the most premium option first because it automatically makes the subsequent options seem more reasonable. Then again, there are people who are premium buyers, and that's OK. Let them convince you, and then ask how they'd like to pay—check, credit card, or bridge loan?

So, once you have the options and the pricing figured out, it's time to create the proposal. I gave you an example in the book of what that looks like. Remember, there is no such thing as a verbal proposal. Everything must be in writing. If there is an issue, you want it to be with the piece of paper or the image on the tablet. That way you and the client are on the same side, and the proposal is the problem. If you've used your solution pick list to collect information about the main repair or equipment solution, additional system enhancements, warranty options, service memberships, and consumables, all that remains is getting it down on the customer option sheet. Remember to create the options as you are doing your diagnosis because the last thing you want to do is disappear into your truck for 20 minutes to do it—it will break the flow of the call.

The good news is that it's easy to be ethical when you are committed to offering your unconditional friendship to the client first and honoring that friendship by staying true to your values and yourself.

For the next step, which is the presentation, you will need to lean on the final Pure Motive Service principle—be determined. Know that even if you're bad at handling objections at first, if you add "What should we do?" at the end of your presentation, you will increase your chances of selling the job.

Be aware of the internal pressure you're experiencing that makes you want to leave before the client has said you're not getting the job. Hang in there because if you bail out early you will just confirm their suspicions that you don't believe in your prices or that what you're offering isn't worth it. Be mentally tough and follow things through to the end. Know that you now have all the tools you need to close the deal.

So, now you have your presentation in hand and you're sitting at the kitchen table with your client. The very next thing you must do is to give the money warning. Remember, there are five parts to the money warning. First, you must get their attention. To do so, use the law of dissonance. Start by saying, "I don't like what I'm seeing here. But don't worry, I've got some solutions." Then, state the main fault in the system that's causing

WHAT SHOULD WE DO?

the problem. Let them know about any other design, installation, safety, or health faults you've found as well.

Next, express your concern by saying, "My greatest fear is ..." and tell them what concerns you about the impact the faults will have on the client and their family.

To ensure you will be presenting to the right person, always ask the client if they would like to include their spouse in the presentation to make sure they both have equal access to the information. Once that's resolved, let the client know you've got some premium, midrange, and economy options to solve these system faults.

Now it's time to give the actual money warning, which sounds something like, "There's the top option, but you might not want it because it might be too premium and have too much service." This is important because it's a way of letting them know it's OK with you if they don't pick that option. To further get in front of their reaction, you can say, "There's no pressure to pick one option over another. Just look at all of them and pick the one that's right for you and your family." After you get a commitment from the client to look at all of your options without getting upset, immediately begin the presentation.

The money warning creates a lot of dissonance, so once it's done you'll want to immediately bring back harmony by telling the client about the top option—without revealing the price. Once you've introduced the top option, the next step is to invite the client to play the price-guess game. This may seem awkward at first, but please do it because it will give you invaluable and immediate feedback on how you're doing when it comes to building value.

It's now time to reveal the price of the top option and say, "What should we do?" In fact, the (perfect) question "What should we do?" is one your client should hear multiple times throughout the presentation. Ask the question, and then be quiet and let the client think.

Two things will happen. Either the client will pick an option and you'll proceed to give it back, or more likely they will make some type of objection. Remember, all objections are not created equal, and some objections, such as statements, are not even really objections. This book provides you with all the tools you need to handle any type of real objection that comes your way. For that reason, you may want to bookmark chapter 27 for reference and review it, particularly the six pack of objection handling, which gives you a system for shifting the focus away from the barrier and toward getting the job done. Most of your efforts should be focused on mastering the objection-handling techniques in chapter 27. For you overachievers, I have provided two heavy-duty techniques for handling objections in chapter 28, but they should only be used if the call is *really* going south.

Congratulations, you've closed the deal! The client is ready to make a purchase. By now you know there is one more step you need to do to make sure the deal you are about to close stays closed and doesn't boomerang back around to bite you.

Doing the post-closing giveback may seem counterintuitive at first, but when done right it does nothing but increase your client's respect and trust. So go ahead and offer them the less expensive options again so you can be extra sure they knew they had those other choices. And after you've received the client's check or credit card or arranged for financing, remember to do a post-selling interview, reminding them of what they liked about their choice.

Be determined to follow this process to completion. At this point, it's not really about the money. It's about respecting your client and not wanting them to go with someone who won't put in the same effort you have to get to know them, their system, and what they really need.

Once again, I want to recognize the effort you have made to read this book. Not everyone would invest this kind of time to learn an entirely new system. I am thankful you saw fit to give me so much of your attention. My goal was to provide a window into a new world of options that you can use to grow your business and serve your clients. Know that even if you only add the question "What should we do?" to all of your client interactions, it will change your business for the better. If you lean into all of these principles and master the system, it will change your life like it has mine and thousands of others.

This may be the end of the book, but it's just the beginning of our relationship. Believe it or not, this book is the Pure Motive Service primer. There's more—way more—where this came from. To join our online community and download tools for your success, please go to servicemvp.com/tools. I'll look forward to seeing you there!

JOIN THE SERVICE MVP COMMUNITY

SERVICE MVP

servicemvp.com

Reach your full potential in our membership-based community. Get coaching, eLearning, revolutionary software, and live training by the legendary Uncle Joe Crisara. It's all created specifically for your home service business managers, technicians, salespeople, customer service representatives, dispatchers, and office staff.

You and your success are our business.

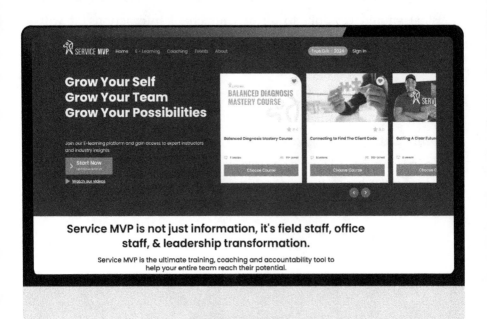

ACKNOWLEDGMENTS

In the journey of authoring *What Should We Do?*, I've been fortunate to receive support, inspiration, and guidance from many remarkable individuals who have touched my life in meaningful ways. Their contributions have been instrumental in shaping the ideas and concepts within this book.

First and foremost, I extend my deepest gratitude to my family. Delores, Joe Crisara Sr., and my sister, Susan Stewart, have been a constant source of love, unconditional care, and unwavering support. They've allowed me to dream big and pursue those dreams with all my heart.

To Dave Muller, I owe a special thank-you. Your guidance on the science of pricing my services has been invaluable. Your wisdom has contributed significantly to the foundation of the concepts presented in this book.

Dr. Stephen R. Covey's groundbreaking book *The 7 Habits of Highly Effective People* changed my paradigm and gave me the priceless gift of responsibility. I am deeply grateful for the transformative impact of his work on my life and for the principles he instilled in me.

I would like to express my appreciation to Kurt Mortensen for his book *Maximum Influence*. This book unveiled the 12 laws of persuasion, which form the bedrock of the materials and concepts presented in this book.

Jack Canfield's teachings have been instrumental in empowering me with actionable behaviors and the courage to take action without fear. Jack, your wisdom and guidance have been a guiding light on my journey.

My friend Rick Picard has been an exemplary source of inspiration and support. His embodiment of Pure Motive Service values is a constant reminder of the importance of living a life of service to my family, team, and friends with unwavering honesty and support.

I also want to acknowledge Tommy Mello, author of *Elevate*. Tommy, your generosity and inclusive spirit, and the fact that you allow everyone to be a part of your dream to help others, have left a lasting impact on my journey.

Thank you to Helena Bouchez, whose effort and expertise in preparing this book were invaluable.

Finally, I extend my heartfelt gratitude to my best friends and immediate family, Joey, Wyatt, and Julie Crisara. Julie, your enduring presence through the darkest times and your unwavering support have been pivotal in getting me to where I am today. Your sacrifices and optimism have made our shared dreams as a family come true, and I am fortunate to have you in my life.

This book is a culmination of the wisdom and inspiration these incredible individuals have shared with me. I am immensely grateful for the positive impact they've had on my life, and I dedicate this work to them with deep appreciation and love.

ABOUT
UNCLE JOE CRISARA

Joe Crisara was once a home service contractor with a failing business. Deeply in debt, he had zero sales skills and undercharged for everything. He assumed the only way to create higher value was to do the same service everyone else did for a lower price.

But when things looked most bleak, Joe had an aha moment. It not only changed his life but also skyrocketed his business.

Since then, Joe and Julie, his wife and business partner, have helped thousands of contractors achieve three to five times

greater revenue by implementing his transformative Pure Motive Service system. Joe's down-to-earth style and direct approach are based on having personally overcome the same pains, troubles, and struggles that all contractors face—all of which are still very real to him. From start-ups to Fortune 1000 companies, scores of owners, managers, technicians, and sales professionals in HVAC, plumbing, and electrical contracting businesses use his principles of persuasion, selling, presentation, and closing.

Today, Joe is known as America's service sales coach—a worldwide sales educator, entrepreneur, and author who helps blue-collar workers live the life they always imagined. His passion and genuine desire to help are evident on live coaching calls, through in-person workshops, or via multimedia resources.

What Should We Do? is Joe's third book, the definitive guide to repackaging, differentiating, and selling services at a higher perceived quality and for more money than anyone else in the market. Joe is also the author of *Whisper Sales Management: Lead, Calm, and Focus the "Wild Mind" of Your Pack* and *Object-o-Matic: Sales Objection Handler.*

Joe and Julie have one son, Wyatt. When they're not coaching, they enjoy traveling as a family, attending Broadway musicals, fine dining, and taking long walks.

Get eLearning, coaching, events, and resources at the Service MVP app, or join the conversation online.

Service MVP | www.servicemvp.com | 877-764-6304

Would you leave an online review?
Your feedback helps spread the word to
other service industry contractors.
Thank you for your support!

WHAT SHOULD WE DO?

Printed in the USA
CPSIA information can be obtained
at www.ICGtesting.com
CBHW071810060324
5024CB00012B/841

9 798989 553415